Literary Theory and Criticism

Edgar Allan Poe

Edited by
LEONARD CASSUTO
Fordham University

DOVER PUBLICATIONS, INC.
Mineola, New York

Copyright

Published in Canada by General Publishing Company, Ltd., 30 Lesmill Road, Don Mills, Toronto, Ontario.

Bibliographical Note

Literary Theory and Criticism, an anthology first published by Dover Publications, Inc., in 1999, is a new selection of essays and reviews by Edgar Allan Poe reprinted from standard sources. An introduction, headnotes and explanatory footnotes have been specially prepared for this edition.

Library of Congress Cataloging-in-Publication Data

Poe, Edgar Allan, 1809–1849.
    Literary theory and criticism / edited by Leonard Cassuto.
       p. cm.
    ISBN 0-486-40155-3
    1. Literature—History and criticism—Theory, etc. 2. Literature—History and criticism. I. Cassuto, Leonard, 1960– . II. Title.
PS2619.A2 C37   1999
809—dc21   99-36639
                                                  CIP

Manufactured in the United States of America
Dover Publications, Inc., 31 East 2nd Street, Mineola, N.Y. 11501

Beyond Originality: Edgar Allan Poe the Critic

Edgar Allan Poe is renowned today as the father of modern horror, but in his own time he was better known as "tomahawk man." He received this nickname not for the gruesomeness of his fiction, but rather for his savagery as a critic. The 1830s and 1840s American literary world that he inhabited was at once genteel and rough-and-tumble, and Poe was its *enfant terrible,* a prolific but unpredictable talent of distinctive opinions and little restraint. While his contemporaries—Ralph Waldo Emerson, Nathaniel Hawthorne, Herman Melville and others—sought their literary fortunes in a relatively sedate fashion, Poe went in a different direction. He was a relentless champion of an eccentric brand of originality, a passionate adherent of his own version of American literary nationalism, a vituperative and often headstrong heckler of the literary coterie that ruled the U.S. publishing business—in short, an aggressive and volatile outsider. For both Poe and his critics, this outsider status was tangled up with his Southern roots and experience. The complex interrelationships of that entanglement are most evident in Poe's voluminous criticism, for although his fiction often seems removed from place and history, his criticism is nearly always of the tumultuous moment, the product of what William Carlos Williams calls " a genius intimately shaped by his locality and time." This anthology presents a selection of this work, organized chronologically, to illustrate Poe's intertwined critical, political, and personal movements over time.

Edgar Allan Poe entered the American publishing scene in the 1830s, a period during which it was distinctly hostile to American writers. There was no international copyright law at the time; therefore United States publishers could pass over all but the best-selling American authors in favor of reprinting the works of established British writers, for which they did not have to pay royalties. American authors, Poe included, found themselves in the unenviable position of having to beg American publishers to issue their works. The publishers treated these requests with disdain, generally demanding financial guarantees against loss—money the authors would supply if they had it; otherwise their manuscripts remained in their desk drawers. Meanwhile, the American publishing business grew and prospered, riding a wave of editions of popular British classics (including novels by Walter Scott, Daniel Defoe, Charles Dickens, and others) along with the odd American work (Washington Irving and James Fenimore Cooper were two of the small number of United States authors with enough name recognition to sell books), and scores of pale (and often plagiarized) imitations of these models that were cranked out to capitalize on their popularity. American literature struggled even as its critics and practitioners consciously sought a coherent identity for it in a country still not far removed from its revolutionary roots.

Facing a catch-22—their work could get published only if they were popular, and they could become popular only if their work were published—American authors courted renown by any means possible. Turning to the magazine trade, many sought to raise their profiles by generating as many favorable reviews of their work as they could. Thus evolved what Charles Frederick Briggs, a contemporary of Poe's, termed "the art of puffing," which was, he said, "the art of all arts at the present day, when nothing will sell that is not first puffed into notice." Magazine editors became valuable friends for writers to have, and cliquish literary scenes coalesced in different regions of the country, with the New York-Boston nexus being the biggest, richest, and most influential. Whom a writer knew was at least as important as what the writer wrote: even an illustrious American author like Hawthorne owed his early smooth path to success to a key endorsement by Henry Wadsworth Longfellow, the respected New England poet, critic, and Harvard professor who also happened to have been Hawthorne's classmate at Bowdoin College.

Poe's rise to fame was considerably rockier. He began his literary career in his twenties. Having provoked his own expulsion from West Point in 1831 after dropping out of the University of Virginia five years earlier, he turned to poetry and fiction, gaining some recognition by the mid-1830s. In 1835, he became editor of the Richmond-based *Southern Literary Messenger*. As a poor Southern writer, Poe was aware that he would have to fight for the prominence he sought in this Northern-dominated business, so he came in with his local colors flying and his rapier pen poised. Already at this early point, and throughout his career, Poe was his own man, a principled reformer who was nonetheless not above betraying his own precepts to advance his interests. With conspicuous wit and vigor, the brash newcomer denounced the unholy alliances among authors, critics, and publishers. He excoriated the practice of indiscriminate reviewing—crucial to the puffing industry—calling it a "flippant, unjust, untenable, and uncritical" activity.

The young firebrand was noticed almost immediately. Less than a year into his tenure at *Southern Literary Messenger*, he published a review of Theodore S. Fay's *Norman Leslie* (see p. 1 in this collection), attacking both the "bepuffed" novel and its puffers with such pointed, sarcastic gusto that he sparked the ire of the New York establishment. Never one to shy away from a fight, Poe continued the exchange in his review of the poetry of Joseph Rodman Drake and Fitz-Greene Halleck (p. 9), wherein he tied the practice of puffery to the degradation of American literature itself. Being American in one's literary sentiments, Poe insisted, should not lead one to elevate bad books to positions of respect purely on the basis of their being homegrown productions. This was simply "misapplied patriotism." American literature, he argued again and again, should feature imaginative vitality, not reflexive nationalism.

Poe's early reviews showcase these aesthetic theories in their first stages of development. One of the most prolific reviewers and commentators of all time, Poe championed both critical independence and authorial originality, but his personal understanding of these virtues was shot through with complex, self-reflective anxiety. As his 1846 essay "The Philosophy of Composition" (p. 100) most clearly shows, Poe measured creativity in terms of effect and affective power—in the case of poetry, "that intense and pure elevation of *soul.*" This emotion-based aesthetic of originality was Poe's replacement for what he calls "the heresy of the didactic" and served as the guiding principle for all of his creative and critical work. But in tying originality to the sublimity of reader response, Poe is essentially saying that originality depends on effect, effect on originality, and both on high artistic quality. He saves himself from pure relativism by insisting that achieving the desired effect depends upon adherence to a set of objective laws and principles: "The highest order of the imaginative intellect," he declares in his review of Griswold, "is always preeminently mathematical." In other words, access to originality—and with it the reader's soul—depends on a creative process that is precise, measured, thoroughly planned and reasoned out. "The Philosophy of Composition," even in its obvious self-aggrandizing parody of this ideal, offers Poe's lesson in how to think, how to create, in this way. This teaching outlines a postulate: to be a good writer is to be original, and to be original is to be a good writer. The corollary follows: bad writing is a failure of originality, and bad writers therefore are imitators, even plagiarists.

The flagrant rip-offs of popular works by American publishers made plagiarism an important economic issue in Poe's day, but in light of his aesthetic theories, it is hardly surprising that for Poe himself, plagiarism became something of a critical and creative obsession. Poe sought what D. H. Lawrence calls "the forming of a new consciousness," but his attempts to free himself from literary and journalistic tradition unavoidably took place within that very tradition. In particular, Poe's appeals for originality followed conventional modes for self-presentation and debate that had evolved in the high-toned British literary magazines; he later incorporated elements of the more populist American magazine business into his own practice.

Poe was calling for newness while wearing old clothes—and he knew it. This tension between innovation and proven formula certainly helped make plagiarism into a running theme in his work and, ironically, a practice that he frequently—and highly self-consciously—engaged in himself. In essence, plagiarism became a way for Poe to think about both his own creative process and those of his rivals. It thus comes as no surprise that Poe's review of Hawthorne's *Twice-Told Tales* (p. 57) would mix praise with accusations of plagiarism, and admiration with barely concealed jealousy of a peer who had clearly made it in the eyes of others. The evidence does not support Poe's accusation in this case (he claims that Hawthorne borrowed elements of his "Howe's Masquerade" from one of Poe's own tales, but Hawthorne's story was actually composed earlier). Nevertheless, this review offers a window into Poe's fraught theory of genius and originality. He sees the true artist as multitalented, gifted with the capacity to create and understand what is beautiful and with the ability to meet the requirements of literary precedent and reader response. Poe's ideal writer is therefore suspended between separation and unity: separation from the artists who came before (to achieve creative freedom) and unity with the reader to follow (to generate the requisite affect). The writer's identity is thus pulled in many directions in Poe's universe. Within this tension, we may glimpse the origins of "William Wilson," Poe's famous tale of an "imaginative and excitable" criminal and his venomous resentment of his virtuous double, a "copy" so accurate as to be a part of him. Poe reflected on creativity and originality throughout his life, combining method, mockery, and endless self-examination in his distinctive critical and artistic signature. His many approaches to these ideas culminate in "The Poetic Principle" (p. 174), a manuscript published posthumously in 1850.

Poe's ideas of originality informed his vision of a national literature. Though a loyal Southerner, Poe attempted to portray himself as a nonregional American literary nationalist. He was aided in this stance by the fact that his editorial talents and career ambitions moved him inexorably northward—toward the literary establishment whose insularity he attacked, yet whose resources he badly wanted to share. Moving from Richmond to Philadelphia (where he edited *Burton's Gentleman's Magazine*) to New York (where he headed *Graham's Lady's and Gentleman's Magazine* and then the *Broadway Journal,* which he also owned before it folded), Poe boosted circulation wherever he went, becoming perhaps the most peripatetic man of letters in the ante-bellum United States. But Poe was not able to separate his critical sensibility from his roots—if indeed he ever wanted to. It is not simply that those roots peek through in an exhortation like "It is high time that the literary South took its own interests into its own charge" (from the "Marginalia," p. 169), or in his attack on James Russell Lowell as "one of the most rabid of the Abolition fanatics," or in his editorial stance (for example, his movement of the *Broadway Journal* away from abolitionism, which incurred the wrath of his coeditor). Poe's critical tastes and preferences are, as many scholars have argued, actually inseparable from his Southernness, and his Southernness inseparable from his crafted self-presentation as a shaper and defender of his own vision of the national literary legacy. In other words, his origins served as both an authentic heritage and a stylized declaration of difference from the Northern establishment. Critics have argued for years over whether Poe wrote the 1836 Paulding-Drayton review (p. 26), which showcases a strong proslavery position consistent with the Southern paternalism of the age. I have included the disputed review here not only because convincing evidence points to Poe as its author (Poe certainly had a hand in it at least), but also because the very argument over the essay's provenance reflects the degree to which Poe's role as outsider is simultaneously ideological and aesthetic. As an involved participant in the literary and critical debates of his time—which were intertwined with national politics and political parties in a way that is scarcely imaginable today—Poe was in no way above the regional fray. His perspective was defined by his position outside the coteries, and his taste (as the Paulding-Drayton review shows most clearly) was shaped by the feudal, sentimentalist, and fundamentally racist culture of the Old South.

Poe tried to keep his critical sentiments, including his vendettas, almost exclusively separate from his feelings about race and slavery (which were themselves expressed obliquely through his fiction in ways that are being explored more deeply by current critics). He usually tried not to be explicitly or stereotypically "Southern" in his views, but as an outsider, a non-New Yorker, and a non-New Englander, Poe deployed a Southern profile selectively constructed out of both fact and fancy. It is a curious but telling aspect of his critical legacy that the Agrarians, the 1930s circle of poets and scholars who idealized the pastoral values of the Old South, adopted Poe as their forbear. Held up by Allen Tate in the essay "Our Cousin, Mr. Poe" as even more Southern that he actually was, Poe became a kind of honorary father of the text-based New Criticism that the Agrarians helped introduce to wide practice. This modern formalism hugely influenced literary study in the United States, with its effects extending to the present day.

Poe called loudly and often for an international copyright law that would level the playing field for American writers and encourage the development of a national literature. But he did so at considerable cost; as a critical gadfly nearly always aligned against the literary establishment upon which he nevertheless depended for his living, Poe made a lot of enemies and never enough money. The combination of the two was fatal for him. His 1845 alliance with Evert Duyckinck and the Young Americans—a New York coterie pushing for a national literature in the name of democratic ideals—was self-serving and pragmatic. The Young Americans linked their literary notions to their wider political worldview, an elitist and expansionist set of positions loosely tethered to the doctrine of manifest destiny. Theirs was a more nativistic vision of American literature than Poe's, but the connection benefited Poe personally in many ways, for Duyckinck was a major player in the publishing world who helped Poe publish his fiction and poetry. But Poe could not be practical for long; in less than a year he had strained the ties of these convenient friendships with a free-swinging critical assault on Longfellow, one of the emerging deans of American letters. Poe attacked Longfellow's work at length as derivative and plagiaristic, inaugurating what Poe himself called "The Little Longfellow War" (see p. 84).

The affair began with Poe's review of Longfellow's *Waif* in the *New York Evening Mirror*, a mixed assessment that balanced admiration of Longfellow's poetry with a complaint about his tendency to "imitate" his American peers without recognizing them. Poe had raised the imitation issue a few years earlier in reviewing Longfellow, but he had never gone so far as to imply, as he did in this case, that the poet was a thief. Poe's attack was answered by various supporters of Longfellow's but one "Outis" (who has never been identified) combined defense with counterattack, charging Poe with the same sort of plagiarism in "The Raven." Given that Poe saw plagiarism as a combined moral and aesthetic failure, it is perhaps not surprising that Outis's accusation set him off, triggering a month-long venting in the pages of the weekly *Broadway Journal* in which he elaborated on his charges against Longfellow and dissected every detail of Outis's indictment of himself. As an exclamation point, Poe then planted an essay in *The Aristidean* in which he reiterated his accusation of Longfellow even more trenchantly. (He published the latter piece anonymously, to create the impression of outside confirmation and independent support of his position.) To call Poe's extended salvos a "war" is somewhat misleading, since neither Longfellow not Outis ever replied to any of his repeated attacks; Poe likely kept the conflict going because it kept his name before the literary public. (Some critics claim, in fact, that Poe *was* Outis, playing both roles in a combined publicity stunt and hoax.) In the end, some of the mud stuck to Longfellow, as some reviewers of the day began to look more critically at his work—but Poe emerged besmeared as well. His testy assault on one of America's most august literary personages lowered his reputation in the country's wealthiest and most influential literary circles.

The Longfellow exchange spotlights the links that bind together Poe's literary theories, his Southern allegiances, and his splenetic attempts to reform the literary business from the outside. His efforts to dedicate poetry to beauty and pleasure rather than the didacticism he saw in Longfellow's work correspond to his efforts to protect the South from Northern progressive (that is, antislavery) thinking, as well as to his continuing struggle to make Longfellow, the consummate New England insider, acknowledge the artistic influence of his less well-connected colleagues. "The Little Longfellow War," framed by "The Philosophy of Composition" and "The Poetic Principle," also stands as Poe's definitive statement of his uniquely mechanistic formalism, an artistic philosophy that was also starkly at odds with the organic, nature-based view of creativity propounded by the New Englander Emerson in such influential essays as "The Poet" (1844).

Emerson's poet is a "natural sayer," a channel for "the impressions of nature." This aesthetic privileges artistic freedom and spontaneity as keys to the eternal. Poe rejected this philosophy on many occasions, seeking beauty not in the "primal warblings" prized by Emerson, but rather in the delicate discipline that he saw as the source of true art. For Emerson, genius operates instinctively. For Poe, it was a matter of craft. Poe's vigorous criticisms of both Emerson's ecstatic sympathy with nature and Longfellow's traditional formalism show how his own aesthetics are informed by opposition to prevailing theories and practices of his time—in other words, by the company he refused to keep.

Poe followed the Longfellow display with a public debacle in Boston, later in 1845. For reasons that will never be fully understood, he embarrassed a distinguished Lyceum audience that had invited him to recite by fobbing off one of his oldest poems as new and then bragging about the deception afterwards. His audience was not amused, and certain of its members pilloried Poe in print. As if this were not enough, Poe was also printing his flirtatious verse exchanges with two married women in the pages of the *Broadway Journal* during that year. Though his intentions clearly were innocent (and his actions even approved by his wife, Virginia) Poe's poor judgment received its own reward, as jealousies erupted into scandal, blame, and—for Poe—degradation and infamy.

As a consequence of these and other carelessnesses, Poe

essentially wore out his welcome in the Northeast corridor. But he had nowhere else to go, especially when his health broke down. Lacking any financial cushion and surrounded by rivals who were sniffing for any weakness he might show, Poe was doubly vulnerable to calamity. When he suffered a nervous breakdown (then called "brain fever"), his situation became grievous, and his career never recovered. His desperate need for money after his illness led him to accept assignments that sensationalized him, turning him into more spectacle than critic. *Godey's* magazine, for example, played on Poe's controversial reputation and nudged him in the direction of self-parody when the publication commissioned "The New York Literati," an 1846 series of prose portraits that seemed designed to exacerbate Poe's troubles in exchange for a handful of change. The sketches (some of which are reprinted here, beginning on p. 111) are delicately satirical, alternating suspicious praise with selective barbs. An exception was the piece on Thomas Dunn English, an obviously unflattering sketch of author as plagiarist. Poe, who was growing more infirm and less productive, got involved in a nasty public exchange of personal insults with English over this portrayal. Eventually Poe sued for libel and won, collecting $225. It was a Pyrrhic victory, however, for the whole affair had made his alcoholic and financial troubles even more public, which made it harder for him to get work. The tailspin continued, eventually leaving Poe literally in the gutter. His death in 1849 remains one of the more infamous in the history of United States literature.

Poe the critic was a melange of imaginative brilliance and the diverse influences of an itinerant life. As an interpreter of the creative imagination and its marketplace, he was a literary theorist before the term was invented. He was also a literary politician, a literary proselytizer, and a literary hothead—an ambitious mixture, as Lowell famously suggested in 1848, of genius and fudge. As a principled champion of causes and a petty avenger of real and imagined wrongs, Poe's power clearly came from both the genius *and* the fudge, and together they supplied him with a source of energy that for a while seemed almost boundless. In just under a decade and a half as a literary professional, Poe produced a large and varied body of work. Though his criticism is far more topical than his imaginative writing, the two pursuits inform each other. One might say that Poe the critic bleeds into Poe the story writer and poet: meditations on originality are present throughout his writings and they are always freighted with meaning and implication. In "The Cask of Amontillado, "for instance, Montresor insists on fiendish, original creativity as a way to finish Fortunato; Roderick Usher's strange pathology is bound up with his original artwork in a self-destructive passage to the crypt in "The Fall of the House of Usher"; the detective Auguste Dupin is a kind of plagiarism detector, locating the letter that a thief is trying to pass off as his own in "The Purloined Letter," and so on. Poe's criticism and imaginative work together showcase his career-long preoccupation with genius, originality, creativity, and national literary identity. His essays offer a path into one of this country's most lively and inventive critical minds, even as they illuminate the works of an American generation casting about for an idea of what American literature was, and what it should be.

Leonard Cassuto,
Fordham University

Acknowledgments

The help I've received from colleagues since beginning this project has proved once again that writing is collaborative. Andrew Delbanco gave direction to this book at the outset. Jonathan Auerbach, Clare Eby, and Robert S. Levine helped at various points in the preparation of the manuscript.

In the latter stages, I've benefited from Julie Nord's careful and thorough editing, George Shea's translations of the classical passages, and Burton R. Pollin's expert aid in tracking down fugitive references as the clock wound down.

A Note on the Text

These readings have been taken from standard sources. The many inconsistencies of spelling and mechanics found in them are typical of publications of Poe's age and have been preserved, for the sake of historical interest and accuracy. In addition, all of Poe's own footnotes (indicated by asterisks or daggers) have been retained. These are not to be confused with the editorial footnotes (indicated by numbers), which were specially prepared for this edition, to help the reader follow Poe's references, allusions, and quotations, many of which are fairly obscure by now.

CONTENTS

Beyond Originality: Edgar Allan Poe the Critic   v

REVIEW
    Theodore S. Fay, *Norman Leslie*   1

REVIEW
    Joseph Rodman Drake, *The Culprit Fay, and other Poems*
    Fitz-Greene Halleck, *Alnwick Castle, with other Poems*   9

REVIEW
    James K. Paulding, *Slavery in the United States*
    William Drayton, *The South Vindicated from the Treason*
      and Fanaticism of the Northern Abolitionists   26

REVIEW
    Charles Dickens, *The Old Curiosity Shop, and other Tales*
      and *Master Humphrey's Clock*   33

REVIEW
    Lambert A. Wilmer, *The Quacks of Helicon: A Satire*   42

Exordium to Critical Notices   51

REVIEW
    Nathaniel Hawthorne, *Twice-Told Tales*   57

REVIEW
    Rufus W. Griswold, *The Poets and Poetry of America*   64

Prospectus of *The Stylus*   71

REVIEW
    James Fenimore Cooper, *Wyandotté*   74

EXCERPT
    "The Little Longfellow War"   84

The Philosophy of Composition   100

EXCERPTS FROM "THE LITERATI OF NEW YORK CITY"   111
   Some Honest Opinions   111
   Thomas Dunn English   114
   Sarah Margaret Fuller   116
   Lydia M. Child   123

The Rationale of Verse   125

REVIEW
   James Russell Lowell, *A Fable for the Critics*   162

Marginalia   169

The Poetic Principle   174

Literary Theory and Criticism

Review

[*Southern Literary Messenger,* December 1835]

Theodore S. Fay, *Norman Leslie. A Tale of the Present Times*
(New York: Harper and Brothers)

Poe's inflammatory review of Theodore Fay's Norman Leslie *was his shot across the bow of the Northern literary establishment. Attacking, even insulting, the novel from every possible angle, Poe deflated the praise Fay's influential friends had manufactured to bring it to notice in the first place. In essence, the young Poe turned his review into a declaration of war on the "puffing" industry. His insistence on "rigid justice and impartiality" in his criticism brought him into immediate conflict first with the New York literary insiders, and later with the Boston clique. These clashes with Northern literary tastemakers were among the major forces that defined Poe's career as a writer—both for better and worse.*

Well!—here we have it! This is *the* book—*the* book *par excellence*—the book bepuffed, beplastered, and be*Mirrored*:[1] the book "attributed to" Mr. Blank, and "said to be from the pen" of Mr. Asterisk: the book which has been "about to appear"—"in press"—"in progress"—"in preparation"—and "forthcoming:" the book "graphic" in anticipation—"talented" *a priori*—and God knows what *in prospectu*. For the sake of every thing puffed, puffing, and puffable, let us take a peep at its contents!

Norman Leslie, gentle reader, a Tale of the Present Times, is, after all, written by nobody in the world but Theodore S. Fay, and Theodore S. Fay is nobody in the world but "one of the Editors of the New York Mirror." The book commences with a Dedication to Colonel Herman Thorn, in which that worthy personage, whoever he may be, is held up, in about a dozen lines, to the admiration of the public, as "hospitable," "generous," "attentive," "benevolent," "kind-hearted," "liberal," "highly-esteemed," and withal "a patron of the arts." But the less we say of this matter the better.

In the Preface Mr. Fay informs us that the most important features

---

[1] The *New York Weekly Mirror,* was a publication of literature and miscellany edited by the poet and lyricist George Pope Morris, with the assistance at times, of Theodore Fay and N. P. Willis. Poe's implication here is that the *Mirror,* (which was published from 1823 until 1857) has been puffing the work of Fay, its recent associate editor.

of his story are founded on fact—that he has availed himself of certain poetical licenses—that he has transformed character, and particularly the character of a young lady, (oh fi! Mr. Fay—oh, Mr. Fay, fi!) that he has sketched certain peculiarities with a mischievous hand—and that the art of novel writing is as dignified as the art of Canova, Mozart or Raphael,—from which we are left to infer, that Mr. Fay himself is as dignified as Raphael, Mozart, and Canova—all three. Having satisfied us on this head, he goes on to say something about an humble student, with a feeble hand, throwing groupings upon a canvass, and standing behind a curtain: and then, after perpetrating all these impertinences, thinks it best "frankly to bespeak the indulgence of the solemn and sapient critics." Body of Bacchus! *we*, at least, are neither solemn nor sapient, and, therefore, do not feel ourselves bound to show him a shadow of mercy. But will any body tell us what is the object of Prefaces in general, and what is the meaning of Mr. Fay's Preface in particular?

As far as we can understand the plot of Norman Leslie, it is this. A certain family reside in Italy—"independent," "enlightened," "affectionate," "happy,"—and all that. Their villa, of course, stands upon the seashore, and their whole establishment is, we are assured, "a scene of Heaven," &c. Mr. Fay says he will not even attempt to describe it—why, therefore, should we? A daughter of this family is nineteen when she is wooed by a young Neapolitan, Rinaldo, of "mean extraction, but of great beauty and talent." The lover, being a man of suspicious character, is rejected by the parents, and a secret marriage ensues. The lady's brother pursues the bridegroom—they fight—and the former is killed. The father and mother die (it is impossible to see for what purpose they ever lived) and Rinaldo flies to Venice. Upon rejoining her husband in that city, the lady (for Mr. Fay has not thought her worth enduing with a specific appellation) discovers him, for the first time, to be a rascal. One fine day he announces his intention of leaving herself and son for an indefinite time. The lady beseeches and finally threatens. "It was the first unfolding," says she, in a letter towards the *dénouement* of the story, "of that character which neither he nor I knew belonged to my nature. It was the first uncoiling of the basilisk within me, (good Heavens, a snake in a lady's stomach!). He gazed on me incredulously, and cooly smiled. You remember that smile—I fainted!!!" Alas! Mr. Davy Crockett,—Mr. Davy Crockett, alas!—thou art beaten hollow—thou art defunct, and undone! thou hast indeed succeeded in grinning a squirrel from a tree, but it surpassed even thine extraordinary abilities to smile a lady into a fainting fit!

"When I recovered"—continues the lady—"he was gone. It was two years before I could trace him. At length I found he had sailed for

America. I followed him in the depth of winter—I and my child. I knew not the name he had assumed, and I was struck mute with astonishment, in your beautiful city, on beholding, surrounded by fair ladies, the form of my husband, still beautiful, and still adored. You know the rest." But as our readers may not be as well informed as the correspondent of the fair forsaken, we will enlighten them with some farther particulars.

Rinaldo, upon leaving his *cara sposa,* had taken shipping for New York, where, assuming the name of "Count Clairmont of the French army," he succeeds in cutting a dash, or, in more proper parlance, in creating a sensation, among the beaux and belles of the city of Gotham. One fair lady, and rich heiress, Miss Flora Temple, is particularly honored by his attentions, and the lady's mother, Mrs. T., fired with the idea of her daughter becoming a real countess, makes no scruple of encouraging his addresses. Matters are in this position when the wife of the adventurer arrives in New York, and is quite bewildered with astonishment upon beholding, one snowy day, her beloved Rinaldo sleighing it to and fro about the streets of New York. In the midst of her amazement she is in danger of being run over by some horses, when a certain personage, by name Norman Leslie, but who might, with equal propriety, be called Sir Charles Grandison,[2] flies to her assistance, whisks herself and child up in the very nick of time, and suddenly rescues them, as Mr. Fay has it, "from the very jaws of Death"—by which we are to understand from the very hoofs of the horses. The lady of course swoons—then recovers—and then—is excessively grateful. Her gratitude, however, being of no service just at that moment, is bottled up for use hereafter, and will no doubt, according to established usage in such cases, come into play towards the close of the second volume. But we shall see.

Having ascertained the address of Rinaldo, *alias* the Count Clairmont, the lady, next morning, is successful in obtaining an interview. Then follows a second edition of entreaties and threats, but, fortunately for the nerves of Mrs. Rinaldo, the Count, upon this occasion, is so forbearing as not to indulge in a smile. She accuses him of a design to marry Miss Temple, and he informs her that it is no concern of hers—that she is not his wife, their marriage having been a feigned one. "She would have cried him through the city for a villain," (Dust ho!—she should have advertised him) but he swears that, in that case, he will never sleep until he has taken the life of both the lady and her child, which assurance puts an end to the debate. "He

---

[2]Title character of Samuel Richardson's 1753 novel. He exemplifies so many laudable qualities that his story is often felt to be a bit dull.

then frankly confesses"—says Mrs. Rinaldo, in the letter which we
have before quoted,—"that his passion for Miss Temple was only a
mask—he loved her not. *Me* he said he loved. It was his intention to
fly when he could raise a large sum of money, and he declared that I
should be his companion." His designs, however, upon Miss Temple
fail—that lady very properly discarding the rascal. Nothing daunted
at this mishap our Count proceeds to make love to a certain Miss
Rosalie Romain, and with somewhat better success. He prevails upon
her to fly, and to carry with her upon her person a number of dia-
monds which the lover hopes to find sufficient for his necessities. He
manages also to engage Mrs. Rinaldo (so we must call her for want of
a better name) in his schemes.

It has so happened that for some time prior to these occurrences,
Clairmont and Norman Leslie, the hero of the novel, have been
sworn foes. On the day fixed for Miss Romain's elopement, that
young lady induces Mr. Leslie to drive her, in a gig, a short distance
out of town. They are met by no less a personage than Mrs. Rinaldo
herself, in another gig, and driving (*proh pudor!*)[3] through the woods
sola. Hereupon Miss Rosalie Romain very deliberately, and to the
great astonishment, no doubt, of Mr. Leslie, gets out of that gentleman's gig, and into the gig of Mrs. Rinaldo. Here's plot! as Vapid says
in the play.[4] Our friend Norman, finding that nothing better can be
done, turns his face towards New York again, where he arrives, in due
time, without farther accident or adventure. Late the same evening
Clairmont sends the ladies aboard a vessel bound for Naples, and
which is to sail in the morning—returning himself, for the present,
to his hotel in Broadway. While here he receives a horse-whipping
from Mr. Leslie on account of certain insinuations in disparagement
of that gentleman's character. Not relishing this treatment he deter-
mines upon revenge, and can think of no better method of accomplishing it than the directing of public suspicion against Mr. Leslie as
the murderer of Miss Romain—whose disappearance has already created much excitement. He sends a message to Mrs. Rinaldo that the
vessel must sail without him, and that he would, by a French ship,
meet them on their landing at Naples. He then flings a hat and feathers belonging to Miss Romain upon a stream, and her handkerchief
in a wood—afterwards remaining some time in America to avert suspicion from himself. Leslie is arrested for the murder, and the proofs
are damning against him. He is, however, to the great indignation of
the populace, acquitted, Miss Temple appearing to testify that she

---

[3]"for shame!"
[4]The play Poe is alluding to is *The Dramatist* (1793) by Frederick M. Reynolds.

actually saw Miss Romain subsequently to her ride with Leslie. Our hero, however, although acquitted, is universally considered guilty, and, through the active malice of Clairmont, is heaped with every species of opprobrium. Miss Temple, who, it appears, is in love with him, falls ill with grief: but is cured, after all other means have failed, by a letter from her lover announcing a reciprocal passion—for the young lady has hitherto supposed him callous to her charms. Leslie himself, however, takes it into his head, at this critical juncture, to travel; and, having packed up his baggage, does actually forget himself so far as to go a-Willising[5] in foreign countries. But we have no reason to suppose that, goose as the young gentleman is, he is silly enough to turn travelling correspondent to any weekly paper. In Rome, having assumed the *alias* of Montfort, he meets with a variety of interesting adventures. All the ladies die for him: and one in particular, Miss Antonia Torrini, the only child of a Duke with several millions of piastres, and a palace which Mr. Fay thinks very much like the City Hall in New York, absolutely throws herself *sans ceremonie* into his arms, and meets—tell it not in Gath![6]—with a flat and positive refusal.

Among other persons whom he encounters is a monk Ambrose, a painter Angelo, another painter Ducci, a Marquis Alezzi, and a Countess D., which latter personage he is convinced of having seen at some prior period of his life. For a page or two we are entertained with a prospect of a conspiracy, and have great hopes that the principal characters in the plot will so far oblige us as to cut one another's throats: but (alas for human expectations!) Mr. Fay having clapped his hands, and cried "Presto!—vanish!" the whole matter ends in smoke, or, as our author beautifully expresses it, is "veiled in impenetrable mystery."

Mr. Leslie now pays a visit to the painter Ducci, and is astonished at there beholding the portrait of the very youth whose life he saved, together with that of his mother, from the horses in New York. Then follows a series of interesting ejaculations, among which we are able to remember only "horrible suspicion!" "wonderful development!" "alack and alas!" with some two or three others. Mr. Leslie is, however, convinced that the portrait of the boy is, as Mr. F. gracefully has it, "inexplicably connected with his own mysterious destiny." He pays a visit to the Countess D., and demands of her if she was, at any time, acquainted with a gentleman called Clairmont. The lady very

---

[5]Nathaniel Parker Willis (1806–1867), as has been mentioned, was an editor at the *Mirror*. Poe is alluding here to Willis's work as a foreign correspondent.

[6]King David's exhortation to his people not to speak of their battle losses lest their enemies rejoice over their sorrow. [II Samuel 1:20]

properly denies all knowledge of that character, and Mr. Leslie's
"mysterious destiny" is in as bad a predicament as ever. He is however fully convinced that Clairmont is the origin of all evil—we do not
mean to say that he is precisely the devil—but the origin of all Mr.
Leslie's evil. Therefore, and on this account, he goes to a masquerade, and, sure enough, Mr. Clairmont, (who has not been heard of
for seven or eight years,) Mr. Clairmont (we suppose through Mr. L's
"mysterious destiny") happens to go, at precisely the same time, to
precisely the same masquerade. But there are surely no bounds to
Mr. Fay's excellent invention. Miss Temple, of course, happens to be
at the same place, and Mr. Leslie is in the act of making love to her
once more, when the "inexplicable" Countess D. whispers into his
ear some ambiguous sentences in which Mr. L. is given to understand
that he must beware of all the Harlequins in the room, one of whom
is Clairmont. Upon leaving the masquerade, somebody hands him a
note requesting him to meet the unknown writer at St. Peter's. While
he is busy reading the paper he is uncivilly interrupted by Clairmont,
who attempts to assassinate him, but is finally put to fight. He hies,
then, to the rendezvous at St. Peter's, where "the unknown" tells him
St. Peter's won't answer, and that he must proceed to the Coliseum.
He goes—why should he not?—and there not only finds the
Countess D. who turns out to be Mrs. Rinaldo, and who now uncorks
her bottle of gratitude, but also Flora Temple, Flora Temple's father,
Clairmont, Kreutzner, a German friend from New York, and, last but
not least, Rosalie Romain herself; all having gone there, no doubt, at
three o'clock in the morning, under the influence of that interesting
young gentleman Norman Leslie's "most inexplicable and mysterious destiny." Matters now come to a crisis. The hero's innocence is
established, and Miss Temple falls into his arms in consequence.
Clairmont, however, thinks he can do nothing better than shoot
Mr. Leslie, and is about to do so, when he is very justly and very dexterously knocked in the head by Mr. Kreutzner. Thus ends the Tale
of the Present Times, and thus ends the most inestimable piece of
balderdash with which the common sense of the good people
of America was ever so openly or so villainously insulted.

We do not mean to say that there is positively *nothing* in Mr. Fay's
novel to commend—but there is indeed very little. One incident is
tolerably managed, in which, at the burning house of Mr. Temple,
Clairmont anticipates Leslie in his design of rescuing Flora. A cotil-
lon scene, too, where Morton, a simple fop, is frequently interrupted
in his attempts at making love to Miss Temple, by the necessity of for-
ward-twoing and *sachezing*, (as Mr. Fay thinks proper to call it) is by
no means very bad, although savoring too much of the farcical. A
duel story told by Kreutzner is really good, but unfortunately not

original, there being a Tale in the *Diary of a Physician,*[7] from which both its matter and manner are evidently borrowed. And here we are obliged to pause; for we can positively think of nothing farther worth even a qualified commendation. The plot, as will appear from the running outline we have given of it, is a monstrous piece of absurdity and incongruity. The characters *have no character*; and, with the exception of Morton, who is, (perhaps) amusing, are, one and all, vapidity itself. No attempt seems to have been made at individualization. All the good ladies and gentlemen are demi-gods and demi-goddesses, and all the bad are—the d—l. The hero, Norman Leslie, "that young and refined man with a leaning to poetry," is a great cox-comb and a great fool. What else must we think of a *bel-esprit* who, in picking up a rose just fallen from the curls of his lady fair, can hit upon no more appropriate phrase with which to make her a presentation of the same, than "Miss Temple, you have dropped your rose—allow me!"—who courts his mistress with a "Dear, dear Flora, how I love you!"—who calls a *buffet* a *bufet,* an *improvisatore* an *improvisitore*—who, before bestowing charity, is always ready with the canting question if the object be *deserving*—who is everlastingly talking of his foe "sleeping in the same red grave with himself," as if American sextons made a common practice of burying two people together—and, who having not a sous in his pocket at page 86, pulls out a handful at page 87, although he has had no opportunity of obtaining a copper in the interim?

As regards Mr. Fay's *style,* it is unworthy of a school-boy. The "Editor of the New York Mirror" has either never seen an edition of Murray's Grammar, or he has been a-Willising so long as to have forgotten his vernacular language. Let us examine one or two of his sentences at random. Page 28, vol. i. "He was doomed to wander through the *far-therest* climes alone and branded." Why not say at once *farthererterest?* Page 150, vol. i. "Yon kindling orb should be hers; and that faint spark close to its side should teach her how dim and yet how near my soul was to her own." What is the meaning of all this? Is Mr. Leslie's soul dim to her own, as well as near to her own?—for the sentence implies as much. Suppose we say "should teach her how dim was my soul, and yet how near to her own." Page 101, vol. i. "You are both right and both wrong—you, Miss Romain, to judge so harshly of all men who are not versed in the easy elegance of the drawing room, and your father in too great lenity towards men of sense, &c." This is really something new, but we are sorry to say, something

---

[7]Passages from *The Diary of a Late Physician,* Samuel Warren (1807–1877). First published in *Blackwood's Magazine,* 1830–1837.

incomprehensible. Suppose we translate it. "You are both right and both wrong—you, Miss Romain, *are both right and wrong* to judge so harshly of all not versed in the elegance of the drawing-room, &c.; and your father *is both right and wrong* in too great lenity towards men of sense."—Mr. Fay, have you ever visited Ireland in your peregrinations? But the book is full to the brim of such absurdities, and it is useless to pursue the matter any farther. There is not a single page of Norman Leslie in which even a schoolboy would fail to detect at least two or three gross errors in Grammar, and some two or three most egregious sins against common-sense.

We will dismiss the "Editor of the Mirror" with a few questions. When did you ever know, Mr. Fay, of any prosecuting attorney behaving so much like a bear as *your* prosecuting attorney in the novel of Norman Leslie? When did you ever hear of an American Court of Justice objecting to the testimony of a witness on the ground that the said witness *had an interest* in the cause at issue? What do you mean by informing us at page 84, vol. i, "that you *think* much faster than you write?" What do you mean by "*the wind roaring in the air?*" see page 26, vol. i. What do you mean by "an *unshadowed* Italian girl?" see page 67, vol. ii. Why are you always talking about "stamping of feet," "kindling and flashing of eyes," "plunging and parrying," "cutting and thrusting," "passes through the body," "gashes open in the cheek," "sculls cleft down," "hands cut off," and blood gushing and bubbling, and doing God knows what else—all of which pretty expressions may be found on page 88, vol. i.? What "mysterious and inexplicable destiny" compels you to the so frequent use, in all its inflections, of that euphonical dyssyllable *blister*? We will call to your recollection some few instances in which you have employed it. Page 185, vol. i. "But an arrival from the city brought the fearful intelligence in all its *blistering* and naked details." Page 193, vol. i. "What but the glaring and *blistering* truth of the charge would select him, &c." Page 39, vol. ii. "Wherever the winds of heaven wafted the English language, the *blistering* story must have been echoed." Page 150, vol. ii. "Nearly seven years had passed away, and here he found himself, as at first, still marked with the *blistering* and burning brand." Here we have a *blistering* detail, a *blistering* truth, a *blistering* story, and a *blistering* brand, to say nothing of innumerable other blisters interspersed throughout the book. But we have done with Norman Leslie,—if ever we saw as silly a thing, may we be—blistered.

Review
[*Southern Literary Messenger,* April 1836]

Joseph Rodman Drake, *The Culprit Fay, and other Poems*
(New York: George Dearborn)

Fitz-Greene Halleck, *Alnwick Castle, with other Poems*
(New York: George Dearborn)

Though Poe almost never signed his magazine writing, he was not trying to hide his identity. His presence on the masthead made it clear to his readers that he was the editor behind the editorial "we." Poe the critic was suspicious of anonymity and took refuge in it only rarely. Accordingly, in this review, he identifies the two authors who have criticized him in other periodicals, and addresses them by name. They themselves have referred to him as, simply, "the critic."

As his response to Col. Stone's criticisms reveals, Poe was likewise suspicious of critics who hid behind unsubstantiated generalities. He demanded extensive substantiation of himself, in fact, when he wrote criticism. In seeking to prove that Joseph Rodman Drake's poetry was fanciful rather than truly imaginative, Poe presented a raft of specific examples—so many that some have been trimmed from this selection in the interest of saving space. Poe pronounced Halleck a weaker poet than Drake, and, he implied, a plagiaristic one as well. In suggesting that Halleck borrowed his images from Wordsworth, Poe gives early voice to his own critical and creative obsession with originality.

Before entering upon the detailed notice which we propose of the volumes before us, we wish to speak a few words in regard to the present state of American criticism.

It must be visible to all who meddle with literary matters, that of late years a thorough revolution has been effected in the censorship of our press. That this revolution is infinitely for the worse we believe. There was a time, it is true, when we cringed to foreign opinion—let us even say when we paid a most servile deference to British critical *dicta*. That an American book could, by any possibility, be worthy perusal, was an idea by no means extensively prevalent in the land; and if we were induced to read at all the productions of our native writers, it was only after repeated assurances from England that such productions were not altogether contemptible. But there was, at all events, a shadow of excuse, and a slight basis of reason for a subserviency so grotesque. Even now, perhaps, it would not be far wrong to assert that such basis of reason may still exist. Let us grant that in many of the abstract sciences—that even in Theology, in Medicine, in Law, in Oratory, in the Mechanical Arts, we have no competitors whatever, still nothing but the most egregious national vanity would assign us a place, in the matter of Polite Literature, upon a level with the elder and riper climes of Europe, the earliest steps of whose children are among the groves of magnificently endowed Academies, and whose innumerable men of leisure, and of consequent learning, drink daily from those august fountains of inspiration which burst around them everywhere from out the tombs of their immortal dead, and from out their hoary and trophied monument of chivalry and song. In paying then, as a nation, a respectful and not undue deference to a supremacy rarely questioned but by prejudice or ignorance, we should, of course, be doing nothing more than acting in a rational manner. The *excess* of our subserviency was blameable—but, as we have before said, this very excess might have found a shadow of excuse in the strict justice, if properly regulated, of the principle from which it issued. Not so, however, with our present follies. We are becoming boisterous and arrogant in the pride of a too speedily assumed literary freedom. We throw off, with the most presumptuous and unmeaning hauteur, *all* deference whatever to foreign opinion—we forget, in the puerile inflation of vanity, that *the world* is the true theatre of the biblical histrio—we get up a hue and cry about the necessity of encouraging native writers of merit—we blindly fancy that we can accomplish this by indiscriminate puffing of good, bad, and indifferent, without taking the trouble to consider that what we choose to denominate encouragement is thus, by its general application, rendered precisely the reverse. In a word, so far from being ashamed of the many disgraceful literary failures to which our own inordinate vanities and misapplied patriotism have lately given birth, and so far from deeply lamenting that these daily puerilities are of home manufacture, we adhere pertinaciously to our original blindly conceived idea, and thus often find ourselves involved in the gross paradox of liking a stupid book the better, because, sure enough, its stupidity is American.*

Deeply lamenting this unjustifiable state of public feeling, it has been our constant endeavor, since assuming the Editorial duties of this Journal, to stem, with what little abilities we possess, a current so disastrously undermining the health and prosperity of our literature. We have seen our efforts applauded by men whose applauses we value. From all quarters we have received abundant private as well as

---

*This charge of indiscriminate puffing will, of course, only apply to the *general* character of our criticism—there are some noble exceptions. We wish also especially to discriminate between those *notices* of new works which are intended merely to call public attention to them, and deliberate criticism on the works themselves.

public testimonials in favor of our *Critical Notices,* and, until very lately, have heard from no respectable source one word impugning their integrity or candor. In looking over, however, a number of the New York Commercial Advertiser, we meet the following paragraph.

> The last number of the Southern Literary Messenger is very readable and respectable. The contributions to the Messenger are much better than the original matter. The critical department of this work— much as it would seem to boast itself of impartiality and discernment,—is in our opinion decidedly *quacky.* There is in it a great assumption of acumen, which is completely unsustained. Many a work has been slashingly condemned therein, of which the critic himself could not write a page, were he to die for it. This affectation of eccentric sternness in criticism, without the power to back one's suit withal, so far from deserving praise, as some suppose, merits the strongest reprehension.—[*Philadelphia Gazette.*]

We are entirely of opinion with the Philadelphia Gazette in relation to the Southern Literary Messenger, and take this occasion to express our total dissent from the numerous and lavish encomiums we have seen bestowed upon its critical notices. Some few of them have been judicious, fair and candid; bestowing praise and censure with judgment and impartiality; but by far the greater number of those we have read, have been flippant, unjust, untenable and uncritical. The duty of the critic is to act as judge, not as enemy, of the writer whom he reviews; a distinction of which the Zoilus of the Messenger seems not to be aware. It is possible to review a book severely, without bestowing opprobrious epithets upon the writer: to condemn with courtesy, if not with kindness. The critic of the Messenger has been eulogized for his scorching and scarifying abilities, and he thinks it incumbent upon him to keep up his reputation in that line, by sneers, sarcasm, and downright abuse; by straining his vision with microscopic intensity in search of faults, and shutting his eyes, with all his might, to beauties. Moreover, we have detected him, more than once, in blunders quite as gross as those on which it was his pleasure to descant.*

In the paragraph from the Philadelphia Gazette, (which is edited by Mr. Willis Gaylord Clark, one of the Editors of the Knickerbocker)

---

*In addition to these things we observe, in the New York Mirror, what follows: "Those who have read the Notices of American books in a certain Southern Monthly, which is striving to gain notoriety by the loudness of its abuse, may find amusement in the sketch on another page, entitled 'The Successful Novel.' The Southern Literary Messenger knows ☞ *by experience* ☜ what it is to write a successless novel." We have, in this case, only to deny, flatly, the assertion of the Mirror. The Editor of the Messenger never in his life wrote or published, or attempted to publish, a novel either successful or *successless.*

we find nothing at which we have any desire to take exception. Mr. C. has a right to think us *quacky* if he pleases, and we do not remember having assumed for a moment that we could write a single line of the works we have reviewed. But there is something equivocal, to say the least, in the remarks of Col. Stone. He acknowledges that "*some* of our notices have been judicious, fair, and candid, bestowing praise and censure with judgment and impartiality." This being the case, how can he reconcile his *total* dissent from the public verdict in our favor, with the dictates of justice? We are accused too of bestowing "opprobrious epithets" upon writers whom we review, and in the paragraph so accusing us we are called nothing less than "flippant, unjust, and uncritical."

But there is another point of which we disapprove. While in our reviews we have at all times been particularly careful *not* to deal in generalities, and have never, if we remember aright, advanced in any single instance an unsupported assertion, our accuser has forgotten to give us any better evidence of our flippancy, injustice, personality, and gross blundering, than the solitary *dictum* of Col. Stone. We call upon the Colonel for assistance in this dilemma. We wish to be shown our blunders that we may correct them—to be made aware of our flippancy, that we may avoid it hereafter—and above all to have our personalities pointed out that we may proceed forthwith with a repentant spirit, to make the *amende honorable.* In default of this aid from the Editor of the Commercial we shall take it for granted that we are neither blunderers, flippant, personal, nor unjust.

Who will deny that in regard to individual poems no definitive opinions can exist, so long as to Poetry in the abstract we attach no definite idea? Yet it is a common thing to hear our critics, day after day, pronounce, with a positive air, laudatory or condemnatory sentences, *en masse,* upon metrical works of whose merits and demerits they have, in the first place, virtually confessed an utter ignorance, in confessing ignorance of all determinate principles by which to regulate a decision. Poetry has never been defined to the satisfaction of all parties. Perhaps, in the present condition of language it never will be. Words cannot hem it in. Its intangible and purely spiritual nature refuses to be bound down within the widest horizon of mere sounds. But it is not, therefore, misunderstood—at least, not by all men is it misunderstood. Very far from it. If, indeed, there be any one circle of thought distinctly and palpably marked out from amid the jarring and tumultuous chaos of human intelligence, it is that evergreen and radiant Paradise which the true poet knows, and knows alone, as the limited realm of his authority—as the circumscribed Eden of his dreams. But a definition is a thing of words—a conception of ideas. And thus while we readily believe that Poesy, the term, it will be troublesome, if not impossible to define—still, with its image vividly existing in the world, we apprehend no difficulty in so describing Poesy, the Sentiment, as to imbue even the most obtuse intellect with a comprehension of it sufficiently distinct for all the purposes of practical analysis.

To look upwards from any existence, material or immaterial, to its *design,* is, perhaps, the most direct, and the most unerring method of attaining a just notion of the nature of the existence itself. Nor is the principle at fault when we turn our eyes from Nature even to Nature's God. We find certain faculties implanted within us, and arrive at a more plausible conception of the character and attributes of those faculties, by considering, with what finite judgment we possess, the *intention* of the Deity in so implanting them within us, than by any actual investigation of their powers, or any speculative deductions from their visible and material effects. Thus, for example, we discover in all men a disposition to look with reverence upon superiority, whether real or supposititious. In some, this disposition is to be recognized with difficulty, and, in very peculiar cases, we are occasionally even led to doubt its existence altogether, until circumstances beyond the common routine bring it accidentally into development. In others again it forms a prominent and distinctive feature of character, and is rendered palpably evident in its excesses. But in all human beings it is, in a greater or less degree, finally perceptible. It has been, therefore, justly considered a primitive sentiment. Phrenologists[1] call it Veneration. It is, indeed, the instinct given to man by God as security for his own worship. And although, preserving its nature, it becomes perverted from its principal purpose, and although, swerving from that purpose, it serves to modify the relations of human society—the relations of father and child, of master and slave, of the ruler and the ruled—its primitive essence is nevertheless the same, and by a reference to primal causes, may at any moment be determined.

Very nearly akin to this feeling, and liable to the same analysis, is the Faculty of Ideality—which is the sentiment of Poesy. This sentiment is the sense of the beautiful, of the sublime, and of the mystical.* Thence spring immediately admiration of the fair flowers, the

---

[1]Phrenology: A now discredited scientific practice, popular in Poe's day, in which the skull was divided into specific areas corresponding to various character traits. Phrenologists held that people's individual qualities could be inferred from the process of mapping the distinctive bumps and ridges on their heads. Initially taken with phrenology, Poe lost his belief in it as a science by the early 1840s.

*We separate the sublime and the mystical—for, despite of high authorities, we are firmly convinced that the latter *may* exist, in the most vivid degree, without giving rise to the sense of the former.

fairer forests, the bright valleys and rivers and mountains of the
Earth—and love of the gleaming stars and other burning glories of
Heaven—and, mingled up inextricably with this love and this admiration of Heaven and of Earth, the unconquerable desire—*to know.*
Poesy is the sentiment of Intellectual Happiness here, and the Hope
of a higher Intellectual Happiness hereafter.* Imagination is its
Soul.† With the *passions* of mankind—although it may modify them
greatly—although it may exalt, or inflame, or purify, or control
them—it would require little ingenuity to prove that it has no
inevitable, and indeed no necessary co-existence. We have hitherto
spoken of Poetry in the abstract: we come now to speak of it in its
every-day acceptation—that is to say, of the practical result arising
from the sentiment we have considered.

And now it appears evident, that since Poetry, in this new sense, *is*
the practical result, expressed in language, of this Poetic Sentiment
in certain individuals, the only proper method of testing the merits
of a poem is by measuring its capabilities of exciting the Poetic

---

*The consciousness of this truth was possessed by no mortal more fully than by Shelley,
although he has only once especially alluded to it. In his *Hymn to Intellectual Beauty* we
find these lines.

> While yet a boy I sought for ghosts, and sped
>   Through many a listening chamber, cave and ruin,
>   And starlight wood, with fearful steps pursuing
> Hopes of high talk with the departed dead:
> I called on poisonous names with which our youth is fed:
>   I was not heard: I saw them not.
>   When musing deeply on the lot
> Of life at that sweet time when birds are wooing
>   All vital things that wake to bring
>   News of buds and blossoming
>   Sudden thy shadow fell on me—
> I shriek'd and clasp'd my hands in ecstacy!

> I vow'd that I would dedicate my powers
>   To thee and thine: have I not kept the vow?
> With beating heart and streaming eyes, even now
> I call the phantoms of a thousand hours
> Each from his voiceless grave: they have in vision'd bowers
>   Of studious zeal or love's delight
>   Outwatch'd with me the envious night:
> They know that never joy illum'd my brow,
>   Unlink'd with hope that thou wouldst free,
>   This world from its dark slavery,
>   That thou, O awful *Loveliness,*
> Wouldst give whate'er these words cannot express.

†Imagination is, possibly, in man, a lesser degree of the creative power in God. What
the Deity imagines, *is,* but *was not* before. What man imagines, *is,* but *was* also. The
mind of man cannot imagine what *is not.* This latter point may be demonstrated.—*See
Les Premiers Traits de L'Erudition Universelle, par M. Le Baron de Bielfield, 1767.*

Sentiment in others. And to this end we have many aids—in observation, in experience, in ethical analysis, and in the dictates of common sense. Hence the *Poeta nascitur*,[2] which is indisputably true if we consider the Poetic Sentiment, becomes the merest of absurdities when we regard it in reference to the practical result. We do not hesitate to say that a man highly endowed with the powers of Causality—that is to say, a man of metaphysical acumen—will, even with a very deficient share of Ideality, compose a finer poem (if we test it, as we should, by its measure of exciting the Poetic Sentiment) than one who, without such metaphysical acumen, shall be gifted, in the most extraordinary degree, with the faculty of Ideality. For a poem is not the Poetic faculty, but *the means* of exciting it in mankind. Now these means the metaphysician may discover by analysis of their effects in other cases than his own, without even conceiving the nature of these effects—thus arriving at a result which the unaided Ideality of his competitor would be utterly unable, except by accident, to attain. It is more than possible that the man who, of all writers, living or dead, has been most successful in writing the purest of all poems—that is to say, poems which excite most purely, most exclusively, and most powerfully the imaginative faculties in men—owed his extraordinary and almost magical pre-eminence rather to metaphysical than poetical powers. We allude to the author of Christabel, of the Rime of the Auncient Mariner, and of Love—to Coleridge—whose head, if we mistake not its character, gave no great phrenological tokens of Ideality, while the organs of Causality and Comparison were most singularly developed.

Perhaps at this particular moment there are no American poems held in so high estimation by our countrymen, as the poems of Drake, and of Halleck. The exertions of Mr. George Dearborn have no doubt a far greater share in creating this feeling than the lovers of literature for its own sake and spiritual uses would be willing to admit. We have indeed seldom seen more beautiful volumes than the volumes now before us. But an adventitious interest of a loftier nature—the interest of the living in the memory of the beloved dead—attaches itself to the few literary remains of Drake. The poems which are now given to us with his name are nineteen in number; and whether all, or whether even the best of his writings, it is our present purpose to speak of these alone, since upon this edition his poetical reputation to all time will most probably depend. . . .

It is more than probable that from among ten readers of the *Culprit Fay*, nine would immediately pronounce it a poem betokening the most extraordinary powers of imagination, and of these nine,

---

[2] "poet is born"

perhaps five or six, poets themselves, and fully impressed with the truth of what we have already assumed, that Ideality is indeed the soul of the Poetic Sentiment, would feel embarrassed between a half-consciousness that they *ought* to admire the production, and a wonder that they *do not.* This embarrassment would then arise from an indistinct conception of the results in which Ideality is rendered manifest. Of these results some few are seen in the *Culprit Fay,* but the greater part of it is utterly destitute of any evidence of imagination whatever. . . . what is so frequently termed the imaginative power of this story, lies especially—we should have rather said is thought to lie—in . . . [passages that] embody, principally, mere specifications of qualities, of habiliments, of punishments, of occupations, of circumstances &c, which the poet has believed in unison with the size, firstly, and secondly with the nature of his Fairies. To all which may be added specifications of other animal existences (such as the toad, the beetle, the lance-fly, the fire-fly and the like) supposed also to be in accordance. An example will best illustrate our meaning upon this point—we take it from page 20.

> He put his acorn helmet on;
> It was plumed of the silk of the thistle down;
> The corslet plate that guarded his breast
> Was once the wild bee's golden vest;
> His cloak of a thousand mingled dyes,
> Was formed of the wings of butterflies;
> His shield was the shell of a lady-bug queen,
> Studs of gold on a ground of green;*
> And the quivering lance which he brandished bright,
> Was the sting of a wasp he had slain in a fight.

We shall now be understood. Were any of the admirers of the *Culprit Fay* asked their opinion of these lines, they would most probably speak in high terms of the *imagination* they display. Yet let the most stolid and the most confessedly unpoetical of these admirers only try the experiment, and he will find, possibly to his extreme surprise, that he himself will have no difficulty whatever in substituting for the equipments of the Fairy, as assigned by the poet, other equipments equally comfortable, no doubt, and equally in unison with the preconceived size, character, and other qualities of the equipped. Why we could accoutre him as well ourselves—let us see.

> His blue-bell helmet, we have heard,
> Was plumed with the down of the humming-bird,

---

*Chestnut color, or more slack,
 Gold upon a ground of black.
                    Ben Jonson

> The corslet on his bosom bold
> Was once the locust's coat of gold,
> His cloak, of a thousand mingled hues,
> Was the velvet violet, wet with dews,
> His target was the crescent shell
> Of the small sea Sidrophel,
> And a glittering beam from a maiden's eye
> Was the lance which he proudly wav'd on high.

The truth is, that the only requisite for writing verses of this nature, *ad libitum,* is a tolerable acquaintance with the qualities of the objects to be detailed, and a very moderate endowment of the faculty of Comparison—which is the chief constituent of *Fancy* or the powers of combination. A thousand such lines may be composed without exercising in the least degree the Poetic Sentiment, which is Ideality, Imagination, or the creative ability. And, as we have before said, the greater portion of the *Culprit Fay* is occupied with these, or similar things, and upon such, depends very nearly, if not altogether, its reputation. We select another example from page 25.

> But oh! how fair the shape that lay
>   Beneath a rainbow bending bright,
> She seem'd to the entranced Fay
>   The loveliest of the forms of light;
> Her mantle was the purple rolled
>   At twilight in the west afar;
> 'Twas tied with threads of dawning gold,
>   And button'd with a sparkling star.
> Her face was like the lily roon
>   That veils the vestal planet's hue;
> Her eyes, two beamlets from the moon
>   Set floating in the welkin blue.
> Her hair is like the sunny beam,
> And the diamond gems which round it gleam
> Are the pure drops of dewy even,
> That ne'er have left their native heaven.

Here again the faculty of Comparison is alone exercised, and no mind possessing the faculty in any ordinary degree would find a difficulty in substituting for the materials employed by the poet other materials equally as good. But viewed as mere efforts of the Fancy and without reference to Ideality, the lines just quoted are much worse than those which were taken from page 20. A congruity was observable in the accoutrements of the Ouphe, and we had no trouble in forming a distinct conception of his appearance when so accoutred. But the most vivid powers of Comparison can attach no definitive idea to even "the loveliest form of light," when habited in a mantle of "rolled purple tied with threads of dawn and buttoned

with a star," and sitting at the same time under a rainbow with "beamlet" eyes and a visage of "lily roon."

But if these things evince no Ideality in their author, do they not
excite it in others?—if so, we must conclude, that without being himself imbued with the Poetic Sentiment, he has still succeeded in writing a fine poem—a supposition as we have before endeavored to
show, not altogether paradoxical. Most assuredly we think not. In the
case of a great majority of readers the only sentiment aroused by compositions of this order is a species of vague wonder at the writer's *ingenuity,* and it is this indeterminate sense of wonder which passes but
too frequently current for the proper influence of the Poetic power.
For our own parts we plead guilty to a predominant sense of the ludicrous while occupied in the perusal of the poem before us—a sense
whose promptings we sincerely and honestly endeavored to quell, perhaps not altogether successfully. . . . That a feeling of this nature is
utterly at war with the Poetic Sentiment, will not be disputed by those
who comprehend the character of the sentiment itself. This character
is finely shadowed out in that popular although vague idea so prevalent throughout all time, that a species of melancholy is inseparably
connected with the higher manifestations of the beautiful. But with
the numerous and seriously-adduced incongruities of the Culprit Fay,
we find it generally impossible to connect other ideas than those of
the ridiculous. We are bidden, in the first place, and in a tone of sentiment and language adapted to the loftiest breathings of the Muse,
to imagine a race of Fairies in the vicinity of West Point. We are told,
with a grave air, of their camp, of their king, and especially of their
sentry, who is a wood-tick. We are informed that an Ouphe of about
an inch in height has committed a deadly sin in falling in love with a
mortal maiden, who may, very possibly, be six feet in her stockings.
The consequence to the Ouphe is—what? Why, that he has "dyed his
wings," "broken his elfin chain," and "quenched his flame-wood
lamp." And he is therefore sentenced to what? To catch a spark from
the tail of a falling star, and a drop of water from the belly of a sturgeon. What are his equipments for the first adventure? An acorn helmet, a thistle-down plume, a butterfly cloak, a lady-bug shield, cockle-
seed spurs, and a fire-fly horse. How does he ride to the second? On
the back of a bull-frog. What are his opponents in the one? "Drizzly
mists," "sulphur and smoke," "shadowy hands" and "flame-shot
tongues." What in the other? "Mailed shrimps," "prickly prongs,"
"blood-red leeches," "jellied quarls," "stony star fishes," "lancing
squabs" and "soldier crabs." Is that all? No—Although only an inch
high he is in imminent danger of seduction from a "sylphid queen,"
dressed in a mantle of "rolled purple," "tied with threads of dawning
gold," "buttoned with a sparkling star," and sitting under a rainbow

with "beamlet eyes" and a countenance of "lily roon." In our account of all this matter we have had reference to the book—and to the book alone. It will be difficult to prove us guilty in any degree of distortion or exaggeration. Yet such are the puerilities we daily find ourselves called upon to admire, as among the loftiest efforts of the human mind, and which not to assign a rank with the proud trophies of the matured and vigorous genius of England, is to prove ourselves at once a fool, a maligner, and no patriot.*

As an instance of what may be termed the sublimely ridiculous we quote the following lines from page 17.

> With sweeping tail and quivering fin,
>   Through the wave the sturgeon flew,
> And like the heaven-shot javelin,
>   He sprung above the waters blue.
>
> Instant as the star-fall light,
>   He plunged into the deep again,
> But left an arch of silver bright
>   The rainbow of the moony main.
>
> *It was a strange and lovely sight*
>   *To see the puny goblin there;*
> *He seemed an angel form of light*
>   *With azure wing and sunny hair,*
> *Throned on a cloud of purple fair*
> *Circled with blue and edged with white*
> *And sitting at the fall of even*
> *Beneath the bow of summer heaven.*

The verses here italicized, if considered without their context, have a certain air of dignity, elegance, and chastity of thought. If however we apply the context, we are immediately overwhelmed with the grotesque. It is impossible to read without laughing, such expressions as "It was a strange and lovely sight"—"He seemed an angel form of light"—"And sitting at the fall of even, beneath the bow of summer heaven" to a Fairy—a goblin—an Ouphe—half an inch high, dressed in an acorn helmet and butterfly-cloak, and sitting on the water in a muscle-shell, with a "brown-backed sturgeon" turning somersets over his head.

In a world where evil is a mere consequence of good, and good a mere consequence of evil—in short where all of which we have any

---

*A review of Drake's poems, emanating from one of our proudest Universities, does not scruple to make use of the following language in relation to the *Culprit Fay. "It is, to say the least, an elegant production, the purest specimen of Ideality we have ever met with, sustaining in each incident a most bewitching interest. Its very title is enough,"* &c. &c. We quote these expressions as a fair specimen of the general unphilosophical and adulatory tenor of our criticism.

conception is good or bad only by comparison—we have never yet
been fully able to appreciate the validity of that decision which would
debar the critic from enforcing upon his readers the merits or
demerits of a work by placing it in juxta-position with another. It
seems to us that an adage based in the purest ignorance has had
more to do with this popular feeling than any just reason founded
upon common sense. Thinking thus, we shall have no scruple in
illustrating our opinion in regard to what *is not* Ideality or the Poetic
Power, by an example of what *is*.* We have already given the description of the Sylphid Queen in the *Culprit Fay*. In the *Queen Mab* of
Shelley a Fairy is thus introduced—

> Those who had looked upon the sight,
>   Passing all human glory,
> Saw not the yellow moon,
> Saw not the mortal scene,
> Heard not the night wind's rush,
> Heard not an earthly sound,
> Saw but the fairy pageant,
> Heard but the heavenly strains
> That filled the lonely dwelling—

and thus described—

> The Fairy's frame was slight; yon fibrous cloud
> That catches but the palest tinge of even,
> And which the straining eye can hardly seize
> When melting into eastern twilight's shadow,
> Were scarce so thin, so slight; but the fair star
> That gems the glittering coronet of morn,
> *Sheds not a light so mild, so powerful,*
> *As that which, bursting from the Fairy's form,*
> *Spread a purpureal halo round the scene,*
>   *Yet with an undulating motion,*
>   *Swayed to her outline gracefully.*

In these exquisite lines the Faculty of mere Comparison is but little exercised—that of Ideality in a wonderful degree. It is probable
that in a similar case the poet we are now reviewing would have
formed the face of the Fairy of the "fibrous cloud," her arms of the
"pale tinge of even," her eyes of the "fair stars," and her body of the

---

*As examples of entire poems of the purest ideality, we would cite the *Prometheus
Vinctus* of Æschylus, the *Inferno* of Dante, Cervantes' *Destruction of Numantia,* the
Comus of Milton, Pope's *Rape of the Lock,* Burns' *Tam O' Shanter,* the *Auncient Mariner,*
the *Christabel,* and the *Kubla Khan* of Coleridge; and most especially the *Sensitive Plant*
of Shelley, and the *Nightingale* of Keats. We have seen American poems evincing the
faculty in the highest degree.

"twilight shadow." Having so done, his admirers would have congratulated him upon his *imagination,* not taking the trouble to think that they themselves could at any moment *imagine* a Fairy of materials equally as good, and conveying an equally distinct idea. Their mistake would be precisely analogous to that of many a schoolboy who admires the imagination displayed in *Jack the Giant-Killer,* and is finally rejoiced at discovering his own imagination to surpass that of the author, since the monsters destroyed by Jack are only about forty feet in height, and he himself has no trouble in imagining some of one hundred and forty. It will be seen that the Fairy of Shelley is not a mere compound of incongruous natural objects, inartificially put together, and unaccompanied by any *moral* sentiment—but a being, in the illustration of whose nature some physical elements are used collaterally as adjuncts, while the main conception springs immediately *or thus apparently springs,* from the brain of the poet, enveloped in the moral sentiments of grace, of color, of motion—of the beautiful, of the mystical, of the august—in short of *the ideal.* *

It is by no means our intention to deny that in the *Culprit Fay* are passages of a different order from those to which we have objected—passages evincing a degree of imagination not to be discovered in the plot, conception, or general execution of the poem. The opening stanza will afford us a tolerable example.

> 'Tis the middle watch of a summer's night—
> *The earth is dark, but the heavens are bright*
> Naught is seen in the vault on high
> But the moon, and the stars, and the cloudless sky,
> And the flood which rolls its milky hue
> A river of light on the welkin blue.
> The moon looks down on old Cronest,
> She mellows the shades of his shaggy breast,
> And seems his huge grey form to throw
> In a silver cone on the wave below;
> His sides are broken by spots of shade,
> By the walnut bough and the cedar made,
> And through their clustering branches dark
> *Glimmers and dies* the fire-fly's spark—
> Like starry twinkles that momently break
> Through the rifts of the gathering tempest rack.

There is Ideality in these lines—but except in the case of the words italicized—it is Ideality *not of a high order.* We have it is true, a

---

*Among things, which not only in our opinion, but in the opinion of far wiser and better men, are to be ranked with the mere prettinesses of the Muse, are the positive similies so abundant in the writings of antiquity, and so much insisted upon by the critics of the reign of Queen Anne.

collection of natural objects, each individually of great beauty, and, if actually seen as in nature, capable of exciting in any mind, through the means of the Poetic Sentiment more or less inherent in all, a certain sense of the beautiful. But to view such natural objects as they exist, and to behold them through the medium of words, are different things. Let us pursue the idea that such a collection as we have here will produce, of necessity, the Poetic Sentiment, and we may as well make up our minds to believe that a catalogue of such expressions as moon, sky, trees, rivers, mountains &c, shall be capable of exciting it,—it is merely an extension of the principle. But in the line "the earth is dark, *but* the heavens are bright" besides the simple mention of the "dark earth" and the "bright heaven," we have, directly, the moral sentiment of the brightness of the sky compensating for the darkness of the earth—and thus, indirectly, of the happiness of a future state compensating for the miseries of a present. All this is effected by the simple introduction of the word *but* between the "dark heaven" and the "bright earth"—this introduction, however, was prompted by the Poetic Sentiment, and by the Poetic Sentiment alone. The case is analogous in the expression "glimmers and dies," where the imagination is exalted by the moral sentiment of beauty heightened in dissolution. . . .

Halleck's poetical powers appear to us essentially inferior, upon the whole, to those of his friend Drake. . . . By the hackneyed phrase, *sportive elegance,* we might possibly designate at once the general character of his writings and the very loftiest praise to which he is justly entitled.

Alnwick Castle is an irregular poem of one hundred and twenty-eight lines—was written, as we are informed, in October 1822—and is descriptive of a seat of the Duke of Northumberland, in Northumberlandshire, England. The effect of the first stanza is materially impaired by a defect in its grammatical arrangement. The fine lines,

> Home of the Percy's high-born race,
>   Home of their beautiful and brave,
> Alike their birth and burial place,
>   Their cradle and their grave!

are of the nature of an invocation, and thus require a continuation of the address to the "Home, &c." We are consequently disappointed when the stanza proceeds with—

> Still sternly o'er the castle gate
> *Their* house's Lion stands in state
>   As in *his* proud departed hours;
> And warriors frown in stone on high,
> And feudal banners "flout the sky"
>   Above *his* princely towers.

The objects of allusion here vary, in an awkward manner, from the castle to the Lion, and from the Lion to the towers. By writing the verses thus the difficulty would be remedied.

> Still sternly o'er the castle gate
> *Thy* house's Lion stands in state,
>   As in his proud departed hours;
> And warriors frown in stone on high,
> And feudal banners "flout the sky"
>   Above *thy* princely towers.

The second stanza, without evincing in any measure the loftier powers of a poet, has that quiet air of grace, both in thought and expression, which seems to be the prevailing feature of the Muse of Halleck.

> A gentle hill its side inclines,
>   Lovely in England's fadeless green,
> To meet the quiet stream which winds
>   Through this romantic scene
> As silently and sweetly still,
> As when, at evening, on that hill,
>   While summer's wind blew soft and low,
> Seated by gallant Hotspur's side
> His Katherine was a happy bride
>   A thousand years ago.

There are one or two brief passages in the poem evincing a degree of rich imagination not elsewhere perceptible throughout the book. For example—

> Gaze on the Abbey's ruined pile:
>   Does not the succoring Ivy keeping,
> Her watch around it seem to smile
>   As o'er a lov'd one sleeping?

and,

> One solitary turret gray
>   Still tells in melancholy glory
> The legend of the Cheviot day.

The commencement of the fourth stanza is of the highest order of Poetry, and partakes, in a happy manner, of that quaintness of expression so effective an adjunct to Ideality, when employed by the Shelleys, the Coleridges and the Tennysons, but so frequently debased, and rendered ridiculous, by the herd of brainless imitators.

> Wild roses by the Abbey towers
>   Are gay in their young bud and bloom:
> *They were born of a race of funeral flowers,*

> That garlanded in long-gone hours,
>   A Templar's knightly tomb.

The tone employed in the concluding portions of Alnwick Castle,
is, we sincerely think, reprehensible, and unworthy of Halleck. No
true poet can unite in any manner the low burlesque with the ideal,
and not be conscious of incongruity and of a profanation. Such
verses as

> Men in the coal and cattle line
>   From Teviot's bard and hero land,
>   From royal Berwick's beach of sand,
>   From Wooller, Morpeth, Hexham, and
>   Newcastle upon Tyne,

may lay claim to oddity—but no more. These things are the defects
and not the beauties of *Don Juan*. They are totally out of keeping with
the graceful and delicate manner of the initial portions of *Alnwick
Castle*, and serve no better purpose than to deprive the entire poem
of all unity of effect. If a poet must be farcical, let him be just that,
and nothing else. To be drolly sentimental is bad enough, as we have
just seen in certain passages of the *Culprit Fay*, but to be sentimental-
ly droll is a thing intolerable to men, and Gods, and columns. . . .

The verses entitled *Burns* consist of thirty eight quatrains—the
three first lines of each quatrain being of four feet, the fourth of
three. This poem has many of the traits of *Alnwick Castle*, and bears
also a strong resemblance to some of the writings of Wordsworth. Its
chief merit, and indeed the chief merit, so we think, of all the poems
of Halleck is the merit of *expression*. In the brief extracts from *Burns*
which follow, our readers will recognize the peculiar character of
which we speak.

> Wild Rose of Alloway! my thanks:
>   Thou mind'st me of *that autumn noon*
> *When first we met upon "the banks*
>   *And braes o' bonny Doon"*—

> Like thine, beneath the thorn-tree's bough,
>   My sunny hour was glad and brief—
> We've crossed the winter sea, *and thou*
>   *Art withered—flower and leaf.*

> *There have been loftier themes than his,*
>   *And longer scrolls and louder lyres*
> *And lays lit up with Poesy's*
>   *Purer and holier fires.*

And when he breathes his master-lay
    Of Alloway's witch-haunted wall
All passions in our frames of clay
    Come thronging at his call.

———

Such graves as his are pilgrim-shrines,
Shrines to no code or creed confined—
The Delphian vales, the Palestines,
    The Meccas of the mind.

———

They linger by the Doon's low trees,
    And pastoral Nith, and wooded Ayr,
And round thy Sepulchres, Dumfries!
    The Poet's tomb is there.

. . . But we must bring our notice to a close. It will be seen that while we are willing to admire in many respects the poems before us, we feel obliged to dissent materially from that public opinion (perhaps not fairly ascertained) which would assign them a very brilliant rank in the empire of Poesy. That we have among us poets of the loftiest order we believe—but we do *not* believe that these poets are Drake and Halleck.

Review

[*Southern Literary Messenger,* April 1836]

James K. Paulding, *Slavery in the United States*
(New York: Harper and Brothers)

William Drayton, *The South Vindicated from the Treason and Fanaticism of the Northern Abolitionists*
(Philadelphia: H. Manly)

Poe's authorship of this review—which contains an approving description of slave-owning paternalism—has been the subject of considerable scholarly dispute. A number of critics claim that the essay was in fact written by Nathaniel Beverly Tucker, a Southern novelist and well known apologist for slavery who was a friend of Poe's. Poe admired Tucker's work and published his essays and poetry in other issues of the Southern Literary Messenger. *The case for Poe's authorship of the Paulding-Drayton review is laid out by Bernard Rosenthal in "Poe, Slavery, and the* Southern Literary Messenger" *(Poe Studies 7(2), December, 1974, pp. 29–38). There have been questions as well about the authorship of* The South Vindicated from the Treason and Fanaticism of the Northern Abolitionists. *Originally published anonymously, it has since been attributed to William Drayton, the dedicatee of Poe's first collection of short fiction,* Tales of the Grotesque and Arabesque *(1839).*

It is impossible to look attentively and understandingly on those phenomena that indicate public sentiment in regard to the subject of these works, without deep and anxious interest. "Nulla vestigia retrorsum,"[1] is a saying fearfully applicable to what is called the "march of mind." It is an unquestionable truth. The absolute and palpable impossibility of ever unlearning what we know, and of returning, even by forgetfulness, to the state of mind in which the knowledge of it first found us, has always afforded flattering encouragement to the hopes of him who dreams about the perfectibility of human nature. Sometimes one scheme, and sometimes another is devised for accomplishing this great end; and these means are so various, and often so opposite, that the different experiments which the world has

---

[1]"No traces [tracks] backward or in the other direction." In other words, "there's no going back." Poe may be referring here to Horace *Epistles* I, i, 75.

countenanced would seem to contradict the maxim we have quoted. At one time human nature is to be elevated to the height of perfection, by emancipating the mind from all the restraints imposed by Religion. At another, the same end is to be accomplished by the universal spread of a faith, under the benign influence of which every son of Adam is to become holy, "even as God is holy." One or the other of these schemes has been a cardinal point in every system of perfectibility which has been devised since the earliest records of man's history began. At the same time the progress of knowledge (subject indeed to occasional interruptions) has given to each successive experiment a seeming advantage over that which preceded it.

But it is lamentable to observe, that let research discover, let science teach, let art practice what it may, man, in all his mutations, never fails to get back to some point at which he has been before. The human mind seems to perform, by some invariable laws, a sort of cycle, like those of the heavenly bodies. We may be unable, (and, for ourselves, we profess to be so) to trace the *causes* of these changes; but we are not sure that an accurate observation of the history of the various nations at different times, may not detect the *laws* that govern them. However eccentric the orbit, the comet's place in the heavens enables the enlightened astronomer to anticipate its future course, to tell when it will pass its perihelion, in what direction it will shoot away into the unfathomable abyss of infinite space, and at what period it will return. But what especially concerns us, is to mark its progress through our planetary system, to determine whether in coming or returning it may infringe upon us, and prove the messenger of that dispensation which, in the end of all things, is to wrap our earth in flames.

Not less eccentric, and far more deeply interesting to us, is the orbit of the human mind. If, as some have supposed, the comet in its upward flight is drawn away by the attraction of some other sun, around which also it bends its course, thus linking another system with our own, the analogy will be more perfect. For while man is ever seen rushing with uncontrollable violence toward one or the other of his opposite extremes, fanaticism and irreligion—at each of these we find placed an attractive force identical in its nature and in many of its effects. At each extreme, we find him influenced by the same prevailing interest—devoting himself to the accomplishment of the same great object. Happiness is his purpose. The sources of that, he may be told, are within himself—but his eye will fix on the external means, and these he will labor to obtain. Foremost among these, and the equivalent which is to purchase all the rest, is property. At this all men aim, and their eagerness seems always proportioned to the excitement, which, from whatever cause, may for the time prevail.

Under such excitement, the many who want, band themselves together against the few that possess; and the lawless appetite of the multitude for the property of others calls itself the spirit of liberty.

In the calm, and, as we would call it, the healthful condition of the public mind, when every man worships God after his own manner, and Religion and its duties are left to his conscience and his Maker, we find each quietly enjoying his own property, and permitting to others the quiet enjoyment of theirs. Under that state of things, those modes and forms of liberty which regulate and secure this enjoyment, are preferred. Peace reigns, the arts flourish, science extends her discoveries, and man, and the sources of his enjoyments, are multiplied. But in this condition things never rest. We have already disclaimed any knowledge of the causes which forbid this—we only know that such exist. We know that men are always passing, with fearful rapidity, between the extremes of fanaticism and irreligion, and that at either extreme, property and all governmental machinery provided to guard it, become insecure. "Down with the Church! Down with the Altar!" is at one time the cry. "Turn the fat bigots out of their styes, sell the property of the Church and give the money to the poor!" "Behold our turn cometh," says the Millenarian. "The kingdoms of this world are to become the kingdoms of God and his Christ. Sell what you have and give to the poor, and let all things be in common!"

It is now about two hundred years since this latter spirit showed itself in England with a violence and extravagance which accomplished the overthrow of all the institutions of that kingdom. With that we have nothing to do; but we should suppose that the striking resemblance between the aspect of a certain party in that country then and now, could hardly escape the English statesmen. Fifty years ago, in France, this eccentric comet, "public sentiment," was in its opposite node. Making allowance for the difference in the characters of the two people, the effects were identical, the apparent causes were the opposites of each other. In the history of the French Revolution, we find a sort of symptomatic phenomenon, the memory of which was soon lost in the fearful exacerbation of the disease. But it should be remembered now, that in that war against property, the first object of attack was property in slaves; that in that war on behalf of the alleged right of man to be discharged from all control of law, the first triumph achieved was in the emancipation of slaves.

The recent events in the West Indies, and the parallel movement here, give an awful importance to these thoughts in our minds. They superinduce a something like despair of success in any attempt that may be made to resist the attack on all our rights, of which that on Domestic Slavery (the basis of all our institutions) is but the precursor. It is a sort of boding that may belong to the family of superstitions. All vague and undefined fears, from causes the nature of which we know not, the operations of which we cannot stay, are of that character. Such apprehensions are alarming in proportion to our estimate of the value of the interest endangered; and are excited by every thing which enhances that estimate. Such apprehensions have been awakened in our minds by the books before us. To Mr. Paulding, as a Northern man, we tender our grateful thanks for the faithful picture he has drawn of slavery as it appeared to him in his visit to the South, and as exhibited in the information he has carefully derived from those most capable of giving it. His work is executed in the very happiest manner of an author in whom America has the greatest reason to rejoice, and will not fail to enhance his reputation immeasurably as a writer of pure and vigorous English, as a clear thinker, as a patriot, and as a man. The other publication, which we take to be from a Southern pen, is more calculated to excite our indignation against the calumnies which have been put forth against us, and the wrongs meditated by those who come to us in the names of our common Redeemer and common country— seeking our destruction under the mask of Christian Charity and Brotherly Love. This, too, is executed with much ability, and may be read with pleasure as well as profit. While we take great pleasure in recommending these works to our readers, we beg leave to add a few words of our own. We are the more desirous to do this, because there is a view of the subject most deeply interesting to us, which we do not think has ever been presented, by any writer, in as high relief as it deserves. We speak of the moral influences flowing from the relation of master and slave, and the moral feelings engendered and cultivated by it. A correspondent of Mr. Paulding's justly speaks of this relation as one partaking of the patriarchal character, and much resembling that of clanship. This is certainly so. But to say this, is to give a very inadequate idea of it, unless we take into consideration the peculiar character (I may say the peculiar nature) of the negro. Let us reason upon it as we may, there is certainly a power, in causes inscrutable to us, which works essential changes in the different races of animals. In their physical constitution this is obvious to the senses. The color of the negro no man can deny, and therefore, it was but the other day, that they who will believe nothing they cannot account for, made this manifest fact an authority for denying the truth of holy writ. Then comes the opposite extreme—they are, like ourselves, the sons of Adam, and must therefore, have like passions and wants and feelings and tempers in all respects. This, we deny, and appeal to the knowledge of all who know. But their authority will be disputed, and their testimony falsified, unless we can devise something to show how a difference might and should have been brought home. Our theory is a short one. It was the will of God it should be so. But the means—how was this effected? We will give the answer to any one who will develop the causes which might and should have blackened the negro's skin and crisped his hair into wool. Until that is done, we shall take leave to speak, as of things *in esse*,[2] in a degree of loyal devotion on the part of the slave to which the white man's heart is a stranger, and of the master's reciprocal feeling of parental attachment to his humble dependant, equally incomprehensible to him who drives a bargain with the cook who prepares his food, the servant who waits at his table, and the nurse who dozes over his sick bed. That these sentiments in the breast of the negro and his master, are stronger than they would be under like circumstances between individuals of the white race, we believe. That they belong to the class of feelings "by which the heart is made better," we know. How come they? They have their rise in the relation between the infant and the nurse. They are cultivated between him and his foster brother. They are cherished by the parents of both. They are fostered by the habit of affording protection and favors to the younger offspring of the same nurse. They grow by the habitual use of the word "my," used in the language of affectionate appropriation, long before any idea of value mixes with it. It is a term of endearment. That is an easy transition by which he who is taught to call the little negro "his," in this sense and *because he loves him,* shall love him *because he is his.* The idea is not new, that our habits and affections are reciprocally cause and effect of each other.

But the great teacher in this school of feeling is sickness. In this school we have witnessed scenes at which even the hard heart of a thorough bred philanthropist would melt. But here, we shall be told, it is not humanity, but interest that prompts. Be it so. Our business is not with the cause but the effect. But is it interest, which, with assiduous care, prolongs the life of the aged and decrepid negro, who has been, for years, a burthen? Is it interest which labors to rear the crippled or deformed urchin, who can never be any thing but a burthen—which carefully feeds the feeble lamp of life that, without any appearance of neglect, might be permitted to expire? Is not the feeling more akin to that parental $\sigma\tau\sigma\rho\gamma\dot{\eta}$,[3] which, in defiance of reason, is most careful of the life which is, all the time, felt to be a curse to the possessor? Are such cases rare? They are as rare as the occasions; but let the occasion occur, and you will see the case. How else is the longevity of the negro proverbial? A negro who does no work for

---

[2]"in its being," in other words, "things *in their essence.*"
[3]storge, "affection."

thirty years! (and we know such examples) is it interest which has lengthened out his existence?

Let the philanthropist think as he may—by the negro himself, his master's care of him in sickness is not imputed to interested feelings. We know an instance of a negress who was invited by a benevolent lady in Philadelphia to leave her mistress. The lady promised to secrete her for a while, and then to pay her good wages. The poor creature felt the temptation and was about to yield. "You are mighty good, madam," said she, "and I am a thousand times obliged to you. And if I am sick or any thing, I am sure you will take care of me, and nurse me, like my good mistress used to do, and bring me something warm and good to comfort me, and tie up my head and fix my pillow." She spoke in the simplicity of her heart, and the tempter had not the heart to deceive her. "No," said she, "all *that* will come out of your wages—for you will have money enough to hire a nurse." The tears had already swelled in the warm hearted creature's eyes, at her own recital of her mistress' kindness. They now gushed forth in a flood, and running to her lady who was a lodger in the house, she threw herself on her knees, confessed her fault, was pardoned, and was happy.

But it is not by the bedside of the sick negro that the feeling we speak of is chiefly engendered. They who would view it in its causes and effects must see him by the sick bed of his master—must see *her* by the sick bed of her *mistress.* We have seen these things. We have seen the dying infant in the lap of its nurse, and have stood with the same nurse by the bed side of her own dying child. Did mighty nature assert her empire, and wring from the mother's heart more and bitterer tears than she had shed over her foster babe? None that the eye of man could distinguish. And he who sees the heart—did he see dissimulation giving energy to the choking sobs that *seemed* to be rendered more vehement by her attempts to repress them? *Philanthropy* may think so if it pleases.

A good lady was on her death bed. Her illness was long and protracted, but hopeless from the first. A servant, (by no means a favorite with her, being high tempered and ungovernable) was advanced in pregnancy, and in bad health. Yet she could not be kept out of the house. She was permitted to stay about her mistress during the day, but sent to bed at an early hour every night. Her reluctance to obey was obvious, and her master found that she evaded his order, whenever she could escape his eye. He once found her in the house late at night, and kindly reproving her, sent her home. An hour after, suddenly going out of the sick room, he stumbled over her in the dark. She was crouched down at the door, listening for the groans of the sufferer. She was again ordered home, and turned to go.

Suddenly she stopped, and bursting into tears, said, "Master, it ain't no use for me to go to bed, Sir. It don't do me no good, I cannot sleep, Sir."

Such instances prove that in reasoning concerning the moral effect of slavery, he who regards man as a unit, the same under all circumstances, leaves out of view an important consideration. The fact that he is not so, is manifest to every body—but the application of the fact to this controversy is not made. The author of "The South Vindicated" quotes at page 228 a passage from Lamartine,[4] on this very point, though he only uses it to show the absurdity of any attempt at amalgamation. . . .

There is much truth here, though certainly not what passes for truth with those who study human nature wholly in the closet, and in reforming the world address themselves exclusively to the faults of *others,* and the evils of which they know the least, and which least concern themselves.

We hope the day has gone by when we are to be judged by the testimony of false, interested, and malignant accusers alone. We repeat that we are thankful to Mr. Paulding for having stepped forward in our defence. Our assailants are numerous, and it is indispensable that we should meet the assault with vigor and activity. Nothing is wanting but manly discussion to convince our own people at least, that in continuing to command the services of their slaves, they violate no law divine or human, and that in the faithful discharge of their reciprocal obligations lies their true duty. Let these be performed, and we believe (with our esteemed correspondent Professor Dew) that society in the South will derive much more of good than of evil from this much abused and partially-considered institution.

---

[4]Alphonse Marie de Lamartine (1790–1869), a French poet, politician, and antislavery agitator in his own country. The use of Lamartine's words in the context of a proslavery argument is intentionally ironic.

Review
[*Graham's Magazine*, May 1841]

Charles Dickens, *The Old Curiosity Shop, and other Tales* and *Master Humphrey's Clock*
(Philadelphia: Lea and Blanchard)

Dickens was wildly popular in the United States, as in England—so much so that the delivery by ship of the last serial installment of The Old Curiosity Shop *caused a near riot which resulted in several drowning deaths among the eager crowd on the dock in Baltimore. Poe's review of Dickens, whose work he respected, shows him fitting England's most popular author into his own critical framework. He was particularly concerned with Dickens's famous exaggerations of character, which he described as a strategy to represent truth to the reader through distortion. This critical assessment highlights the importance of reader response to Poe's creative aesthetic.*

What we here give in Italics is the duplicate title, on two separate title-pages, of an octavo volume of three hundred and sixty two pages. Why this method of nomenclature should have been adopted is more than we can understand—although it arises, *perhaps*, from a certain confusion and hesitation observable in the whole structure of the book itself. Publishers have an idea, however, (and no doubt they are the best judges in such matters) that a complete work obtains a readier sale than one "to be continued;" and we see plainly that it is with the design of intimating the *entireness* of the volume now before us, that *"The Old Curiosity Shop and other Tales,"* has been made not only the primary and main title, but the name of the whole publication as indicated by the back. This may be quite fair in trade, but is morally wrong not the less. The volume is only one of a series—only part of a whole; and the title has no right to *insinuate otherwise.* So obvious is this intention to misguide, that it has led to the absurdity of putting the inclusive, or general, title of the series, as a secondary instead of a primary one. Anybody may see that if the wish had been fairly to represent the plan and extent of the volume, something like this would have been given on a single page—

"Master Humphrey's Clock. By Charles Dickens. Part I. Containing The Old Curiosity Shop, and other Tales, with Numerous Illustrations, &c. &c."

This would have been better for all parties, a good deal more honest, and a vast deal more easily understood. In fact, there is sufficient

uncertainty of purpose in the book itself, without resort to mystification in the matter of title. We do not think it altogether impossible
that the rumors in respect to the sanity of Mr. Dickens which were so
prevalent during the publication of the first numbers of the work,
had some slight—some very slight foundation in truth. By this, we
mean merely to say that the mind of the author, at the time, might
possibly have been struggling with some of those manifold and multiform *aberrations* by which the nobler order of genius is so frequently beset—but which are still so very far removed from disease.

There are some facts in the physical world which have a really wonderful analogy with others in the world of thought, and seem thus to
give some color of truth to the (false) rhetorical dogma, that
metaphor or simile may be made to strengthen an argument, as well
as to embellish a description. The principle of the *vis inertiæ*, for
example, with the amount of *momentum* proportionate with it and
consequent upon it, seems to be identical in physics and metaphysics. It is not more true, in the former, that a large body is with
more difficulty set in motion than a smaller one, and that its subsequent impetus is commensurate with this difficulty, than it is, in the
latter, that intellects of the vaster capacity, while more forcible, more
constant, and more extensive in their movements than those of inferior grade, are yet the less readily moved, and are more embarrassed
and more full of hesitation in the first few steps of their progress.
While, therefore, it is not impossible, as we have just said, that some
slight mental aberration might have given rise to the hesitancy and
indefinitiveness of purpose which are so very perceptible in the first
pages of the volume before us, we are still the more willing to believe
these defects the result of the moral fact just stated, since we find the
work itself of an unusual order of excellence, even when regarded as
the production of the author of "Nicholas Nickleby." That the evils
we complain of are not, and were not, fully perceived by Mr. Dickens
himself, cannot be supposed for a moment. Had his book been published in the old way, we should have seen no traces of them
whatever.

The design of the general work, "Humphrey's Clock," is simply the
common-place one of putting various tales into the mouths of a
social party. The meetings are held at the house of Master
Humphrey—an antique building in London, where an old-fashioned
clock-case is the place of deposit for the M.S.S. Why such designs
have become common is obvious. One half the pleasure experienced
at a theatre arises from the spectator's sympathy with the rest of the
audience, and, especially, from his belief in their sympathy with him.
The eccentric gentleman who not long ago, at the Park, found himself the solitary occupant of box, pit, and gallery, would have derived

but little enjoyment from his visit, had he been suffered to remain. It was an act of mercy to turn him out. The present absurd rage for lecturing is founded in the feeling in question. Essays which we would not be hired to read—so trite is their subject—so feeble is their execution—so much easier is it to get better information on similar themes out of any Encyclopædia in Christendom—we are brought to tolerate, and alas, even to applaud in their tenth and twentieth repetition, through the sole force of our sympathy with the throng. In the same way we listen to a story with greater zest when there are others present at its narration beside ourselves. Aware of this, authors without due reflection have repeatedly attempted, by supposing a circle of listeners, to imbue their narratives with the interest of sympathy. At a cursory glance the idea seems plausible enough. But, in the one case, there is an actual, personal, and palpable sympathy, conveyed in looks, gestures and brief comments—a sympathy of real individuals, all with the matters discussed to be sure, but then especially, *each with each.* In the other instance, we, alone in our closet, are required to sympathise *with* the sympathy of fictitious listeners, who, so far from being present in body, are often studiously kept out of sight and out of mind for two or three hundred pages at a time. This is sympathy double-diluted—the shadow of a shade. It is unnecessary to say that the design invariably fails of its effect.

In his preface to the present volume, Mr. Dickens seems to feel the necessity for an apology in regard to certain portions of his commencement, without seeing clearly what apology he should make, or for what precise thing he should apologise. He makes an effort to get over the difficulty, by saying something about its never being "his intention to have the members of 'Master Humphrey's Clock' active agents in the stories they relate," and about his "picturing to himself the various sensations of his hearers—thinking how Jack Redburn might incline to poor Kit—how the deaf gentleman would have his favorite, and Mr. Miles his," &c. &c.—but we are quite sure that all this is as pure a fiction as "The Curiosity Shop" itself. Our author is deceived. Occupied with little Nell and her grandfather, he had forgotten the very existence of his interlocutors until he found himself, at the end of his book, under the disagreeable necessity of saying a word or two concerning them, by way of winding them up. The simple truth is that, either for one of the two reasons at which we have already hinted, or else because the work was begun in a hurry, Mr. Dickens did not precisely know his own plans when he penned the five or six first chapters of the "Clock."

The wish to preserve a certain degree of unity between various narratives naturally unconnected, is a more obvious and a better reason for employing interlocutors. But such unity as may be thus had is scarcely worth having. It may, in some feeble measure, satisfy the judgment by a sense of completeness; but it seldom produces a pleasant effect; and if the speakers are made to take part in their own stories (as has been the case here) they become injurious by creating confusion. Thus, in "The Curiosity Shop," we feel displeased to find Master Humphrey commencing the tale in the first person, dropping this for the third, and concluding by introducing himself as the "single gentleman" who figures in the story. In spite of all the subsequent explanation we are forced to look upon him as two. All is confusion, and what makes it worse, is that Master Humphrey is painted as a lean and sober personage, while his second self is a fat, bluff and boisterous old bachelor.

Yet the species of connexion in question, besides preserving the unity desired, *may* be made, if well managed, a source of consistent and agreeable interest. It has been so made by Thomas Moore—the most skilful literary artist of his day—perhaps of any day—a man who stands in the singular and really wonderful predicament of being undervalued on account of the profusion with which he has scattered about him his good things. The brilliancies on any one page of Lalla Rookh[1] would have sufficed to establish that very reputation which has been in a great measure self-dimmed by the galaxied lustre of the entire book. It seems that the horrid laws of political economy cannot be evaded even by the inspired, and that a perfect versification, a vigorous style, and a never-tiring fancy, may, like the water we drink and die without, yet despise, be so plentifully set forth as to be absolutely of no value at all.

By far the greater portion of the volume now published, is occupied with the tale of "The Curiosity Shop," narrated by Master Humphrey himself. The other stories are brief. The "Giant Chronicles" is the title of what appears to be meant for a series within a series, and we think this design doubly objectionable. The narrative of "The Bowyer," as well as of "John Podgers," is not altogether worthy of Mr. Dickens. They were probably sent to press to supply a demand for copy, while he was occupied with the "Curiosity Shop." But the "Confession Found in a Prison in the Time of Charles the Second" is a paper of remarkable power, truly original in conception, and worked out with great ability.

The story of "The Curiosity Shop" is very simple. Two brothers of England, warmly attached to each other, love the same lady, without

---

[1]Published in 1817, this narrative poem was one of the most popular works of the very popular Irish Romantic poet Thomas Moore (1779–1852). The publisher, Longmans, agreed to pay Moore the spectacular sum of 3,000 pounds for the work even before having seen it.

each other's knowledge. The younger at length discovers the elder's secret, and, sacrificing himself to fraternal affection, quits the country and resides for many years in a foreign land, where he amasses great wealth. Meantime his brother marries the lady, who soon dies, leaving an infant daughter—her perfect resemblance. In the widower's heart the mother lives again through the child. This latter grows up, marries unhappily, has a son and a daughter, loses her husband, and dies herself shortly afterward. The grandfather takes the orphans to his home. The boy spurns his protection, falls into bad courses, and becomes an outcast. The girl—in whom a third time lives the object of the old man's early choice—dwells with him alone, and is loved by him with a most doting affection. He has now become poor, and at length is reduced to keeping a shop for antiquities and curiosities. Finally, through his dread of involving the child in want, his mind becomes weakened. He thinks to redeem his fortune by gambling, borrows money for this purpose of a dwarf, who, at length, discovering the true state of the old man's affairs, seizes his furniture and turns him out of doors. The girl and himself set out, without farther object than to relieve themselves of the sight of the hated city, upon a weary pilgrimage, whose events form the basis or body of the tale. In fine, just as a peaceful retirement is secured for them, the child, wasted with fatigue and anxiety, dies. The grandfather, through grief, immediately follows her to the tomb. The younger brother, meantime, has received information of the old man's poverty, hastens to England, and arrives only in time to be at the closing scene of the tragedy.

This plot is the best which could have been constructed for the main object of the narrative. This object is the depicting of a fervent and dreamy love for the child on the part of the grandfather—such a love as would induce devotion to himself on the part of the orphan. We have thus the conception of a childhood, educated in utter ignorance of the world, filled with an affection which has been, through its brief existence, the sole source of its pleasures, and which has no part in the passion of a more mature youth for an object of its own age—we have the idea of this childhood, full of ardent hopes, leading by the hand, forth from the heated and wearying city, into the green fields, to seek for bread, the decrepid imbecillity of a doting and confiding old age, whose stern knowledge of man, and of the world it leaves behind, is now merged in the sole consciousness of receiving love and protection from that weakness it has loved and protected.

This conception is indeed most beautiful. It is simply and severely grand. The more fully we survey it, the more thoroughly are we convinced of the lofty character of that genius which gave it birth. That

in its present simplicity of form, however, it was first entertained by
Mr. Dickens, may well be doubted. That it was *not*, we are assured by
the title which the tale bears. When in its commencement he called
it "The Old Curiosity Shop," his design was far different from what
we see it in its completion. It is evident that had he now to name the
story he would not so term it; for the shop itself is a thing of an altogether collateral interest, and is spoken of merely in the beginning.
This is only one among a hundred instances of the disadvantage
under which the periodical novelist labors. When his work is done,
he never fails to observe a thousand defects which he might have
remedied, and a thousand alterations, in regard to the book as a
whole, which might be made to its manifest improvement.

But if the conception of this story deserves praise, its execution is
beyond all—and here the subject naturally leads us from the gener-
alisation which is the proper province of the critic, into details
among which it is scarcely fitting that he should venture.

The Art of Mr. Dickens, although elaborate and great, seems only
a happy modification of Nature. In this respect he differs remarkably
from the author of "Night and Morning."[2] The latter, by excessive
care and by patient reflection, aided by much rhetorical knowledge,
and general information, has arrived at the capability of producing
books which might be mistaken by ninety-nine readers out of a hundred for the genuine inspirations of genius. The former, by the
promptings of the truest genius itself, has been brought to compose,
and evidently without effort, works which have effected a long-sought
consummation—which have rendered him the idol of the people,
while defying and enchanting the critics. Mr. Bulwer, through art, has
almost created a genius. Mr. Dickens, through genius, has perfected
a standard from which Art itself will derive its essence, in rules.

When we speak in this manner of the "Old Curiosity Shop," we
speak with entire deliberation, and know quite well what it is we
assert. We do not mean to say that it is perfect, as a whole—this could
not well have been the case under the circumstances of its composition. But we know that, in all the higher elements which go to make
up literary greatness, it is supremely excellent. We think, for instance,
that the introduction of Nelly's brother (and here we address those
who have read the work) is supererogatory—that the character of
Quilp would have been more in keeping had he been confined to
petty and grotesque acts of malice—that his death should have been

---

[2]E. G. Bulwer-Lytton (1803–1873), British novelist, poet, dramatist, politician, and orator, whose work Poe admired. In an 1841 review, Poe asserts that Bulwer-Lytton constructed the plot of *Night and Day* backwards—a method Poe champions in "The
Philosophy of Composition."

made the *immediate* consequence of his attempt at revenge upon Kit; and that after matters had been put fairly in train for this poetical justice, he should not have perished by an accident inconsequential upon his villainy. We think, too, that there is an air of *ultra*-accident in the finally discovered relationship between Kit's master and the bachelor of the old church—that the sneering politeness put into the mouth of Quilp, with his manner of commencing a question which he wishes answered in the affirmative, with an affirmative interrogatory, instead of the ordinary negative one—are fashions borrowed from the author's own Fagin—that he has repeated himself in many other instances—that the practical tricks and love of mischief of the dwarf's boy are too nearly consonant with the traits of the master—that so much of the propensities of Swiveller as relate to his inapposite appropriation of odds and ends of verse, is stolen from the generic loafer of our fellow-townsman, Neal—and that the writer has suffered the overflowing kindness of his own bosom to mislead him in a very important point of art, when he endows so many of his *dramatis personæ* with a warmth of feeling so very rare in reality. Above all, we acknowledge that the death of Nelly is excessively painful—that it leaves a most distressing oppression of spirit upon the reader—and should, therefore, have been avoided.

But when we come to speak of the excellences of the tale these defects appear really insignificant. It embodies more *originality* in every point, but in character especially, than any single work within our knowledge. There is the grandfather—a truly profound conception; the gentle and lovely Nelly—we have discoursed of her before; Quilp, with mouth like that of the panting dog—(a bold idea which the engraver has neglected to embody) with his hilarious antics, his cowardice, and his very petty and spoilt-child-like malevolence; Dick Swiveller, that prince of good-hearted, good-for-nothing, lazy, luxurious, poetical, brave, romantically generous, gallant, affectionate, and not over-and-above honest, "glorious Apollos;" the marchioness, his bride; Tom Codlin and his partner; Miss Sally Brass, that "fine fellow;" the pony that had an opinion of its own; the boy that stood upon his head; the sexton; the man at the forge; not forgetting the dancing dogs and baby Nubbles. There are other admirably drawn characters—but we note these for their remarkable originality, as well as for their wonderful keeping, and the glowing colors in which they are painted. We have heard some of them called caricatures—but the charge is grossly ill-founded. No critical principle is more firmly based in reason than that a certain amount of exaggeration is essential to the proper depicting of truth itself. We do not paint an object to be true, but to appear true to the beholder. Were we to copy nature with accuracy the object copied would seem unnatural. The columns of the Greek temples, which convey the idea of absolute proportion, are very considerably thicker just beneath the capital than at the base. We regret that we have not left ourselves space in which to examine this whole question as it deserves. We must content ourselves with saying that caricature seldom exists (unless in so gross a form as to disgust at once) where the component parts are *in keeping;* and that the laugh excited by it, in any case, is radically distinct from that induced by a properly artistical *incongruity*—the source of all mirth. Were these creations of Mr. Dickens' really caricatures they would not live in public estimation beyond the hour of their first survey. We regard them as *creations*—(that is to say as original combinations of character) only not all of the highest order, because the elements employed are not always of the highest. In the instances of Nelly, the grandfather, the Sexton, and the man of the furnace, the force of the creative intellect could scarcely have been engaged with nobler material, and the result is that these personages belong to the most august regions of the *Ideal*.

In truth, the great feature of the "Curiosity Shop" is its chaste, vigorous, and glorious *imagination*. This is the one charm, all potent, which alone would suffice to compensate for a world more of error than Mr. Dickens ever committed. It is not only seen in the conception, and general handling of the story, or in the invention of character; but it pervades every sentence of the book. We recognise its prodigious influence in every inspired word. It is this which induces the reader who is at all ideal, to pause frequently, to re-read the occasionally quaint phrases, to muse in uncontrollable delight over thoughts which, while he wonders he has never hit upon them before, he yet admits that he never has encountered. In fact it is the wand of the enchanter.

Had we room to particularise, we would mention as points evincing most distinctly the ideality of the "Curiosity Shop"—the picture of the shop itself—the newly-born desire of the worldly old man for the peace of green fields—his whole character and conduct, in short—the schoolmaster, with his desolate fortunes, seeking affection in little children—the haunts of Quilp among the wharf-rats—the tinkering of the Punch-men among the tombs—the glorious scene where the man of the forge sits poring, at deep midnight, into that dread fire—again the whole conception of this character; and, last and greatest, the stealthy approach of Nell to her death—her gradual sinking away on the journey to the village, so skilfully indicated rather than described—her pensive and prescient meditation—the fit of strange musing which came over her when the house *in which she was to die* first broke upon her sight—the description of this house, of the old church, and of the church-yard—every thing in rigid consonance with the one impression to be conveyed—that deep meaningless well—the comments of the Sexton upon death, and upon his own secure life—this whole world of mournful yet peaceful idea merging, at length, into the decease of the child Nelly, and the uncomprehending despair of the grandfather. These concluding scenes are so drawn that human language, urged by human thought, could go no farther in the excitement of human feelings. And the pathos is of that best order which is relieved, in great measure, by ideality. Here the book has never been equalled,—never approached except in one instance, and that is in the case of the "Undine" of De La Motte Fouqué. The imagination is perhaps as great in this latter work, but the pathos, although truly beautiful and deep, fails of much of its effect through the material from which it is wrought. The chief character, being endowed with purely fanciful attributes, cannot command our full sympathies, as can a simple denizen of earth. In saying, a page or so above, that the death of the child left too painful an impression, and should therefore have been avoided, we must, of course, be understood as referring to the work as a whole, and in respect to its general appreciation and popularity. The death, as recorded, is, we repeat, of the highest order of literary excellence—yet while none can deny this fact, there are few who will be willing to read the concluding passages a second time.

Upon the whole we think the "Curiosity Shop" very much the best of the works of Mr. Dickens. It is scarcely possible to speak of it too well. It is in all respects a tale which will secure for its author the enthusiastic admiration of every man of genius.

The edition before us is handsomely printed, on excellent paper. The designs by Cattermole and Browne are many of them excellent—some of them outrageously bad. Of course it is difficult for us to say how far the American engraver is in fault. In conclusion, we must enter our solemn protest against the final page full of little angles in smock frocks, or dimity chemises.

Review

[Graham's Magazine, August 1841]

Lambert A. Wilmer, *The Quacks of Helicon: A Satire*
(Philadelphia: Printed by J. W. Maclefield)

Poe appreciated Wilmer's Quacks of Helicon *because the sentiments of the poem agreed with his own. Wilmer aimed his satiric barbs at the evils of literary cliques, which Poe described elsewhere as having the same people "first write all our books and then review them." Like Poe, Wilmer is courageous enough to attack the offenders by name, and Poe shows his appreciation of Wilmer's willingness to join him in the same critical wilderness.*

A satire, professedly such, at the present day, and especially by an American writer, is a welcome novelty, indeed. We have really done very little in the line upon this side of the Atlantic—nothing, certainly, of importance—Trumbull's clumsy poem and Halleck's "Croakers" to the contrary notwithstanding. Some things we have produced, to be sure, which were excellent in the way of burlesque, without intending a syllable that was not utterly solemn and serious. Odes, ballads, songs, sonnets, epics, and epigrams, possessed of this unintentional excellence, we would have no difficulty in designating by the dozen; but, in the matter of directly-meant and genuine satire, it cannot be denied that we are sadly deficient. Although, as a literary people, however, we are not exactly Archilocuses—although we have no pretensions to the ηχεηντες ιαμβοι[1]—although, in short, we are no satirists ourselves, there can be no question that we answer sufficiently well as subjects for satire.

We repeat, that we are glad to see this book of Mr. Wilmer's; first, because it is something new under the sun; secondly, because, in many respects, it is well executed; and, thirdly, because, in the universal corruption and rigmarole amid which we gasp for breath, it is really a pleasant thing to get even one accidental whiff of the unadulterated air of *truth.*

The "Quacks of Helicon," as a poem and otherwise, has many defects, and these we shall have no scruple in pointing out—

---

[1] *echeentes iamboi* "echoing iambics." Archilochus, a Greek satirist, originated the use of iambic meter. Poe presumably means "we will not echo his meter, since we do not presume to pattern ourselves after him."

although Mr. Wilmer is a personal friend of our own,* and we are happy and proud to say so—but it has also many remarkable merits— merits which it will be quite useless for those aggrieved by the satire—quite useless for any *clique,* or set of *cliques,* to attempt to frown down, or to affect not to see, or to feel, or to understand.

Its prevalent blemishes are referrible chiefly to the leading sin of *imitation.* Had the work been composed professedly in paraphrase of the whole manner of the sarcastic epistles of the times of Dryden and Pope, we should have pronounced it the most ingenious and truthful thing of the kind upon record. So close is the copy, that it extends to the most trivial points—for example to the old forms of punctuation. The turns of phraseology, the tricks of rhythm, the arrangement of the paragraphs, the general conduct of the satire—everything— all—are Dryden's. We cannot deny, it is true, that the satiric model of the days in question is insusceptible of improvement, and that the modern author who deviates therefrom, must necessarily sacrifice something of merit at the shrine of originality. Neither can we shut our eyes to the fact, that the imitation, in the present case, has conveyed, in full spirit, the higher qualities, as well as, in rigid letter, the minor elegances and general peculiarities of the author of "Absalom and Achitophel."[2] We have here the bold, vigorous, and sonorous verse, the biting sarcasm, the pungent epigrammatism, the unscrupulous directness, as of old. Yet it will not do to forget that Mr. Wilmer has been *shown how* to accomplish these things. He is thus only entitled to the praise of a close observer, and of a thoughtful and skilful copyist. The images are, to be sure, his own. They are neither Pope's, nor Dryden's, nor Rochester's, nor Churchill's—but they are moulded in the identical mould used by these satirists.

This servility of imitation has seduced our author into errors which his better sense should have avoided. He sometimes mistakes intention; at other times he copies faults, confounding them with beauties. In the opening of the poem, for example, we find the lines—

> Against usurpers, Olney, I declare
> A righteous, just, and patriotic war.

The rhymes *war* and *declare* are here adopted from Pope, who employs them frequently; but it should have been remembered that the modern relative pronunciation of the two words differs materially from the relative pronunciation of the era of the "Dunciad."[3]

We are also sure that the gross obscenity, the filth—we can use no

---

*Of Mr. Poe's.

[2] A two-part satire in verse, published in 1681. The first part was by John Dryden, the second by Nahum Tate, revised by Dryden.

[3] (1728) Literally, the "dunce-epic," a satire in verse by Alexander Pope.

gentler name—which disgraces the "Quacks of Helicon," cannot be
the result of innate impurity in the mind of the writer. It is but a part
of the slavish and indiscriminating imitation of the Swift and
Rochester school. It has done the book an irreparable injury, both in
a moral and pecuniary view, without effecting anything whatever on
the score of sarcasm, vigor or wit. "Let what is to be said, be said
plainly." True; but let nothing vulgar be *ever* said, or conceived.

In asserting that this satire, even in its mannerism, has imbued
itself with the full spirit of the polish and of the pungency of Dryden,
we have already awarded it high praise. But there remains to be mentioned the far loftier merit of speaking fearlessly the truth, at an
epoch when truth is out of fashion, and under circumstances of
social position which would have deterred almost any man in our
community from a similar Quixotism. For the publication of the
"Quacks of Helicon,"—a poem which brings under review, by name,
most of our prominent *literati,* and treats them, generally, as they
deserve (what treatment could be more bitter?)—for the publication
of this attack, Mr. Wilmer, whose subsistence lies in his pen, has little
to look for—apart from the silent respect of those at once honest and
timid—but the most malignant open or covert persecution. For this
reason, and because it is the truth which he has spoken, do we say to
him from the bottom of our hearts, "God speed!"

We repeat it:—*it is* the truth which he has spoken, and who shall
contradict us? He has said unscrupulously what every reasonable
man among us has long known to be "as true as the Pentateuch"—
that, as a literary people, we are one vast perambulating humbug. He
has asserted that we are *clique*-ridden, and who does not smile at the
obvious truism of that assertion? He maintains that chicanery is, with
us, a far surer road than talent to distinction in letters. Who gainsays
this? The corrupt nature of our ordinary criticism has become noto-
rious. Its powers have been prostrated by its own arm. The inter-
course between critic and publisher, as it now almost universally
stands, is comprised either in the paying and pocketing of black mail,
as the price of a simple forbearance, or in a direct system of petty and
contemptible bribery, properly so called—a system even more injurious than the former to the true interests of the public, and more
degrading to the buyers and sellers of good opinion, on account
of the more positive character of the service here rendered for the
consideration received. We laugh at the idea of any denial of our
assertions upon this topic; they are infamously true. In the charge of
general corruption there are undoubtedly many noble exceptions to
be made. There are, indeed, some very few editors, who, maintaining
an entire independence, will receive no books from publishers at all,
or who receive them with a perfect understanding, on the part of

these latter, that an unbiassed *critique* will be given. But these cases are insufficient to have much effect on the popular mistrust: a mistrust heightened by late exposure of the machinations of *coteries* in New York—*coteries* which, at the bidding of leading booksellers, manufacture, as required from time to time, a pseudo-public opinion by wholesale, for the benefit of any little hanger on of the party, or pettifogging protector of the firm.

We speak of these things in the bitterness of scorn. It is unnecessary to cite instances, where one is found in almost every issue of a book. It is needless to call to mind the desperate case of Fay—a case where the pertinacity of the effort to gull—where the obviousness of the attempt at forestalling a judgment—where the wofully over-done be-Mirrorment of that man-of-straw, together with the pitiable platitude of his production, proved a dose somewhat too potent for even the well-prepared stomach of the mob. We say it is supererogatory to dwell upon "Norman Leslie," or other by-gone follies, when we have, before our eyes, hourly instances of the machinations in question. To so great an extent of methodical assurance has the *system* of puffery arrived, that publishers, of late, have made no scruple of keeping on hand an assortment of commendatory notices, prepared by their men of all work, and of sending these notices around to the multitudinous papers within their influence, done up within the fly-leaves of the book. The grossness of these base attempts, however, has not escaped indignant rebuke from the more honorable portion of the press; and we hail these symptoms of restiveness under the yoke of unprincipled ignorance and quackery (strong only in combination) as the harbinger of a better era for the interests of real merit, and of the national literature as a whole.

It has become, indeed the plain duty of each individual connected with our periodicals, heartily to give whatever influence he possesses, to the good cause of integrity and the truth. The results thus attainable will be found worthy his closest attention and best efforts. We shall thus frown down all conspiracies to foist inanity upon the public consideration at the obvious expense of every man of talent who is not a member of a *clique* in power. We may even arrive, in time, at that desirable point from which a distinct view of our men of letters may be obtained, and their respective pretensions adjusted, by the standard of a rigorous and self-sustaining criticism alone. That their several positions are as yet properly settled; that the posts which a vast number of them now hold are maintained by any better tenure than that of the chicanery upon which we have commented, will be asserted by none but the ignorant, or the parties who have best right to feel an interest in the "good old condition of things." No two matters can be more radically different than the reputation of some of our prominent *litterateurs,* as gathered from the mouths of the people, (who glean it from the paragraphs of the papers,) and the same reputation as deduced from the private estimate of intelligent and educated men. We do not advance this fact as a new discovery. Its truth, on the contrary, is the subject, and has long been so, of every-day witticism and mirth.

Why not? Surely there can be few things more ridiculous than the general character and assumptions of the ordinary critical notices of new books! An editor, sometimes without the shadow of the commonest attainment—often without brains, always without time—does not scruple to give the world to understand that he is in the *daily* habit of critically reading and deciding upon a flood of publications one tenth of whose title-pages he may possibly have turned over, three fourths of whose contents would be Hebrew to his most desperate efforts at comprehension, and whose entire mass and amount, as might be mathematically demonstrated, would be sufficient to occupy, in the most cursory perusal, the attention of some ten or twenty readers for a month! What he wants in plausibility, however, he makes up in obsequiousness; what he lacks in time he supplies in temper. He is the most easily pleased man in the world. He admires everything, from the big Dictionary of Noah Webster to the last diamond edition of Tom Thumb. Indeed his sole difficulty is in finding tongue to express his delight. Every pamphlet is a miracle—every book in boards is an epoch in letters. His phrases, therefore, get bigger and bigger every day, and, if it were not for talking Cockney, we might call him a "regular swell."

Yet in the attempt at getting definite information in regard to any one portion of our literature, the merely general reader, or the foreigner, will turn in vain from the lighter to the heavier journals. But it is not our intention here to dwell upon the radical, antique, and systematized rigmarole of our Quarterlies. The articles here are anonymous. Who writes?—who causes to be written? Who but an ass will put faith in tirades which *may* be the result of personal hostility, or in panegyrics which nine times out of ten may be laid, directly or indirectly, to the charge of the author himself? It is in the favor of these saturnine pamphlets that they contain, now and then, a good essay *de omnibus rebus et quibusdam aliis,*[4] which may be looked into, without decided somnolent consequences, at any period not immediately subsequent to dinner. But it is useless to expect criticism from periodicals called "Reviews" from never reviewing. Besides, all men know, or should know, that these books are sadly given to verbiage. It is a part of their nature, a condition of their being, a point of their

---

[4]"about all things and certain other things."

faith. A veteran reviewer loves the safety of generalities, and is therefore rarely particular. "Words, words, words" are the secret of his strength. He has one or two ideas of his own, and is both wary and fussy in giving them out. His wit lies with his truth, in a well, and there is always a world of trouble in getting it up. He is a sworn enemy to all things simple and direct. He gives no ear to the advice of the giant Moulineau— *"Belier, mon ami, commencez au commencement."*[5] He either jumps at once into the middle of his subject, or breaks in at a back door, or sidles up to it with the gait of a crab. No other mode of approach has an air of sufficient profundity. When fairly into it, however, he becomes dazzled with the scintillations of his own wisdom, and is seldom able to see his way out. Tired of laughing at his antics, or frightened at seeing him flounder, the reader at length shuts him up, with the book. "What song the Syrens sang," says Sir Thomas Browne, "or what name Achilles assumed when he hid himself among women, though puzzling questions, are not beyond *all* conjecture"—but it would puzzle Sir Thomas, backed by Achilles and all the Syrens in Heathendom, to say, in nine cases out of ten, *what is the object* of a thorough-going Quarterly Reviewer.

Should the opinions promulgated by our press at large be taken, in their wonderful aggregate, as an evidence of what American literature absolutely is, (and it may be said that, in general, they are really so taken,) we shall find ourselves the most enviable set of people upon the face of the earth. Our fine writers are legion. Our very atmosphere is redolent of genius; and we, the nation, are a huge, well-contented chameleon, grown pursy by inhaling it. We are *teretes et rotundi*—enwrapped in excellence. All our poets are Miltons, neither mute nor inglorious; all our poetesses are "American Hemanses;" nor will it do to deny that all our novelists are great Knowns or great Unknowns, and that every body who writes, in every possible and impossible department, is the admirable Crichton, or at least the admirable Crichton's ghost.[6] We are thus in a glorious condition, and will remain so until forced to disgorge our ethereal honors. In truth, there is some danger that the jealousy of the Old World will interfere. It cannot long submit to that outrageous monopoly of "all the decency and all the talent" in which the gentlemen of the press give such undoubted assurance of our being so busily engaged.

---

[5]"Ram, my friend, begin at the beginning." (Rabelais, *Gargantua and Pantagruel*.) Moulineau is one of many giants encountered in this work.

[6]James Crichton (1560–c. 1582), a Scottish prodigy who in his brief life achieved great distinction in the sciences, languages, arts, and swordsmanship. Often referred to as "the Admirable Crichton," he reputedly wrote Latin verse and was enormously successful in debating the great Italian scholars of his day, often convincing them that their views on Aristotle, mathematics and other subjects, were erroneous.

But we feel angry with ourselves for the jesting tone of our observations upon this topic. The prevalence of the spirit of puffery is a subject far less for merriment than for disgust. Its truckling, yet dogmatical character—its bold, unsustained, yet self-sufficient and wholesale laudation—is becoming, more and more, an insult to the common sense of the community. Trivial as it essentially is, it has yet been made the instrument of the grossest abuse in the elevation of imbecility, to the manifest injury, to the utter ruin, of true merit. Is there any man of good feeling and of ordinary understanding—is there one single individual among all our readers—who does not feel a thrill of bitter indignation, apart from any sentiment of mirth, as he calls to mind instance after instance of the purest, of the most unadulterated quackery in letters, which has risen to a high post in the apparent popular estimation, and which still maintains it, by the sole means of a blustering arrogance, or of a busy wriggling conceit, or of the most barefaced plagiarism, or even through the simple immensity of its assumptions—assumptions not only unopposed by the press at large, but absolutely supported in proportion to the vociferous clamor with which they are made—in exact accordance with their utter baselessness and untenability? We should have no trouble in pointing out, today, some twenty or thirty so-called literary personages, who, if not idiots, as we half think them, or if not hardened to all sense of shame by a long course of disingenuousness, will now blush, in the perusal of these words, through consciousness of the shadowy nature of that purchased pedestal upon which they stand—will now tremble in thinking of the feebleness of the breath which will be adequate to the blowing it from beneath their feet. With the help of a hearty good will, even *we* may yet tumble them down.

So firm, through a long endurance, has been the hold taken upon the popular mind (at least so far as we may consider the popular mind reflected in ephemeral letters) by the laudatory system which we have deprecated, that what is, in its own essence, a vice, has become endowed with the appearance, and met with the reception of a virtue. Antiquity, as usual, has lent a certain degree of speciousness even to the absurd. So continuously have we puffed, that we have at length come to think puffing the duty, and plain speaking the dereliction. What we began in gross error, we persist in through habit. Having adopted, in the earlier days of our literature, the untenable idea that this literature, as a whole, could be advanced by an indiscriminate approbation bestowed on its every effort—having adopted this idea, we say, without attention to the obvious fact that praise of all was bitter although negative censure to the few alone deserving, and that the only result of the system, in the fostering way, would be the fostering of folly—we now continue our vile practices through the supineness of custom, even while, in our national self-conceit, we repudiate that necessity for patronage and protection in which originated our conduct. In a word, the press throughout the country has not been ashamed to make head against the very few bold attempts at independence which have, from time to time, been made in the face of the reigning order of things. And if, in one, or perhaps two, insulated cases, the spirit of severe truth, sustained by an unconquerable will, was not to be so put down, then, forthwith, were private chicaneries set in motion; then was had resort, on the part of those who considered themselves injured by the severity of criticism, (and who were so, if the just contempt of every ingenuous man is injury,) resort to arts of the most virulent indignity, to untraceable slanders, to ruthless assassination in the dark. We say these things were done, while the press in general looked on, and, with a full understanding of the wrong perpetrated, spoke not against the wrong. The idea had absolutely gone abroad—had grown up little by little into toleration—that attacks however just, upon a literary reputation however obtained, however untenable, were well retaliated by the basest and most unfounded traduction of personal fame. But is this an age—is this a day—in which it can be necessary even to advert to such considerations as that the book of the author is the property of the public, and that the issue of the book is the throwing down of the gauntlet to the reviewer—to the reviewer whose duty is the plainest; the duty not even of approbation, or of censure, or of silence, at his own will, but at the sway of those sentiments and of those opinions which are derived from the author himself, through the medium of his written and published words? True criticism is the reflection of the thing criticised upon the spirit of the critic.

But *à nos moutons*[7]—to the "Quacks of Helicon." This satire has many faults besides those upon which we have commented. The title, for example, is not sufficiently distinctive, although otherwise good. It does not confine the subject to *American* quacks, while the work does. The two concluding lines enfeeble instead of strengthening the *finale*, which would have been exceedingly pungent without them. The individual portions of the thesis are strung together too much at random—a natural sequence is not always preserved—so that although the lights of the picture are often forcible, the whole has what, in artistical parlance, is termed an accidental and spotty appearance. In truth, the parts of the poem have evidently been composed each by each, as separate themes, and afterwards fitted into the general satire, in the best manner possible.

---

[7]Literally, "to our sheep;" in this context, "back to the subject."

But a more reprehensible sin than any or than all of these is yet to be mentioned—the sin of indiscriminate censure. Even here Mr. Wilmer has erred through imitation. He has held in view the sweeping denunciations of the Dunciad, and of the later (abortive) satire of Byron. No one in his senses can deny the justice of the general charges of corruption in regard to which we have just spoken from the text of our author. But are there *no* exceptions? We should indeed blush if there were not. And is there *no* hope? Time will show. We cannot do everything in a day—*Non se gano Zamora en un ora.*[8] Again, it cannot be gainsaid that the greater number of those who hold high places in our poetical literature are absolute nincompoops—fellows alike innocent of reason and of rhyme. But neither are we *all* brainless, nor is the devil himself so black as he is painted. Mr. Wilmer must read the chapter in Rabelais' *Gargantua, "de ce qu' est signifié par les couleurs blanc et bleu"*[9]—for there is *some* difference after all. It will not do in a civilized land to run a-muck like a Malay. Mr. Morris *has* written good songs. Mr. Bryant is not *all* a fool. Mr. Willis is not *quite* an ass. Mr. Longfellow *will* steal, but perhaps he cannot help it, (for we have heard of such things,) and then it must not be denied that *nil tetigit quod non ornavit.*[10]

The fact is that our author, in the rank exuberance of his zeal, seems to think as little of discrimination as the Bishop of Autun* did of the Bible. Poetical "things in general" are the windmills at which he spurs his rosinante. He as often tilts at what is true as at what is false; and thus his lines are like the mirrors of the temples of Smirna, which represent the fairest images as deformed. But the talent, the fearlessness, and especially the *design* of this book, will suffice to save it even from that dreadful damnation of "silent contempt" to which editors throughout the country, if we are not very much mistaken, will endeavor, one and all, to consign it.

---

[8]"Zamora is not won in an hour." Cervantes, *Don Quixote*, II, 71.

[9]"of what is meant by the colors white and blue." François Rabelais, *Gargantua and Pantagruel* (1532–1552), Book i, ix and x. In this work, white connotes joy, and blue, heaven. Poe may mean to suggest that even a satire as legendary as this one contains coverage of things that are praiseworthy.

[10]"He touched nothing which he did not grace," Samuel Johnson's epitaph on Oliver Goldsmith.

*Talleyrand.

Exordium to Critical Notices
[*Graham's Magazine*, January 1842]

In this inaugural notice of a new year of critical remonstration, Poe took the opportunity to articulate his theory of criticism. Inveighing against "the cant of generality," Poe took the position that a work of criticism is sui generis: *not necessarily an essay, but a precise analytical evaluation of a literary work by a critic who, scorning anonymity, stands accountable for all that he writes. The tendency toward self-portraiture here is, of course, hardly a coincidence.*

In commencing, with the New Year, a New Volume, we shall be permitted to say a very few words by way of *exordium* to our usual chapter of Reviews, or, as we should prefer calling them, of Critical Notices. Yet we speak *not* for the sake of the *exordium,* but because we have really something to say, and know not when or where better to say it.

That the public attention, in America, has, of late days, been more than usually directed to the matter of literary criticism, is plainly apparent. Our periodicals are beginning to acknowledge the importance of the science (shall we so term it?) and to disdain the flippant *opinion* which so long has been made its substitute.

Time was when we imported our critical decisions from the mother country. For many years we enacted a perfect farce of subserviency to the *dicta* of Great Britain. At last a revulsion of feeling, with self-disgust, necessarily ensued. Urged by these, we plunged into the opposite extreme. In throwing *totally* off that "authority," whose voice had so long been so sacred, we even surpassed, and by much, our original folly. But the watchword now was, "a national literature!"—as if any true literature *could be* "national"—as if the world at large were not the only proper stage for the literary *histrio.* We became, suddenly, the merest and maddest *partizans* in letters. Our papers spoke of "tariffs" and "protection." Our Magazines had habitual passages about that "truly native novelist, Mr. Cooper," or that "staunch American genius, Mr. Paulding." Unmindful of the spirit of the axioms that "a prophet has no honor in his own land" and that "a hero is never a hero to his *valet-de-chambre*"—axioms founded in reason and in truth—our reviews urged the propriety—our booksellers the necessity, of strictly "American" themes. A foreign subject, at this epoch, was a weight more than enough to drag down into the very depths of critical damnation the finest writer owning nativity in the States; while, on the reverse, we found ourselves daily in the paradoxical dilemma of liking, or pretending to like, a stupid book the better because (sure enough) its stupidity was of our own growth, and discussed our own affairs.

It is, in fact, but very lately that this anomalous state of feeling has shown any signs of subsidence. Still it *is* subsiding. Our views of literature in general having expanded, we begin to demand the use—to inquire into the offices and provinces of criticism—to regard it more as an art based immoveably in nature, less as a mere system of fluctuating and conventional dogmas. And, with the prevalence of these ideas, has arrived a distaste even to the home-dictation of the book-seller-*coteries*. If our editors are not as yet *all* independent of the will of a publisher, a majority of them scruple, at least, *to confess* a subservience, and enter into no positive combinations against the minority who despise and discard it. And this is a *very* great improvement of exceedingly late date.

Escaping these quicksands, our criticism is nevertheless in some danger—some very little danger—of falling into the pit of a most detestable species of cant—the cant of *generality*. This tendency has been given it, in the first instance, by the onward and tumultuous spirit of the age. With the increase of the thinking-material comes the desire, if not the necessity, of abandoning particulars for masses. Yet in our individual case, as a nation, we seem merely to have adopted this bias from the British Quarterly Reviews, upon which our own Quarterlies have been slavishly and pertinaciously modelled. In the foreign journal, the review or criticism properly so termed, has gradually yet steadily degenerated into what we see it at present—that is to say into anything but criticism. Originally a "review," was not so called as *lucus a non lucendo*.[1] Its name conveyed a just idea of its design. It reviewed, or surveyed the book whose title formed its text, and, giving an analysis of its contents, passed judgment upon its merits or defects. But, through the system of anonymous contribution, this natural process lost ground from day to day. The name of a writer being known only to a few, it became to him an object not so much to write well, as to write fluently, at so many guineas per sheet. The analysis of a book is a matter of time and of mental exertion. For many classes of composition there is required a deliberate perusal, with notes, and subsequent generalization. An easy substitute for this labor was found in a digest or compendium of the work noticed, with copious extracts—or a still easier, in random comments upon such passages as accidentally met the eye of the critic, with the passages themselves copied at full length. The mode of reviewing most in favor, however, because carrying with it the greatest *semblance* of care, was that of diffuse essay upon the subject matter of the publication,

---

[1]"an illumination from one who does not illuminate."

the reviewer (?) using the facts alone which the publication supplied, and using them as material for some theory, the sole concern, bearing, and intention of which, was mere difference of opinion with the author. These came at length to be understood and habitually practised as the customary or conventional *fashions* of review; and although the nobler order of intellects did not fall into the full heresy of these fashions—we may still assert that even Macaulay's nearest approach to criticism in its legitimate sense, is to be found in his article upon Ranke's "History of the Popes"—an article in which the whole strength of the reviewer is put forth *to account* for a single fact—the progress of Romanism—which the book under discussion has established.[2]

Now, while we do not mean to deny that a good essay is a good thing, we yet assert that these papers on general topics have nothing whatever to do with that *criticism* which their evil example has nevertheless infected *in se*.[3] Because these dogmatising pamphlets, which *were once* "Reviews," have lapsed from their original faith, it does not follow that the faith itself is extinct—that "there shall be no more cakes and ale"—that criticism, in its old acceptation, does not exist. But we complain of a growing inclination on the part of our lighter journals to believe, on such grounds, that such is the fact—that because the British Quarterlies, through supineness, and our own, through a degrading imitation, have come to merge all varieties of vague generalization in the one title of "Review," it therefore results that criticism, being everything in the universe, is, consequently, nothing whatever in fact. For to this end, and to none other conceivable, is the tendency of such propositions, for example, as we find in a late number of that very clever monthly magazine, Arcturus.[4]

"But *now*" (the emphasis on the *now* is our own)—"But *now*," says Mr. Mathews, in the preface to the first volume of his journal, "criticism has a wider scope and a universal interest. It dismisses errors of grammar, and hands over an imperfect rhyme or a false quantity to

---

[2]Thomas Babington Macaulay (1800–1859), British statesman, poet, historian, essayist, and biographer. Poe had previously reviewed the widely admired Macaulay volume that included this essay on Leopold von Ranke's 3-volume *History of the Popes* (published in English in 1840). He had praised Macaulay's style and rhetoric, but stated, "in the way of criticism there is nothing [in this essay] worth the name."

[3]"in itself."

[4]A short-lived but influential monthly magazine sponsored by the New York-based coterie of U.S. literary nationalists known as the Young Americans (with whom Poe later briefly allied himself). Edited by Cornelius Mathews and Evert A. Duyckinck, the *Arcturus* published many of the best known American writers of the day, including Nathaniel Hawthorne, Henry Wadsworth Longfellow, and James Russell Lowell. Despite the presence of these luminaries in its pages, the magazine lasted just a year and a half, from December 1840 until May 1842.

the proof-reader; it looks *now* to the heart of the subject and the author's design. It is a test of opinion. Its acuteness is not pedantic, but philosophical; it unravels the web of the author's mystery to interpret his meaning to others; it detects his sophistry, because sophistry is injurious to the heart and life; it promulgates his beauties with liberal, generous praise, because this is its true duty as the servant of truth. Good criticism may be well asked for, since it is the type of the literature of the day. It gives method to the universal inquisitiveness on every topic relating to life or action. A criticism, *now,* includes every form of literature, except perhaps the imaginative and the strictly dramatic. It is an essay, a sermon, an oration, a chapter in history, a philosophical speculation, a prose-poem, an art-novel, a dialogue; it admits of humor, pathos, the personal feelings of autobiography, the broadest views of statesmanship. As the ballad and the epic were the productions of the days of Homer, the review is the native characteristic growth of the nineteenth century."

We respect the talents of Mr. Mathews, but must dissent from nearly all that he here says. The species of "review" which he designates as the "characteristic growth of the nineteenth century" is only the growth of the last twenty or thirty years *in Great Britain.* The French Reviews, for example, which are *not* anonymous, are very different things, and preserve the *unique* spirit of true criticism. And what need we say of the Germans?—what of Winkelmann, of Novalis, of Schelling, of Göethe, of Augustus William, and of Frederick Schlegel?—that their magnificent *critiques raisonnées* differ from those of Kaimes, of Johnson, and of Blair, in principle not at all, (for the principles of these artists will not fail until Nature herself expires,) but solely in their more careful elaboration, their greater thoroughness, their more profound analysis and application of the principles themselves. That a criticism *"now"* should be different in spirit, as Mr. Mathews supposes, from a criticism at any previous period, is to insinuate a charge of variability in laws that cannot vary—the laws of man's heart and intellect—for these are the sole basis upon which the true critical art is established. And this art *"now"* no more than in the days of the "Dunciad," can, without neglect of its duty, "dismiss errors of grammar," or "hand over an imperfect rhyme or a false quantity to the proof-reader." What is meant by a "test of opinion" in the connexion here given the words by Mr. M., we do not comprehend as clearly as we could desire. By this phrase we are as completely enveloped in doubt as was Mirabeau in the castle of *If.*[5] To our imperfect appreciation it seems to form a portion of that general vagueness

---

[5]Honoré Mirabeau (1749–1791), French revolutionary orator and defender of the constitutional monarchy. He was imprisoned for several years in the Chateau d'If.

which is the *tone* of the whole philosophy at this point:—but all that which our journalist describes a criticism to be, is all that which we sturdily maintain it *is not*. Criticism is *not*, we think, an essay, nor a sermon, nor an oration, nor a chapter in history, nor a philosophical speculation, nor a prose-poem, nor an art novel, nor a dialogue. In fact, it *can be* nothing in the world but—a criticism. But if it were all that Arcturus imagines, it is not very clear why it might not be equally "imaginative" or "dramatic"—a romance or a melo-drama, or both. That it would be a farce cannot be doubted.

It is against this frantic spirit of *generalization* that we protest. We have a word, "criticism," whose import is sufficiently distinct, through long usage, at least; and we have an art of high importance and clearly-ascertained limit, which this word is quite well enough understood to represent. Of that conglomerate science to which Mr. Mathews so eloquently alludes, and of which we are instructed that it is anything and everything at once—of this science we know nothing, and really wish to know less; but we object to our contemporary's appropriation in its behalf, of a term to which we, in common with a large majority of mankind, have been accustomed to attach a certain and very definitive idea. Is there no word but "criticism" which may be made to serve the purposes of "Arcturus?" Has it any objection to Orphicism, or Dialism, or Emersonism, or any other pregnant compound indicative of confusion worse confounded?[6]

Still, we must not pretend a total misapprehension of the idea of Mr. Mathews, and we should be sorry that he misunderstood *us*. It may be granted that we differ only in terms—although the difference will yet be found not unimportant in effect. Following the highest authority, we would wish, in a word, to limit literary criticism to comment upon *Art*. A book is written—and it is only *as the book* that we subject it to review. With the opinions of the work, considered otherwise than in their relation to the work itself, the critic has really nothing to do. It is his part simply to decide upon *the mode* in which these opinions are brought to bear. Criticism is thus no "test of opinion." For this test, the work, divested of its pretensions as an *art-product*, is turned over for discussion to the world at large—and first, to that class which it especially addresses—if a history, to the historian—if a metaphysical treatise, to the moralist. In this, the only true and intelligible sense, it will be seen that criticism, the test or

---

[6]Poe is alluding here to "Orphic Sayings" by Bronson Alcott, to *The Dial,* the magazine of the New England Transcendentalists, and to Ralph Waldo Emerson, the movement's leading avatar. Transcendentalism was a New England-based social and intellectual movement that advocated an individualistic, spontaneous approach to the world of people and nature. Poe, with his emphasis on a finely crafted aesthetic, was generally hostile to Transcendentalism and its proponents.

analysis of *Art,* (*not* of opinion,) is only properly employed upon pro-ductions which have their basis in art itself, and although the jour-nalist (whose duties and objects are multiform) may turn aside, at pleasure, from the *mode* or vehicle of opinion to discussion of the opinion conveyed—it is still clear that he is *"critical"* only in so much as he deviates from his true province not at all.

And of the critic himself what shall we say?—for as yet we have spo-ken only the *proem* to the true *epopea.* What *can* we better say of him than, with Bulwer, that "he must have courage to blame boldly, mag-nanimity to eschew envy, genius to appreciate, learning to compare, an eye for beauty, an ear for music, and a heart for feeling." Let us add, a talent for analysis and a solemn indifference to abuse.

Review
[*Graham's Magazine*, May 1842]

Nathaniel Hawthorne, *Twice-Told Tales*
(Boston: James Munroe & Co.)

Poe's review of Hawthorne's Twice-Told Tales *reveals at least as much about Poe as about the book he is discussing. Although he expresses admiration for Hawthorne's genius, Poe also suggests here that Hawthorne has plagiarized Poe's own "William Wilson" in one of his tales. (The accusation is groundless, as Poe's tale was composed after the Hawthorne story in question.) Poe's finger-pointing highlights his definition of originality and the crucial role it plays in his critical and creative practice.*

We said a few hurried words about Mr. Hawthorne in our last number, with the design of speaking more fully in the present. We are still, however, pressed for room, and must necessarily discuss his volumes more briefly and more at random than their high merits deserve.

The book professes to be a collection of *tales*, yet is, in two respects, misnamed. These pieces are now in their third republication, and, of course, are thrice-told. Moreover, they are by no means *all* tales, either in the ordinary or in the legitimate understanding of the term. Many of them are pure essays, for example, "Sights from a Steeple," "Sunday at Home," "Little Annie's Ramble," "A Rill from the Town-Pump," "The Toll-Gatherer's Day," "The Haunted Mind," "The Sister Years," "Snow-Flakes," "Night Sketches," and "Foot-Prints on the Sea-Shore." We mention these matters chiefly on account of their discrepancy with that marked precision and finish by which the body of the work is distinguished.

Of the Essays just named, we must be content to speak in brief. They are each and all beautiful, without being characterised by the polish and adaptation so visible in the tales proper. A painter would at once note their leading or predominant feature, and style it *repose*. There is no attempt at effect. All is quiet, thoughtful, subdued. Yet this repose may exist simultaneously with high originality of thought; and Mr. Hawthorne has demonstrated the fact. At every turn we meet with novel combinations; yet these combinations never surpass the limits of the quiet. We are soothed as we read; and withal is a calm astonishment that ideas so apparently obvious have never occurred

or been presented to us before. Herein our author differs materially
from Lamb or Hunt or Hazlitt—who, with vivid originality of manner
and expression, have less of the true novelty of thought than is generally supposed, and whose originality, at best, has an uneasy and
meretricious quaintness, replete with startling effects unfounded in
nature, and inducing trains of reflection which lead to no satisfactory result. The Essays of Hawthorne have much of the character of
Irving, with more of originality, and less of finish; while, compared
with the Spectator, they have a vast superiority at all points. The
Spectator, Mr. Irving, and Mr. Hawthorne have in common that tranquil and subdued manner which we have chosen to denominate
repose; but, in the case of the two former, this repose is attained rather
by the absence of novel combination, or of originality, than otherwise, and consists chiefly in the calm, quiet, unostentatious expression of commonplace thoughts, in an unambitious unadulterated
Saxon. In them, by strong effort, we are made to conceive the
absence of all. In the essays before us the absence of effort is too obvious to be mistaken, and a strong undercurrent of *suggestion* runs continuously beneath the upper stream of the tranquil thesis. In short,
these effusions of Mr. Hawthorne are the product of a truly imaginative intellect, restrained, and in some measure repressed, by fastidi-
ousness of taste, by constitutional melancholy and by indolence.

But it is of his tales that we desire principally to speak. The tale
proper, in our opinion, affords unquestionably the fairest field for
the exercise of the loftiest talent, which can be afforded by the wide
domains of mere prose. Were we bidden to say how the highest
genius could be most advantageously employed for the best display
of its own powers, we should answer, without hesitation—in the composition of a rhymed poem, not to exceed in length what might be
perused in an hour. Within this limit alone can the highest order of
true poetry exist. We need only here say, upon this topic, that, in
almost all classes of composition, the unity of effect or impression is
a point of the greatest importance. It is clear, moreover, that this
unity cannot be thoroughly preserved in productions whose perusal
cannot be completed at one sitting. We may continue the reading of
a prose composition, from the very nature of prose itself, much
longer than we can persevere, to any good purpose, in the perusal of
a poem. This latter, if truly fulfilling the demands of the poetic sentiment, induces an exaltation of the soul which cannot be long sustained. All high excitements are necessarily transient. Thus a long
poem is a paradox. And, without unity of impression, the deepest
effects cannot be brought about. Epics were the offspring of an
imperfect sense of Art, and their reign is no more. A poem *too* brief
may produce a vivid, but never an intense or enduring impression.

Without a certain continuity of effort—without a certain duration or repetition of purpose—the soul is never deeply moved. There must be the dropping of the water upon the rock. De Béranger[1] has wrought brilliant things—pungent and spirit-stirring—but, like all immassive bodies, they lack *momentum,* and thus fail to satisfy the Poetic Sentiment. They sparkle and excite, but, from want of continuity, fail deeply to impress. Extreme brevity will degenerate into epigrammatism; but the sin of extreme length is even more unpardonable. *In medio tutissimus ibis.*[2]

Were we called upon however to designate that class of composition which, next to such a poem as we have suggested, should best fulfil the demands of high genius—should offer it the most advantageous field of exertion—we should unhesitatingly speak of the prose tale, as Mr. Hawthorne has here exemplified it. We allude to the short prose narrative, requiring from a half-hour to one or two hours in its perusal. The ordinary novel is objectionable, from its length, for reasons already stated in substance. As it cannot be read at one sitting, it deprives itself, of course, of the immense force derivable from *totality.* Worldly interests intervening during the pauses of perusal, modify, annul, or counteract, in a greater or less degree, the impressions of the book. But simple cessation in reading would, of itself, be sufficient to destroy the true unity. In the brief tale, however, the author is enabled to carry out the fulness of his intention, be it what it may. During the hour of perusal the soul of the reader is at the writer's control. There are no external or extrinsic influences—resulting from weariness or interruption.

A skilful literary artist has constructed a tale. If wise, he has not fashioned his thoughts to accommodate his incidents; but having conceived, with deliberate care, a certain unique or single *effect* to be wrought out, he then invents such incidents—he then combines such events as may best aid him in establishing this preconceived effect. If his very initial sentence tend not to the outbringing of this effect, then he has failed in his first step. In the whole composition there should be no word written, of which the tendency, direct or indirect, is not to the one pre-established design. And by such means, with such care and skill, a picture is at length painted which leaves in the mind of him who contemplates it with a kindred art, a sense of the fullest satisfaction. The idea of the tale has been presented unblemished, because undisturbed; and this is an end unattainable by the

---

[1]Pierre Jean De Béranger (1780–1857) was a French poet, very popular and much cited in the 1830s and 1840s. His work was often political in nature. Translations of his writings into English were published by Griswold. See Burton R. Pollin, *Discoveries in Poe,* pp. 54–74.

[2]"You will go most safely in the middle (road)."

novel. Undue brevity is just as exceptionable here as in the poem; but undue length is yet more to be avoided.

We have said that the tale has a point of superiority even over the poem. In fact, while the *rhythm* of this latter is an essential aid in the development of the poem's highest idea—the idea of the Beautiful—the artificialities of this rhythm are an inseparable bar to the development of all points of thought or expression which have their basis in *Truth*. But Truth is often, and in very great degree, the aim of the tale. Some of the finest tales are tales of ratiocination. Thus the field of this species of composition, if not in so elevated a region on the mountain of Mind, is a table-land of far vaster extent than the domain of the mere poem. Its products are never so rich, but infinitely more numerous, and more appreciable by the mass of mankind. The writer of the prose tale, in short, may bring to his theme a vast variety of modes or inflections of thought and expression—(the ratiocinative, for example, the sarcastic or the humorous) which are not only antagonistical to the nature of the poem, but absolutely forbidden by one of its most peculiar and indispensable adjuncts; we allude of course, to rhythm. It may be added, here, *par parenthèse*, that the author who aims at the purely beautiful in a prose tale is laboring at great disadvantage. For Beauty can be better treated in the poem. Not so with terror, or passion, or horror, or a multitude of such other points. And here it will be seen how full of prejudice are the usual animadversions against those *tales of effect* many fine examples of which were found in the earlier numbers of Blackwood. The impressions produced were wrought in a legitimate sphere of action, and constituted a legitimate although sometimes an exaggerated interest. They were relished by every man of genius: although there were found many men of genius who condemned them without just ground. The true critic will but demand that the design intended be accomplished, to the fullest extent, by the means most advantageously applicable.

We have very few American tales of real merit—we may say, indeed, none, with the exception of "The Tales of a Traveller" of Washington Irving, and these "Twice-Told Tales" of Mr. Hawthorne. Some of the pieces of Mr. John Neal abound in vigor and originality; but in general, his compositions of this class are excessively diffuse, extravagant, and indicative of an imperfect sentiment of Art. Articles at random are, now and then, met with in our periodicals which might be advantageously compared with the best effusions of the British Magazines; but, upon the whole, we are far behind our progenitors in this department of literature.

Of Mr. Hawthorne's Tales we would say, emphatically, that they belong to the highest region of Art—an Art subservient to genius of a very lofty order. We had supposed, with good reason for so supposing, that he had been thrust into his present position by one of the impudent *cliques* which beset our literature, and whose pretensions it is our full purpose to expose at the earliest opportunity; but we have been most agreeably mistaken. We know of few compositions which the critic can more honestly commend then these "Twice-Told Tales." As Americans, we feel proud of the book.

Mr. Hawthorne's distinctive trait is invention, creation, imagination, originality—a trait which, in the literature of fiction, is positively worth all the rest. But the nature of originality, so far as regards its manifestation in letters, is but imperfectly understood. The inventive or original mind as frequently displays itself in novelty of *tone* as in novelty of matter. Mr. Hawthorne is original at *all* points.

It would be a matter of some difficulty to designate the best of these tales; we repeat that, without exception, they are beautiful. "Wakefield" is remarkable for the skill with which an old idea—a well-known incident—is worked up or discussed. A man of whims conceives the purpose of quitting his wife and residing *incognito,* for twenty years, in her immediate neighborhood. Something of this kind actually happened in London. The force of Mr. Hawthorne's tale lies in the analysis of the motives which must or might have impelled the husband to such folly, in the first instance, with the possible causes of his perseverance. Upon this thesis a sketch of singular power has been constructed.

"The Wedding Knell" is full of the boldest imagination—an imagination fully controlled by taste. The most captious critic could find no flaw in this production.

"The Minister's Black Veil" is a masterly composition of which the sole defect is that to the rabble its exquisite skill will be *caviare.* The *obvious* meaning of this article will be found to smother its insinuated one. The *moral* put into the mouth of the dying minister will be supposed to convey the *true* import of the narrative; and that a crime of dark dye, (having reference to the "young lady") has been committed, is a point which only minds congenial with that of the author will perceive.

"Mr. Higginbotham's Catastrophe" is vividly original and managed most dexterously.

"Dr. Heidegger's Experiment" is exceedingly well imagined, and executed with surpassing ability. The artist breathes in every line of it.

"The White Old Maid" is objectionable, even more than the "Minister's Black Veil," on the score of its mysticism. Even with the thoughtful and analytic, there will be much trouble in penetrating its entire import.

"The Hollow of the Three Hills" we would quote in full, had we space;—not as evincing higher talent than any of the other pieces, but as affording an excellent example of the author's peculiar ability. The subject is common-place. A witch subjects the Distant and the Past to the view of a mourner. It has been the fashion to describe, in such cases, a mirror in which the images of the absent appear; or a cloud of smoke is made to arise, and thence the figures are gradually unfolded. Mr. Hawthorne has wonderfully heightened his effect by making the ear, in place of the eye, the medium by which the fantasy is conveyed. The head of the mourner is enveloped in the cloak of the witch, and within its magic folds there arise sounds which have an all-sufficient intelligence. Throughout this article also, the artist is conspicuous—not more in positive than in negative merits. Not only is all done that should be done, but (what perhaps is an end with more difficulty attained) there is nothing done which should not be. Every word *tells*, and there is not a word which does *not* tell.

In "Howe's Masquerade" we observe something which resembles a plagiarism—but which *may be* a very flattering coincidence of thought. We quote the passage in question.

> "*With a dark flush of wrath* upon his brow they saw the general *draw his sword* and *advance to meet* the figure *in the cloak* before the latter had stepped one pace upon the floor.
>
> "'*Villain, unmuffle yourself,*' cried he, 'you pass no farther!'
>
> "The figure, without blenching a hair's breadth from the sword which was pointed at his breast, made a solemn pause, and *lowered the cape of the cloak* from his face, yet not sufficiently for the spectators to catch a glimpse of it. But Sir William Howe had evidently seen enough. The sternness of his countenance gave place to a look of wild amazement, if not horror, while he recoiled several steps from the figure, *and let fall his sword* upon the floor."—See vol. 2, page 20.

The idea here is, that the figure in the cloak is the phantom or reduplication of Sir William Howe; but in an article called "William Wilson," one of the "Tales of the Grotesque and Arabesque," we have not only the same idea, but the same idea similarly presented in several respects. We quote two paragraphs, which our readers may compare with what has been already given. We have italicized, above, the immediate particulars of resemblance.

> "The brief moment in which I averted my eyes had been sufficient to produce, apparently, a material change in the arrangement at the upper or farther end of the room. A large mirror, it appeared to me, now stood where none had been perceptible before: and as I stepped up to it in extremity of terror, mine own image, but with features all pale and dabbled in blood, *advanced* with a feeble and tottering gait to meet me.
>
> "Thus it appeared I say, but was not. It was Wilson, who then stood

before me in the agonies of dissolution. Not a line in all the marked and singular lineaments of that face which was not even identically mine own. *His mask and cloak lay where he had thrown them, upon the floor.*"—Vol. 2. p. 57.

Here it will be observed that, not only are the two general conceptions identical, but there are various *points* of similarity. In each case the figure seen is the wraith or duplication of the beholder. In each case scene is a masquerade. In each case the figure is cloaked. In each, there is a quarrel—that is to say, angry words pass between the parties. In each the beholder is enraged. In each the cloak and sword fall upon the floor. The "villain, unmuffle yourself," of Mr. H. is precisely paralleled by a passage at page 56 of "William Wilson."

In the way of objection we have scarcely a word to say of these tales. There is, perhaps, a somewhat too general or prevalent *tone*—a tone of melancholy and mysticism. The subjects are insufficiently varied. There is not so much of *versatility* evinced as we might well be warranted in expecting from the high powers of Mr. Hawthorne. But beyond these trivial exceptions we have really none to make. The style is purity itself. Force abounds. High imagination gleams from every page. Mr. Hawthorne is a man of the truest genius. We only regret that the limits of our Magazine will not permit us to pay him that full tribute of commendation, which, under other circumstances, we should be so eager to pay.

Review

[*Boston Miscellany*, November 1842]

Rufus W. Griswold, *The Poets and Poetry of America, with a Historical Introduction.*
(Second Edition. Philadelphia: Carey & Hart)

Poe parlays his favorable review of this early anthology of American poetry into a chance to meditate on the state of the national literature. However, this compliment did not win him the loyalty of the volume's compiler, Rufus Wilmot Griswold. Griswold, a member of the New York literary coterie that Poe attacked so often, somehow gained the position of literary executor of Poe's writings. Presumably acting in revenge for Poe's attacks on his friend Lewis Gaylord Clark, Griswold included in his edition of Poe's edited works a vicious and deliberately distorted account of Poe's life, death, and writing. This posthumous character assassination was mainly successful. Poe's American reputation became moribund, and remained so until the French Symbolist poets began to export Poe back to his native literary canon.

That we are not a poetical people has been asserted so often and so roundly, both at home and abroad, that the slander, through mere dint of repetition, has come to be received as truth. Yet nothing can be farther removed from it. The mistake is but a portion, or corollary, of the old dogma, that the calculating faculties are at war with the ideal; while, in fact, it may be demonstrated that the two divisions of mental power are never to be found, in perfection, apart. The *highest* order of the imaginative intellect is always preëminently mathematical; and the converse.

The idiosyncrasy of our political position has stimulated into early action whatever practical talent we possessed. Even in our national infancy we evinced a degree of utilitarian ability which put to shame the mature skill of our forefathers. While yet in leading-strings we proved ourselves adepts in all the arts and sciences which promote the *comfort* of the animal man. But the arena of exertion, and of consequent distinction, into which our first and most obvious wants impelled us, has been regarded as the field of our deliberate choice. Our necessities have been mistaken for our propensities. Having been forced to make rail-roads, it has been deemed impossible that we should make verse. Because it suited us to construct an engine in the first instance, it has been denied that we could compose an epic in the second. Because we were not all Homers in the beginning, it has been somewhat too rashly taken for granted that we shall be all Jeremy Benthams to the end.

But this is the purest insanity. The principles of the poetic senti-ment lie deep within the immortal nature of man, and have little nec-essary reference to the worldly circumstances which surround him. The poet in Arcady is, in Kamschadtka, the poet still. The self-same Saxon current animates the British and the American heart; nor can any social, or political, or moral, or physical conditions do more than momentarily repress the impulses which glow in our own bosoms as fervently as in those of our progenitors.

Those who have taken most careful note of our literature for the last ten or twelve years, will be most willing to admit that *we are* a poet-ical people; and in no respect is the fact more plainly evinced than in the eagerness with which books professing to compile or select from the productions of our native bards, are received and appreciated by the public. Such books meet with success, at least with sale, at peri-ods when the general market for literary wares is in a state of stagna-tion; and even the ill taste displayed in some of them has not sufficed to condemn. The "Specimens of American Poetry," by Kettell; the "Common-place Book of American Poetry," by Cheever; a Selection by General Morris; another by Mr. Bryant; the "Poets of America," by Mr. Keese—all these have been widely disseminated and well received. In some measure, to be sure, we must regard their success as an affair of personalities. Each individual, honored with a niche in the compiler's memory, is naturally anxious to possess a copy of the book so honoring him; and this anxiety will extend, in some cases, to ten or twenty of the immediate friends of the complimented; while, on the other hand, purchasers will arise, in no small number, from among a very different class—a class animated by very different feel-ings. I mean the omitted—the large body of those who, supposing themselves entitled to mention, have yet been unmentioned. These buy the unfortunate book as a matter of course, for the purpose of abusing it with a clear conscience and at leisure. But holding these deductions in view, we are still warranted in believing that the demand for works of the kind in question, is to be attributed, main-ly, to the general interest of the subject discussed. The public have been desirous of obtaining a more distinct view of our poetical liter-ature than the scattered effusions of our bards and the random crit-icisms of our periodicals, could afford. But, hitherto, nothing has been accomplished in the way of supplying the *desideratum*. The "specimens" of Kettell were specimens of nothing but the ignorance and ill taste of the compiler. A large proportion of what he gave to the world as American poetry, to the exclusion of much that was

really so, was the doggerel composition of individuals unheard of and
undreamed of, except by Mr. Kettell himself. Mr. Cheever's book did
not belie its title, and was excessively "Common-place." The selection
by General Morris was in so far good, that it accomplished its object
to the full extent. This object looked to nothing more than single,
brief extracts from the writings of every one in the country who had
established even the slightest reputation as poet. The extracts, so far
as our truer poets were concerned, were tastefully made; but the
proverbial kind feeling of the General seduced him into the admission of an inordinate quantity of the purest twattle. It was gravely
declared that we had more than *two hundred* poets in the land. The
compilation of Mr. Bryant, from whom much was expected, proved a
source of mortification to his friends, and of astonishment and dis-
appointment to all; merely showing that a poet is, necessarily, neither
a critical nor an unpartial judge of poetry. Mr. Keese succeeded
much better. He brought to his task, if not the most rigorous impartiality, at least a fine taste, a sound judgment, and a more thorough
acquaintance with our poetical literature than had distinguished
either of his predecessors.

Much, however, remained to be done; and here it may be right to
inquire—"What should be the aim of every compilation of the character now discussed?" The object, in general terms, may be stated, as
the conveying, within moderate compass, a distinct view of our poetry and of our poets. This, in fact, is the demand of the public. A book
is required, which shall not so much be the reflection of the compiler's peculiar views and opinions upon poetry in the abstract, as of the
popular judgment upon such poetical works as have come immediately within its observation. It is not the author's business to insist
upon his own theory, and, in its support, to rake up from the by-ways
of the country the "inglorious Miltons" who may, possibly, there
abound; neither, because ill according with this theory, is it his duty
to dethrone and reject those who have long maintained supremacy
in the estimation of the people. In this view, it will be seen that regard
must be paid to the mere *quantity* of a writer's effusions. He who has
published much, is not to be omitted because, in the opinion of the
compiler, he has written nothing fit for publication. On the other
hand, he who has extemporized a single song, which has met the eye
of no one but our bibliographer, is not to be set forth among the
poetical magnates, even although the one song itself be esteemed
equal to the very best of Béranger.[1]

Of the two classes of sins—the negative and the positive—those of
omission and those of commission—obvious ones of the former class

---

[1]See fn. 1 on p. 59.

are, beyond doubt, the more unpardonable. It is better to introduce half a dozen "great unknowns," than to give the "cut direct" to a single individual who has been fairly acknowledged as known. The public, in short, seem to demand *such a compendium of our poetical literature as shall embrace specimens from those works alone, of our recognised poets; which, either through accident, or by dint of merit, have been most particularly the subjects of public discussion.* We wish this, that we may be put in condition to decide for ourselves upon the justice or injustice of the reputation attained. In critical opinion much diversity exists; and, although there is but one true and tenable critical opinion, there are still a thousand, upon all topics, which, being only the shadows, have all the outlines, and assume all the movements, of the substance, of truth. Thus any critic who should exclude from the compendium all which tallied not with his individual ideas of the Muse, would be found to exclude nine hundred and ninety-nine thousandths of that which the public at large, embracing *all* varieties of opinion, has been accustomed to acknowledge as poesy.

These remarks apply only to the admission or rejection of poetical specimens. The public being put fairly in possession of the matter debated, with the provisions above-mentioned, the analysis of individual claims, *so far as the specimens extend,* is not only not unbecoming in the compiler, but a thing to be expected and desired. To this department of his work he should bring analytical ability; a distinct impression of the nature, the principles, and the aims of poetry; a thorough contempt for all prejudice at war with principle; a poetic sense of the poetic; sagacity in the detection, and audacity in the exposure of demerit; in a word talent *and faith*; the lofty honor which places mere courtesy beneath its feet; the boldness to praise an enemy, and the more unusual courage to damn a friend.

It is, in fact, by the criticism of the work, that the public voice will, in the end, decide upon its merits. In proportion to the ability or incapacity here displayed, will it, sooner or later, be approved or condemned. Nevertheless, the mere *compilation* is a point, perhaps, of greater importance. With the meagre published *aids* existing previously to Mr. Griswold's book, the labor of such an undertaking must have been great; and not less great the industry and general information in respect to our literary affairs, which have enabled him so successfully to prosecute it.

The work before us is indeed so vast an improvement upon those of a similar character which have preceded it, that we do its author some wrong in classing all together. Having explained, somewhat minutely, our views of the proper mode of compilation, and of the general aims of the species of book in question, it but remains to say that these views have been very nearly fulfilled in the "Poets and Poetry of America," while altogether unsatisfied by the earlier publications.

The volume opens with a preface, which, with some little super-erogation, is addressed "To the Reader;" inducing very naturally the query, whether the whole book is not addressed to the same individual. In this preface, which is remarkably well written and strictly to the purpose, the author thus evinces a just comprehension of the nature and objects of true poesy:

"He who looks on Lake George, or sees the sun rise on Mackinaw, or listens to the grand music of a storm, is divested, certainly for a time, of a portion of the alloy of his nature. The elements of power in all sublime sights and heavenly harmonies, should live in the poet's song, to which they can be transferred only by him who possesses the creative faculty. The sense of beauty, next to the miraculous divine suasion, is the means through which the human character is purified and elevated. *The creation of beauty, the manifestation of the real by the ideal, 'in words that move in metrical array,' is poetry.*"

The italics are our own; and we quote the passage because it embodies the *sole true* definition of what has been a thousand times erroneously defined.

The earliest specimens of poetry presented in the body of the work, are from the writings of Philip Freneau, "one of those worthies who, both with lyre and sword, aided in the achievement of our independence." But, in a volume professing to treat, generally, of the "Poets and Poetry of America," some mention of those who versified before Freneau, would of course, be considered desirable. Mr. Griswold has included, therefore, most of our earlier votaries of the Muse, with many specimens of their powers, in an exceedingly valuable "Historical Introduction;" his design being to exhibit as well "*the progress* as the condition of poetry in the United States."

The basis of the compilation is formed of short biographical and critical notices, with selections from the works of Philip Freneau, John Trumbull, Timothy Dwight, David Humphreys, Joel Barlow, Richard Alsop, St. John Honeywood, William Cliffton, Robert Treat Paine, Washington Allston, James Kirke Paulding, Levi Frisbie, John Pierpont, Andrews Norton, Richard H. Dana, Richard Henry Wilde, James A. Hillhouse, Charles Sprague, Hannah F. Gould, Carlos Wilcox, Henry Ware, Jr., William Cullen Bryant, John Neal, Joseph Rodman Drake, Maria Brooks, James Gates Percival, Fitz-Green Halleck, John G. C. Brainard, Samuel Griswold Goodrich, Isaac Clason, Lydia H. Sigourney, George Washington Doane, William B. O. Peabody, Robert C. Sands, Grenville Mellen, George Hill, James G. Brooks, Albert G. Greene, William Leggett, Edward C. Pinckney, Ralph Waldo Emerson, Sumner Lincoln Fairfield, Rufus Dawes,

Edmund D. Griffin, J. H. Bright, George D. Prentice, William Croswell, Walter Colton, Charles Fenno Hoffman, Mrs. Seba Smith, N. P. Willis, Edward Sanford, J. O. Rockwell, Thomas Ward, John H. Bryant, Henry Wadsworth Longfellow, William Gilmore Simms, George Lunt, Jonathan Lawrence, Elizabeth Hall, Emma C. Embury, John Greenleaf Whittier, Oliver Wendell Holmes, Albert Pike, Park Benjamin, Willis Gaylord Clark, William D. Gallagher, James Freeman Clarke, Elizabeth F. Ellett, James Aldrich, Anna Peyre Dinnies, Edgar Allan Poe, Isaac McLellan, Jr., Jones Very, Alfred B. Street, William H. Burleigh, William Jewett Pabodie, Louis Legrand Noble, C. P. Cranch, Henry Theodore Tuckerman, Epes Sargent, Lucy Hooper, Arthur Cleveland Coxe, James Russell Lowell, Amelia B. Welby, Lucretia and Margaret Davidson—in all, eighty-seven, chronologically arranged. In an appendix at the end of the volume, are included specimens from the works of sixty authors, whose compositions have either been too few, or in the editor's opinion too *mediocres,* to entitle them to more particular notice. To each of these specimens are appended foot notes, conveying a brief biographical summary, without anything of critical disquisition.

Of the general plan and execution of the work we have already expressed the fullest approbation. We know no one in America who could, or *who would,* have performed the task here undertaken, at once so well in accordance with the judgment of the critical, and so much to the satisfaction of the public. The labors, the embarrassments, the great difficulties of the achievement are not easily estimated by those before the scenes.

The writer of this article, in saying that, individually, he disagrees with many of the opinions expressed by Mr. Griswold, is merely suggesting what, in itself, would have been obvious without the suggestion. It rarely happens that any two persons thoroughly agree upon any one point. It would be mere madness to imagine that any two could coincide in every point of a case where exists a multiplicity of opinions upon a multiplicity of points. There is no one who, reading the volume before us, will not in a thousand instances, be tempted to throw it aside, because its prejudices and partialities are, in a thousand instances, altogether at war with his own. But when so tempted, he should bear in mind, that had the work been that of Aristarchus[2] himself, the discrepancies of opinion would still have startled him and vexed him as now.

We disagree then, with Mr. Griswold in *many* of his critical

---

[2]Aristarchus of Samothrace (c. 217–145 BCE), a leading Homeric scholar in his day and one of antiquity's greatest philologists. His work on the *Iliad* and the *Odyssey* has been integral to studies of Homer in later centuries.

estimates; although in general, we are proud to find his decisions our own. He has omitted from the body of his book, some one or two whom we should have been tempted to introduce. On the other hand, he has scarcely made us amends by introducing some one or two dozen whom we should have treated with contempt. We might complain too of a prepossession, evidently unperceived by himself, for the writers of New England. We might hint also, that in two or three cases, he has rendered himself liable to the charge of personal partiality; it is often so *very* difficult a thing to keep separate in the mind's eye, our conceptions of the poetry of a friend, from our impressions of his good fellowship and our recollections of the flavor of his wine.

But having said thus much in the way of fault-finding, we have said all. The book should be regarded as *the most important addition which our literature has for many years received.* It fills a void which should have been long ago supplied. It is written with judgment, with dignity and candor. Steering with a dexterity not to be sufficiently admired, between the Scylla of Prejudice on the one hand, and the Charybdis of Conscience on the other, Mr. Griswold in the "Poets and Poetry of America," has entitled himself to the thanks of his countrymen, while showing himself a man of taste, talent, *and tact.*

Prospectus of *The Stylus*
[*Philadelphia Saturday Museum*, **March 1843**]

Throughout his career Poe sought a secure purchase in the literary world, a perch from which he might have full editorial and financial autonomy to write and publish what he saw fit. (He briefly enjoyed this authority when he purchased the Broadway Journal *with borrowed money in 1845, but the magazine folded less than a year later.) Poe tried to get "The Stylus" off the ground for years without success. His vision for the magazine—"A Monthly Journal of General Literature to be Edited by Edgar A. Poe and Published in the City of Philadelphia, by Clarke & Poe"—as expressed in this prospectus, reflects his sense of "the general interests of the Republic of Letters."*

————unbending that all men
Of thy firm TRUTH may say—"Lo! this is writ
With the antique *iron pen.*
Launcelot Canning.

To the public.—The Prospectus of a Monthly Journal to have been called "THE PENN MAGAZINE," has already been partially circulated. Circumstances, in which the public have no interest, induced a suspension of the project, which is now, under the best auspices, resumed, with no other modification than that of the title. "The Penn Magazine," it has been thought, was a name somewhat too local in its suggestions, and "THE STYLUS" has been finally adopted.

It has become obvious, indeed, to even the most unthinking, that the period has at length arrived when a journal of the character here proposed, is demanded and will be sustained. The late movements on the great question of International Copy-Right, are but an index of the universal *disgust* excited by what is quaintly termed the *cheap* literature of the day:—as if that which is utterly worthless in itself, can be cheap at any price under the sun.

"The Stylus" will include about one hundred royal octavo pages, in single column, per month; forming two thick volumes per year. In its mechanical appearance—in its typography, paper and binding—it will far surpass all American journals of its kind. Engravings, when used, will be in the highest style of Art, but are promised only in obvious illustration of the text, and in strict keeping with the Magazine character. Upon application to the proprietors, by any agent of repute who may desire the work, or by any other individual who may feel interested, a specimen sheet will be forwarded. As, for many reasons, it is inexpedient to commence a journal of this kind at any other period than at the beginning or middle of the year, the first number of "The Stylus" will not be regularly issued until the first of July, 1843. In the meantime, to insure its perfect and permanent success, no means will be left untried which long experience, untiring energy, and the amplest capital, can supply. The price will be *Five Dollars* per annum, or *Three Dollars* per single volume, in advance. Letters which concern only the Editorial management may be addressed to Edgar A. Poe, individually; all others to Clarke & Poe.

The necessity for any very rigid definition of the literary character or aims of "The Stylus," is, in some measure, obviated by the general knowledge, on the part of the public, of the editor's connexion, formerly, with the two most successful periodicals in the country—"The Southern Literary Messenger," and "Graham's Magazine." Having no proprietary right, however, in either of these journals; his objects, too, being, in many respects, at variance with those of their very worthy owners; he found it not only impossible to effect anything, on the score of taste, for the mechanical appearance of the works, but exceedingly difficult, also, to stamp, upon their internal character, that *individuality* which he believes essential to the full success of all similar publications. In regard to their extensive and permanent influence, it appears to him that continuity, definitiveness, and a marked certainty of purpose, are requisites of vital importance; and he cannot help thinking that these requisites are attainable, only where a single mind has at least *the general* direction of the enterprise. Experience, in a word, has distinctly shown him—what, indeed, might have been demonstrated *à priori*—that in founding a Magazine wherein his interest should be not merely editorial, lies his sole chance of carrying out to completion whatever peculiar intentions he may have entertained.

In many important points, then, the new journal will differ widely from either of those named. It will endeavor to be at the same time more varied and more *unique,*—more vigorous, more pungent, more original, more individual, and more independent. It will discuss not only the Belles-Lettres, but, very thoroughly, the Fine Arts, with the Drama: and, more in brief, will give, each month, a Retrospect of our Political History. It will enlist the loftiest talent, but employ it not always in the loftiest—at least not always in the most pompous or Puritanical way. It will aim at affording a fair and not dishonorable field for the *true* intellect of the land, without reference to the mere *prestige* of celebrated names. It will support the general interests of the Republic of Letters, and insist upon regarding the world at large as the sole proper audience for the author. It will resist the dictation of Foreign Reviews. It will eschew the stilted dulness of our own Quarterlies, and while it *may*, if necessary, be no less learned, will deem it wiser to be less anonymous, and difficult to be more dishonest, than they.

An important feature of the work, and one which will be introduced in the opening number, will be a series of *Critical* and *Biographical Sketches* of *American Writers*. These sketches will be accompanied with full length and characteristic portraits; will include every person of literary note in America; and will investigate carefully, and with rigorous impartiality, the individual claims of each.

It shall, in fact, be the *chief purpose* of "The Stylus" to become known as a journal wherein may be found, at all times, upon all subjects within its legitimate reach, a sincere and a fearless opinion. It shall be a leading object to assert in precept, and to maintain in practice, the rights, while, in effect, it demonstrates the advantages, of an absolutely independent criticism;—a criticism self-sustained; guiding itself only by the purest rules of Art; analyzing and urging these rules as it applies them; holding itself aloof from all personal bias; and acknowledging no fear save that of outraging the Right.

CLARKE & POE.

N. B. Those friends of the Proprietors, throughout the country, who may feel disposed to support "The Stylus," will confer an important favor by sending in their names *at once.*

The provision in respect to payment *'in advance,'* is intended only as a general rule, and has reference to the Magazine *when established.* In the commencement, the subscription money will not be demanded untill the issue of the second number.

C. & P.

Review

[*Graham's Magazine*, November 1843]

James Fenimore Cooper, *Wyandotté, or The Hutted Knoll.* A Tale, by the Author of *The Pathfinder, Deerslayer, Last of the Mohicans, Pioneers, Prairie, &c., & c.*
(Philadelphia: Lea & Blanchard)

"With Indians or Nature," D.H. Lawrence wrote, "Poe has no truck." James Fenimore Cooper, on the other hand, may be fairly credited with popularizing the frontier novel, a genre invented in the United States. Cooper's Leather-stocking, the mythical hero of five such novels of the American wilderness written between 1823 and 1841, remains the basis for the novelist's reputation today. Highly successful in his time, Cooper was one of the scant few Americans who could publish books in a market ungoverned by international copyright laws, a situation which favored the reprinting of British works. Though not above soliciting contributions to the Southern Literary Messenger *from him, Poe nevertheless considered Cooper to be a vulgar popularizer, and he debunks Cooper's success in this review of* Wyandotté *(1843).*

"Wyandotté, or The Hutted Knoll" is, in its general features, precisely similar to the novels enumerated in the title. It is a forest subject; and, when we say this, we give assurance that the story is a good one; for Mr. Cooper has never been known to fail, either in the forest or upon the sea. The interest, as usual, has no reference to *plot,* of which, indeed, our novelist seems altogether regardless, or incapable, but depends, first, upon the nature of the theme; secondly, upon a Robinson-Crusoe-like detail in its management; and thirdly, upon the frequently repeated portraiture of the half-civilized Indian. In saying that the interest depends, *first,* upon the nature of the theme, we mean to suggest that this theme—life in the Wilderness—is one of intrinsic and universal interest, appealing to the heart of man in all phases; a theme, like that of life upon the ocean, so unfailingly omniprevalent in its power of arresting and absorbing attention, that while success or popularity is, with such a subject, expected as a matter of course, a failure might be properly regarded as conclusive evidence of imbecility on the part of the author. The two theses in question have been handled *usque ad nauseam*—and this through the instinctive perception of the universal interest which appertains to them. A writer, distrustful of his powers, can scarcely do better than discuss either one or the other. A man of genius will rarely, and should never, undertake either; first, because both are excessively hackneyed; and, secondly, because the reader never fails, in forming his opinion of a book, to make discount, either wittingly or unwittingly, for that intrinsic interest which is inseparable from the subject and independent of the manner in which it is treated. Very few and very dull indeed are those who do not instantaneously perceive the distinction; and thus there are two great classes of fictions,—a popular and widely circulated class, read with pleasure, but without admiration—in which the author is lost or forgotten; or remembered, if at all, with something very nearly akin to contempt; and then, a class not so popular, nor so widely diffused, in which, at every paragraph, arises a distinctive and highly pleasurable interest, springing from our perception and appreciation of the skill employed, of the genius evinced in the composition. After perusal of the one class, we think solely of the book—after reading the other, chiefly of the author. The former class leads to popularity—the latter to fame. In the former case, the books sometimes live, while the authors usually die; in the latter, even when the works perish, the man survives. Among American writers of the less generally circulated, but more worthy and more artistical fictions, we may mention Mr. Brockden Brown, Mr. John Neal, Mr. Simms,[1] Mr. Hawthorne; at the head of the more popular division we may place Mr. Cooper.

"The Hutted Knoll," without pretending to detail facts, gives a narrative of fictitious events, similar, in nearly all respects, to occurrences which actually happened during the opening scenes of the Revolution, and at other epochs of our history. It pictures the dangers, difficulties, and distresses of a large family, living, completely insulated, in the forest. The tale commences with a description of the "region which lies in the angle formed by the junction of the Mohawk with the Hudson, extending as far south as the line of Pennsylvania, and west to the verge of that vast rolling plain which composes Western New York"—a region of which the novelist has already frequently written, and the whole of which, with a trivial exception, was a wilderness before the Revolution. Within this district, and on a creek running into the Unadilla, a certain Captain Willoughby purchases an estate, or "patent," and there retires, with

---

[1]Charles Brockden Brown (1771–1810), one of America's first novelists, wrote seven novels in five years at the end of the eighteenth century, including *Wieland, or The Transformation* (1798), considered the first American Gothic novel, and *Edgar Huntly, or Memoirs of a Sleepwalker* (1799); Maine native John Neal (1793–1876) was prolific in a great variety of genres; William Gilmore Simms (1806–1870), a prominent proslavery intellectual, wrote many novels portraying the society, history and politics of South Carolina.

his family and dependents, to pass the close of his life in agricultural pursuits. He has been an officer in the British army, but, after serving many years, has sold his commission, and purchased one for his only son, Robert, who alone does not accompany the party into the forest. This party consists of the captain himself; his wife; his daughter, Beulah; an adopted daughter, Maud Meredith; an invalid sergeant, Joyce, who had served under the captain; a Presbyterian preacher, Mr. Woods; a Scotch mason, Jamie Allen; an Irish laborer, Michael O'Hearn; a Connecticut man, Joel Strides; four negroes, Old Plin and Young Plin, Big Smash and Little Smash; eight axe-men; a house-carpenter; a millwright, &c., &c. Besides these, a Tuscarora Indian called Nick, or *Wyandotté*, accompanies the expedition. This Indian, who figures largely in the story, and gives it its title, may be considered as the principal character—the one chiefly elaborated. He is an outcast from his tribe, has been known to Captain Willoughby for thirty years, and is a compound of all the good and bad qualities which make up the character of the half-civilized Indian. He does not remain with the settlers; but appears and re-appears at intervals upon the scene.

Nearly the whole of the first volume is occupied with a detailed account of the estate purchased, (which is termed "The Hutted Knoll" from a natural mound upon which the principal house is built) and of the progressive arrangements and improvements. Toward the close of the volume the Revolution commences; and the party at the "Knoll" are besieged by a band of savages and "rebels," with whom an understanding exists, on the part of Joel Strides, the Yankee. This traitor, instigated by the hope of possessing Captain Willoughby's estate, should it be confiscated, brings about a series of defections from the party of the settlers, and finally, deserting himself, reduces the whole number to six or seven, capable of bearing arms. Captain Willoughby resolves, however, to defend his post. His son, at this juncture, pays him a clandestine visit, and, endeavoring to reconnoitre the position of the Indians, is made captive. The captain, in an attempt at rescue, is murdered by Wyandotté, whose vindictive passions had been aroused by ill-timed allusions, on the part of Willoughby, to floggings previously inflicted, by his orders, upon the Indian. Wyandotté, however, having satisfied his personal vengeance, is still the ally of the settlers. He guides Maud, who is beloved by Robert, to the hut in which the latter is confined, and effects his escape. Aroused by this escape, the Indians precipitate their attack upon the Knoll, which, through the previous treachery of Strides in ill-hanging a gate, is immediately carried. Mrs. Willoughby, Beulah, and others of the party, are killed. Maud is secreted and thus saved by Wyandotté. At the last moment, when all is apparently lost, a reinforcement appears, under command of Evert Beekman, the husband of Beulah; and the completion of the massacre is prevented. Woods, the preacher, had left the Knoll, and made his way through the enemy, to inform Beekman of the dilemma of his friends. Maud and Robert Willoughby are, of course, happily married. The concluding scene of the novel shows us Wyandotté repenting the murder of Willoughby, and converted to Christianity through the agency of Woods.

It will be at once seen that there is nothing *original* in this story. On the contrary, it is even excessively common-place. The lover, for example, rescued from captivity by the mistress; the Knoll carried through the treachery of an inmate; and the salvation of the besieged, at the very last moment, by a reinforcement arriving, in consequence of a message borne to a friend by one of the besieged, without the cognizance of the others; these, we say, are incidents which have been the common property of every novelist since the invention of letters. And as for *plot*, there has been no attempt at any thing of the kind. The tale is a mere succession of events, scarcely any one of which has any necessary dependence upon any one other. Plot, however, is, at best, an artificial effect, requiring, like music, not only a natural bias, but long cultivation of taste for its full appreciation; some of the finest narratives in the world—"Gil-Blas" and "Robinson Crusoe," for example—have been written without its employment; and "The Hutted Knoll," like all the sea and forest novels of Cooper, has been made deeply interesting, although depending upon this peculiar source of interest not at all. Thus the absence of plot can never be critically regarded as a *defect*; although its judicious use, in all cases aiding and in no case injuring other effects, must be regarded as of a very high order of merit.

There are one or two points, however, in the mere *conduct* of the story now before us, which may, perhaps, be considered as defective. For instance, there is too much *obviousness* in all that appertains to the hanging of the large gate. In more than a dozen instances, Mrs. Willoughby is made to allude to the delay in the hanging; so that the reader is too positively and pointedly forced to perceive that this delay is to result in the capture of the Knoll. As we are never in doubt of the fact, we feel diminished interest when it actually happens. A single vague allusion, well-managed, would have been in the true artistical spirit.

Again; we see too plainly, from the first, that Beekman is to marry Beulah, and that Robert Willoughby is to marry Maud. The killing of Beulah, of Mrs. Willoughby, and Jamie Allen, produces, too, a painful impression which does not properly appertain to the right fiction. Their deaths affect us as revolting and supererogatory; since the

purposes of the story are not thereby furthered in any regard. To
Willoughby's murder, however distressing, the reader makes no similar objection; merely because in his decease is fulfilled a species of
poetical justice. We may observe here, nevertheless, that his repeated
references to his flogging the Indian seem unnatural, because we
have otherwise no reason to think him a fool, or a madman, and these
references, under the circumstances, are absolutely insensate. We
object, also, to the manner in which the general interest is dragged
out, or suspended. The besieging party are kept before the Knoll so
long, while so little is done, and so many opportunities of action are
lost, that the reader takes it for granted that nothing of consequence
will occur—that the besieged will be finally delivered. He gets so
accustomed to the presence of danger that its excitement, at length,
departs. The action is not sufficiently rapid. There is too much pro-
crastination. There is too much mere talk for talk's sake. The inter-
minable discussions between Woods and Captain Willoughby are,
perhaps, the worst feature of the book, for they have not even the
merit of referring to the matters on hand. In general, there is quite
too much colloquy for the purpose of manifesting character, and too
little for the explanation of motive. The characters of the drama
would have been better made out by action; while the motives to
action, the reasons for the different courses of conduct adopted by
the *dramatis personæ*, might have been made to proceed more satisfactorily from their own mouths, in casual conversations, than from that
of the author in person. To conclude our remarks upon the head of
ill-conduct in the story, we may mention occasional incidents of the
merest melodramatic absurdity: as, for example, at page 156, of the
second volume, where "Willoughby had an arm round the waist of
Maud, and bore her forward with a rapidity to which her own strength
was entirely unequal." We may be permitted to doubt whether a
young lady of sound health and limbs, exists, within the limits of
Christendom, who could not run faster, on her own proper feet, for
any considerable distance, than she could be carried upon *one arm* of
either the Cretan Milo or of the Hercules Farnese.

On the other hand, it would be easy to designate many particulars
which are admirably handled. The love of Maud Meredith for Robert
Willoughby is painted with exquisite skill and truth. The incident of
the tress of hair and box is naturally and effectively conceived. A fine
collateral interest is thrown over the whole narrative by the connection of the theme with that of the Revolution; and, especially, there
is an excellent dramatic point, at page 124 of the second volume,
where Wyandotté, remembering the stripes inflicted upon him by
Captain Willoughby, is about to betray him to his foes, when his purpose is arrested by a casual glimpse, through the forest, of the hut

which contains Mrs. Willoughby, who had preserved the life of the Indian, by inoculation for the small-pox.

In the depicting of character, Mr. Cooper has been unusually successful in "Wyandotté." One or two of his personages, to be sure, must be regarded as little worth. Robert Willoughby, like most novel heroes, is a nobody; that is to say, there is nothing about him which may be looked upon as distinctive. Perhaps he is rather silly than otherwise; as, for instance, when he confuses all his father's arrangements for his concealment, and bursts into the room before Strides—afterward insisting upon accompanying that person to the Indian encampment, without any possible or impossible object. Woods, the parson, is a sad bore, upon the Dominie Sampson[2] plan, and is, moreover, caricatured. Of Captain Willoughby we have already spoken—he is too often on stilts. Evert Beekman and Beulah are merely episodical. Joyce is nothing in the world but Corporal Trim—or, rather, Corporal Trim and water. Jamie Allen, with his prate about Catholicism, is insufferable. But Mrs. Willoughby, the humble, shrinking, womanly wife, whose whole existence centres in her affections, is worthy of Mr. Cooper. Maud Meredith is still better. In fact, we know no female portraiture, even in Scott, which surpasses her; and yet the world has been given to understand, by the enemies of the novelist, that he is incapable of depicting a woman. Joel Strides will be recognized by all who are conversant with his general prototypes of Connecticut. Michael O'Hearn, the County Leitrim man, is an Irishman all over, and his portraiture abounds in humor; as, for example, at page 31, of the first volume, where he has a difficulty with a skiff, not being able to account for its revolving upon its own axis, instead of moving forward! or, at page 132, where, during divine service, to exclude at least a portion of the heretical doctrine, he stops *one* of his ears with his thumb; or, at page 195, where a passage occurs so much to our purpose that we will be pardoned for quoting it in full. Captain Willoughby is drawing his son up through a window, from his enemies below. The assistants, placed at a distance from this window to avoid observation from without, are ignorant of what burthen is at the end of the rope:

"The men did as ordered, raising their load from the ground a foot or two at a time. In this manner the burthen approached, yard after yard, until it was evidently drawing near the window.

"'It's the captain hoisting up the big baste of a hog, for provisioning the hoose again a saige,' whispered Mike to the negroes, who

---

[2]Character from Sir Walter Scott's *Guy Mannering* (1815), described as "a poor, modest, humble scholar, who had won his way through the classics, but fallen to the leeward in the voyage of life."

grinned as they tugged; 'and, when the craitur squails, see to it, that ye do not squail yourselves.'

"At that moment, the head and shoulders of a man appeared at the window. Mike let go the rope, seized a chair, and was about to knock the intruder upon the head; but the captain arrested the blow.

"'It 's one o' the vagabone Injins that has undermined the hog and come up in its stead,' roared Mike.

"'It 's my son,' said the captain; 'see that you are silent and secret.'"

The negroes are, without exception, admirably drawn. The Indian, Wyandotté, however, is the great feature of the book, and is, in every respect, equal to the previous Indian creations of the author of "The Pioneer." Indeed, we think this "forest gentleman" superior to the other noted heroes of his kind—the heroes which have been immortalized by our novelist. His keen sense of the distinction, in his own character, between the chief, Wyandotté, and the drunken vagabond, Sassy Nick; his chivalrous delicacy toward Maud, in never disclosing to her that knowledge of her real feelings toward Robert Willoughby, which his own Indian intuition had discovered; his enduring animosity toward Captain Willoughby, softened, and for thirty years delayed, through his gratitude to the wife; and then, the vengeance consummated, his pity for that wife conflicting with his exultation at the deed—these, we say, are all traits of a lofty excellence indeed. Perhaps the most effective passage in the book, and that which, most distinctively, brings out the character of the Tuscarora, is to be found at pages 50, 51, 52 and 53 of the second volume, where, for some trivial misdemeanor, the captain threatens to make use of the whip. The manner in which the Indian *harps* upon the threat, returning to it again and again, in every variety of phrase, forms one of the finest pieces of mere character-painting with which we have any acquaintance.

The most obvious and most unaccountable faults of "The Hutted Knoll," are those which appertain to the *style*—to the mere grammatical construction;—for, in other and more important particulars of style, Mr. Cooper, of late days, has made a very manifest improvement. His sentences, however, are arranged with an awkwardness so remarkable as to be matter of absolute astonishment, when we consider the education of the author, and his long and continual practice with the pen. In minute descriptions of localities, any verbal inaccuracy, or confusion, becomes a source of vexation and misunderstanding, detracting very much from the pleasure of perusal; and in these inaccuracies "Wyandotté" abounds. Although, for instance, we carefully read and re-read that portion of the narrative which details the situation of the Knoll, and the construction of the buildings and walls about it, we were forced to proceed with the story without any exact or definite impressions upon the subject. Similar difficulties, from similar causes, occur *passim* throughout the book. For example: at page 41, vol. I:

"The Indian gazed at the house, with that fierce intentness which sometimes glared, in a manner that had got to be, in its ordinary aspects, dull and besotted." This it is utterly impossible to comprehend. We presume, however, the intention is to say that although the Indian's ordinary manner (of gazing) had "got to be" dull and besotted, he occasionally gazed with an intentness that glared, and that he did so in the instance in question. The "got to be" is atrocious—the whole sentence no less so.

Here, at page 9, vol. I., is something excessively vague: "Of the latter character is the face of most of that region which lies in the angle formed by the junction of the Mohawk with the Hudson," &c. &c. The Mohawk, joining the Hudson, forms *two* angles, of course,—an acute and an obtuse one; and, without farther explanation, it is difficult to say which is intended.

At page 55, vol. I., we read:—"The captain, owing to his English education, had avoided straight lines, and formal paths; giving to the little spot the improvement on nature which is a consequence of embellishing her works without destroying them. On each side of this lawn was an orchard, thrifty and young, and which *were* already beginning to show signs of putting forth their blossoms." Here we are tautologically informed that improvement is a consequence of embellishment, and supererogatorily told that the rule holds good only where the embellishment is not accompanied by destruction. Upon the "each orchard *were*" it is needless to comment.

At page 30, vol. I., is something similar, where Strides is represented as "never doing any thing that required a particle more than the exertion and strength that were absolutely necessary to effect his object." Did Mr. C. ever hear of any labor that *required* more exertion than was *necessary*? He means to say that Strides exerted himself no farther than was necessary—that 's all.

At page 59, vol. I., we find this sentence—"He was advancing by the only road that was ever traveled by the stranger as he approached the Hut; or, he came up the valley." This is merely a vagueness of speech. "Or" is intended to imply "that is to say." The whole would be clearer thus—"He was advancing by the valley—the only road traveled by a stranger approaching the Hut." We have here sixteen words, instead of Mr. Cooper's twenty-five.

At page 8, vol. II., is an unpardonable awkwardness, although an awkwardness strictly grammatical. "I was a favorite, I believe, with, certainly was much petted by, both." Upon this we need make no farther observation. It speaks for itself.

We are aware, however, that there is a certain air of unfairness, in this quoting detached passages, for animadversion of this kind; for, however strictly at random our quotations may really be, we have, of course, no means of proving the fact to our readers; and there are *no* authors, from whose works individual inaccurate sentences may not be culled. But we mean to say that Mr. Cooper, no doubt through haste or neglect, is *remarkably* and *especially* inaccurate, as a general rule; and, by way of demonstrating this assertion, we will dismiss our extracts at random, and discuss some entire page of his composition. More than this: we will endeavor to select that particular page upon which it might naturally be supposed he would bestow the most careful attention. The reader will say at once—"Let this be his *first* page— the first page of his Preface." This page, then, shall be taken of course.

"The history of the borders is filled with legends of the sufferings of isolated families, during the troubled scenes of colonial warfare. Those which we now offer to the reader, are distinctive in many of their leading facts, if not rigidly true in the details. The first alone is necessary to the legitimate objects of fiction."

"*Abounds* with legends," would be better than "is filled with legends;" for it is clear that if the history were *filled* with legends, it would be all legend and no history. The word "of," too, occurs, in the first sentence, with an unpleasant frequency. The *"those"* commencing the second sentence, grammatically refers to the noun "scenes," immediately preceding, but is intended for "legends." The adjective *"distinctive"* is vaguely and altogether improperly employed. Mr. C. we believe means to say, merely, that although the details of his legends may not be strictly true, facts similar to his leading ones have actually occurred. By use of the word *"distinctive,"* however, he has contrived to convey a meaning nearly converse. In saying that his legend is *"distinctive"* in many of the leading facts, he has said what he, clearly, did not wish to say—viz.: that his legend contained facts which distinguished it from all other legends—in other words, facts never before discussed in other legends, and belonging peculiarly to his own. That Mr. C. *did* mean what we suppose, is rendered evident by the third sentence—"The first alone is necessary to the legitimate objects of fiction." This third sentence itself, however, is very badly constructed. "The first" can refer, grammatically, only to "facts;" but no such reference is intended. If we ask the question—what is meant by "the first?"—*what* "alone is necessary to the legitimate objects of fiction?"—the natural reply is, "that facts similar to the leading ones have actually happened." This circumstance is alone to be cared for—this consideration "alone is necessary to the legitimate objects of fiction."

"One of the misfortunes of a nation is to hear nothing besides its own praises." This is the fourth sentence, and is by no means lucid. The design is to say that individuals composing a nation, and living altogether within the national bounds, hear from each other only praises of the nation, and that this is a misfortune to the individuals, since it misleads them in regard to the actual condition of the nation. Here it will be seen that, to convey the intended idea, we have been forced to make distinction between the nation and its individual members; for it is evident that a nation is considered as such only in reference to other nations; and thus, *as a nation,* it hears *very* much "besides its own praises;" that is to say, it hears the detractions of other rival nations. In endeavoring to compel his meaning within the compass of a brief sentence, Mr. Cooper has completely sacrificed its intelligibility.

The fifth sentence runs thus:—"Although the American Revolution was probably as just an effort as was ever made by a people to resist the first inroads of oppression, the cause had its evil aspects, as well as all other human struggles."

The American Revolution is here improperly called an "effort." The effort was the cause, of which the Revolution was the result. A rebellion is an "effort" to effect a revolution. An "inroad of oppression" involves an untrue metaphor; for "inroad" appertains to *aggres*sion, to attack, to active assault. "The cause had its evil aspects, as well as all other human struggles," implies that the cause had not only its evil aspects, but had, also, all other human struggles. If the words must be retained at all, they should be thus arranged—"The cause like [or as well as] all other human struggles, had its evil aspects;" or better thus—"The cause had its evil aspect, as have all human struggles." "Other" is superfluous.

The sixth sentence is thus written:—"We have been so much accustomed to hear every thing extolled, of late years, that could be dragged into the remotest connection with that great event, and the principles which led to it, that there is danger of overlooking truth in a pseudo patriotism." The "of late years," here, should follow the "accustomed," or precede the "We have been;" and the Greek "pseudo" is objectionable, since its exact equivalent is to be found in the English "false." "Spurious" would be better, perhaps, than either.

Inadvertences such as these sadly disfigure the style of "The Hutted Knoll;" and every true friend of its author must regret his inattention to the minor morals of the Muse. But these "minor morals," it may be said, are trifles at best. Perhaps so. At all events, we should never have thought of dwelling so pertinaciously upon the unessential demerits of "Wyandotté," could we have discovered any more momentous upon which to comment.

Excerpt from "The Little Longfellow War"
Omnibus review of Henry Wadsworth Longfellow
[*Aristidean*, April 1845]

Poems on Slavery, **Second edition**
Voices of the Night, **Tenth edition**
Ballads and other Poems, **Eighth edition**
The Waif: a collection of Poems, **Second edition**
(**Cambridge: John Owen**)

"The Little Longfellow War," Poe's name for his protracted attack on Henry Wadsworth Longfellow, took place in a variety of publications between January and April, 1845. Poe's original review of The Waif, *an anthology of contemporary poetry edited by Longfellow, accused the latter of "imitation" in stronger terms than Poe had yet used for this respected writer. Poe charged the distinguished New England poet and professor with nothing less than venality, "a very careful avoidance of all American poets who may be supposed especially to interfere with the claims of Mr. Longfellow. These men Mr. Longfellow can continuously* imitate *(is that the word?) and yet never incidentally commend." A number of Longfellow's friends rose to defend him, but the sharpest counter came from "Outis" ("Nobody"), whose reply accused Poe of plagiarism in turn. Many critics believe that Outis was really Poe himself, playing the trickster by torching his own tailfeathers in order to keep public attention on the affair. Such a hoax would have served to justify the prolonged blast from Poe that followed, an elaboration of the original charges against Longfellow along with a point-by-point refutation of Outis's accusations that spread across four issues of the weekly* Broadway Journal. *Shortly after unleashing that attack, Poe supported it by planting an anonymous essay in the* Aristidean *that summarized the case he had made against the foremost poet in the United States at the time. This last salvo, which many scholars believe Poe composed, is reprinted here.*

We will never fully understand what motivated Poe's quixotic attack on one of the foremost men of letters in the United States at the time, and many critics have weighed in on the subject. Kenneth Alan Hovey is one who has argued that the episode shows how Poe's aesthetics were inseparable from his Southern politics. That is, Poe's rage at Longfellow's "borrowing" from less well known poets and his resentment of Longfellow's didacticism (which Poe abhorred as artless and which he attacks again in his 1850 essay "The Poetic Principle") were intertwined with his sectional opposition to New England's moralistic antislavery thinking.

The poetical reputation of Mr. Longfellow is, no doubt, in some measure well-deserved; but it may be questioned whether, without the adventitious influence of his social position as Professor of Modern Languages and Belles Lettres at Harvard, and an access of this influence by marriage with an heiress, he would even have acquired his present celebrity—such as it is.

We really feel no little shame in being forced, not into the expression, but into the entertainment of opinions such as these—the only shame we feel in respect to the matter of their expression, is shame for others and not for ourselves—shame that we in the infancy of our journalism, should have been permitted to take the lead in the utterance of a thought so long common with the *literati* of the land. In no literary circle out of Boston—or, indeed, out of the small coterie of abolitionists, transcendentalists and fanatics in general, which is the Longfellow junto—have we heard a seriously dissenting voice on this point. It is universally, in private conversation—out of the knot of rogues and madmen aforesaid—admitted that the poetical claims of Mr. Longfellow have been vastly overrated, and that the individual himself would be esteemed little without the accessaries of wealth and position. It is usually said, that he has a sufficient scholarship, a fine taste, a keen appreciation of the beautiful, a happy memory, a happier tact at imitation or transmutation, felicity of phrase and some fancy. A few insist on his imagination—thus proving the extent of their own—and showing themselves to be utterly unread in the old English and modern German literature, to one or other of which, the author of "Outre Mer" is unquestionably indebted for whatever imagination or traces of invention his works may display. No phrenologist, indeed, would require to be told that Mr. Longfellow was not the man of genius his friends would have us believe him—his head giving no indication of ideality.[1] Nor, when we speak of phrenologists, do we mean to insist on implicit faith in the marvels and inconsistencies of the Fowlers *et id genus omne.* Common observation, independently of either Gall or Spurzheim,[2] would suffice to teach all mankind that very many of the salient points of phrenological science are undisputable truths—whatever falsity may be detected in the principles kindly furnished to the science by hot-headed and asinine votaries. Now, one of these salient points, is the fact that what men term "poetical genius," and what the phrenologists generally term the organ of ideality, are always

---

[1] See fn. 1 on p. 13.

[2] Orson Squier Fowler and Lorenzo N. Fowler, prominent phrenologists; *et id genus omne:* "and that whole group"; Franz Josef Gall and Johann Gaspar Spurzheim were German phrenologists. Poe also mentions them in the story "Some Words with a Mummy."

found co-existent in the same individual. We should as soon expect
to see our old friend, Satan, presiding at a temperance meeting, as
to see a veritable poem—of his own—composed by a man whose
head was flattened at the temples, like that of Professor Longfellow.
Holding these views, we confess that we were not a little surprised to
hear Mr. Poe, in a late lecture, on the Poetry of America, claim for
the Professor a pre-eminence over all poets of this country on the
score of the "loftiest poetical quality—imagination." There is no
doubt in our minds, that an opinion so crude as this, must arise
from a want of leisure or inclination to compare the works of the
writer in question with the sources from which they were stolen. A
defensive letter written by an unfortunate wight who called himself
"Outis," seems to have stirred up the critic to make the proper examination, and we will make an even wager of a pound avoirdupois of
nothing against Longfellow's originality, that the rash opinion
would not be given again. The simple truth is, that, whatever may be
the talents of Professor Longfellow, he is the Great Mogul of the
Imitators. There is, perhaps, no other country than our own, under
the sun, in which it would have been possible for him to have
attained his present eminence; and no other, certainly, in which,
after having attained it by accident or chicanery, he would not have
been hurled from it in a very brief period after its attainment.

We have now before us all the collected poems of Mr. Longfellow;
and the first question which forces itself upon us as we look at them,
is, how much of their success may be attributed to the luxurious manner in which, as merely physical books, they have been presented to
the public. Of course we cannot pretend to answer our own question
with precision; but that the *physique* has had vast influence upon the
morale, no reflecting person of common honesty will be willing to deny.

We intend nothing in the shape of digested review; but as the subject has derived great interest of late through a discussion carried on
in the pages of "The Broadway Journal," we propose to turn over
these volumes, in a cursory manner, and make a few observations, in
the style of the marginal note, upon each one of the poems in each.

The first volume is entitled "Poems on Slavery," and is intended for
the especial use of those negrophilic old ladies of the north, who
form so large a part of Mr. Longfellow's friends. The first of this collection is addressed to William Ellery Channing, the great essayist,
and not the very little poet of the same name. There is much force in
the concluding line of the succeeding extract:—

> "Well done! thy words are great and bold;
>   At times they seem to me
> Like Luther's, in the days of old,
>   *Half-battles for the free.*"

In the second poem—"The Slave's Dream"—there is also a particularly beautiful close to one of the stanzas:—

> "At night he heard the lion roar,
>   And the hyæna scream,
> And the river-horse as he crushed the reeds
>   Beside some hidden stream;
> And it passed *like a glorious roll of drums,*
>   *Through the triumph of his dream.*"

This is certainly very fine; although we do not exactly understand *what* is like the glorious roll of drums, whether it be the stream, or the various sounds aforesaid. This embarrassment in future will be prevented, if the poet will only affix a note to the next edition, declaring what he does mean, if he know himself.

The third poem—"The Good Part that shall not be taken away"—has two very effective lines:—

> "And musical as silver bells
>   Their falling chains shall be."

The whole poem is in praise of a certain lady, who

> "——was rich and gave up all
> To break the iron bands
> Of those who waited in her hall
> And labored in her lands."

No doubt, it is a very commendable and very comfortable thing, in the Professor, to sit at ease in his library chair, and write verses instructing the southerners how to give up their all with a good grace, and abusing them if they will not; but we have a singular curiosity to know how much of his own, under a change of circumstances, the Professor himself would be willing to surrender. Advice of this character looks well only in the mouth of those who have entitled themselves to give it, by setting an example of the self-sacrifice.

The fourth is "The Slave in the Dismal Swamp." This is a shameless medley of the grossest misrepresentation. When did Professor Longfellow ever *know* a slave to be hunted with bloodhounds in the Dismal Swamp? Because he has heard that runaway slaves are so treated in Cuba, he has certainly no right to change the locality, and by insinuating a falsehood in lieu of a fact, charge his countrymen with barbarity. What makes the matter worse, he is one of those who insist upon truth as one of the elements of poetry.

The fifth—"The Slave singing at midnight," embodies some good and novel rhymes—for example—

> "In that hour when night is *calmest,*
>   Sang he from the Hebrew *psalmist.*"

"Angel" and "evangel," however, are inadmissible because identical—just as "excision" and "circumcision" would be—that is to say: the ear, instead of being gratified with a variation of a sound—the principle of rhyme—is positively displeased by its bare repetition. The commencement of the rhyming words, or—equally—of the rhyming portions of words, must always be different.

The sixth is "The witnesses," and is exceedingly feeble throughout. We cannot conceive how any artist could in two distinct stanzas of so brief a poem, admit such a termination as "witness*es*"—rhyming it too with "abyss."

The seventh, "The Quadroon Girl," is the old abolitionist story—worn threadbare—of a slaveholder selling his own child—a thing which may be as common in the South as in the East, is the infinitely worse crime of making matrimonial merchandise—or even less legitimate merchandise—of one's daughter.

The eighth—"The Warning," contains at least one stanza of absolute truth—as follows.

> "There is a poor, blind Sampson in this land,
>   Shorn of his strength and bound in bonds of steel,
> Who may, in some grim revel, raise his hand,
>   And shake the pillars of the common weal,
> Till the vast temple of our Liberties,
> A shapeless mass of wreck and rubbish lies."

One thing is certain:—if this prophecy be *not* fulfilled, it will be through no lack of incendiary doggrel on the part of Professor Longfellow and his friends. We dismiss this volume with no more profound feeling than that of contempt.

The next volume we have is—"The Voices of the Night." "The Prelude," in this, is indistinct, but contains some noble passages. For example:—

> A slumberous sound—a sound that brings
>   The feelings of a dream—
> As of innumerable wings,
> As when a bell no longer swings,
> Faint the hollow murmur rings
>   O'er meadow lake and stream.

And again:

> The lids of Fancy's sleepless eyes
> Are gates unto that Paradise.

The last stanza commences with a plagiarism from Sir Philip Sidney:

> Look then into thine heart and write!

In the "Astrophel and Stella"[3] we find it thus:—"Foole, said then my muse unto me, looke into thy heart and write!" The versification of the *Prelude* is weak, if not exactly erroneous:—we allude especially to the penultimate verse of each stanza.

The "Hymn to the Night" is one of the best of Mr. Longfellow's poems. There is a very inartistical fluctuation of thought, however, in the opening quotation:

> I heard the trailing garments of the Night
> Sweep through her marble Halls!
> I saw her sable skirts all fringed with light
> From the celestial walls!

In the first two lines, the Night is personified as a woman in trailing garments passing through a marble palace: in the third and fourth by the use of the epithet "celestial" we are brought back to the real or unpersonified Night—and this too only in an imperfect manner, for the "sable skirts" of the personified Night are still retained. This vacillation pervades the whole poem and seriously injures its effect. Speaking of the first quatrain—what are we to understand by the notes of admiration at the closes of the second and fourth lines? They are called for by no rhetorical rules, and seem to be meant as expressive merely of the Professor's own admiration of his own magnificence. The concluding stanza is majestic, but liable to misapprehension upon a first reading. The "Peace! Peace!" of the first line will be mistaken by nine readers out of ten for an injunction of silence, rather than an invocation of the divinity, Peace. An instance occurs in this poem of Mr. Longfellow's strong tendency to imitation:—so strong, indeed, that he not unfrequently imitates himself. He here speaks of "the sounds of sorrow and delight" that "fill the chambers of the Night," and just before, in the *Prelude,* he has

> "All forms of sorrow and delight
> All solemn voices of the Night."

"A Psalm of Life," is German throughout, in manner and spirit, and otherwise is chiefly remarkable for its containing one of the most palpable plagiarisms ever perpetrated by an author of equal character. We allude to the well-known lines:

> "Art is long and time is fleeting
> And our *hearts,* tho' stout and brave,
> Still like *muffled drums are beating*
> Funeral marches to the grave."

---

[3]Elizabethan sonnet sequence by Sir Philip Sidney (1554–1586), published in 1591.

Mr. Longfellow has, unfortunately, derived from these very lines, a *full half* of his poetical reputation. But they are by no means his own—the first line being an evident translation of the well-known Latin sentence—

"Ârs longa, vita brêvis"—

and the remaining part pillaged from an old English writer. Mr. Poe first detected this. It appears that in "Headley's collection of old British Ballads," there is to be found, "An Exequy on the death of his wife, by Henry King, Bishop of Chichester," and in this Exequy the following verses:

> "But hark! my *pulse, like a soft drum,*
> *Beats* my approach—tells thee I come—
> And slow howe'er my *marches* be
> I shall at last sit down by thee."

Dr. King is here speaking of soon following his wife *to the grave.* We have thus, in each poem, the identical ideas of a pulse (or heart)—of its beating like a drum—like a soft (or muffled) drum—of its beating a march; and of its beating a march to the grave:—all this identity of idea expressed in identical phraseology, and all in the compass of four lines. Now it was the seeming *originality* of this fine image which procured for it so wide a popularity in the lines of Longfellow; we presume, then, that not even the most desperate friends of his fine fortune, will attempt to defend him on the ground of this image's being one which would naturally arise in the mind of every poet—the common cant of those interested in the justification of a plagiarism. In larcenies of this kind it will always be found that an improvement is effected in externals—that is to say in point, flow of diction, etc., while there is a deterioration of the original in the higher merits of freshness, appositeness, and application of the thought to the general subject. How markedly is all this observable in the present instance!

"The Reaper and the Flowers" has nothing in it beyond common thoughts very gracefully expressed.

"The Light of Stars," opens with a very singularly silly stanza:

> "The night is come, but not too soon,
> And, sinking silently,
> All silently, the *little* moon
> Drops down behind the sky."

Why *will* Mr. Longfellow persist in supposing that *ly* is a rhyme for sky?—why will he adhere to a conventionality, which has no meaning whatever? And what does he propose to himself in calling the moon *little*? The far-fetchedness of the phrase becomes at once obvious when we consider that *all* men agree in being struck with the apparent *increase* in the size of the setting moon. The first man who ever talked of its littleness under such circumstances is Professor Longfellow himself:—here at least and at last is he original.

"Footsteps of Angels." Mr. Poe, in his late *exposé*, has given some very decisive instances of what he too modestly calls *imitations* on the part of Mr. Longfellow from himself (Mr. Poe.) Here is one, however, which he has overlooked:

> "And, like *phantoms* grim and tall,
> *Shadows* from the fitful fire-light
> *Dance upon the parlor wall.*"

In a poem called "The Sleeper," by E. A. Poe, and which we first saw a great many years ago in the "Southern Literary Messenger," we have a distinct recollection of these lines:

> "The wanton airs from the tree-top
> Laughingly through the lattice drop,
> And wave this crimson canopy
> So fitfully—so fearfully—
> Above the closed and fringéd lid
> 'Neath which thy slumbering soul lies hid,
> That o'er the floor and *down the wall*
> *Like ghosts the shadows rise and fall.*"

"Flowers"—is merely a weak amplification of the idea of a German poet, that flowers are the stars of earth. The versification is of a bad class, and of its class, bad.

"The Beleaguered City" was published in the "Southern Literary Messenger" just about six weeks after the appearance in Brooks' "Museum" (a five-dollar Baltimore Monthly) of Mr. Poe's "Haunted Palace," and is a palpable imitation of the latter in matter and manner. Mr. Longfellow's title is, indeed, merely a paraphrase of Mr. Poe's. "The Beleaguered City" is designed to imply a mind beset with lunatic fancies; and this is, identically, the intention of "The Haunted Palace." Mr. Longfellow says, speaking of a "broad *valley*" that in it,

> "——an army of phantoms vast and wan
> Beleaguer the human soul,
> Encamped beside Life's rushing *stream*
> In Fancy's mystic light
> *Gigantic shapes* and shadows gleam
> Portentous through the night."

Mr. Poe says:

> "And travellers, now, within that *valley,*
> Through the red-litten windows see
> *Vast forms,* that move fantastically
> To a discordant melody,

> While, *like a ghastly rapid river*
> Through the pale door
> A hideous throng rush out forever
> And laugh—but smile no more."

The "Midnight Mass for the Dying Year" is a singular admixture of Cordelia's death scene in "Lear" and Tennyson's "Death of the Old Year." A more palpable plagiarism was never committed. At the time of the original publication of Professor Longfellow's poem, Tennyson, was comparatively unknown, and we believe that no collection of his works had ever been reprinted in this country. The "Midnight Mass" concludes the later poems of the "Voices of the Night," which are noticeable, in general, as imitative of the German poetry, or of poetry imbued with the German spirit. The rest of the volume is occupied with "Earlier Poems" and "Translations." Of these the former are Bryant,[4] and nothing beyond. They were written in the author's youth, before his acquaintance with German Letters—and yet it was necessary that he should imitate something. In minds such as his, this imitation is, indeed, as imperious a necessity as any animal function.

"An April Day" has nothing observable *beyond* the obvious imitation of the American model.

"Autumn" might absolutely be read *through*, in mistake for Bryant's "Thanatopsis." The similarity of conclusion in the two poems is so close as to carry with it an air of parody. Mr. Bryant says:

> "So live, that when thy summons comes to join
> The innumerable caravan that moves
> To that mysterious realm where each shall take
> His chamber in the silent halls of Death
> Thou go not, like the quarry slave at night,
> Scourged to his dungeon; but sustained and soothed
> By an unfaltering trust, approach thy grave
> Like one who wraps the drapery of his couch
> About him, and lies down to pleasant dreams."

Mr. Longfellow says:

> "To him the wind, aye and the yellow leaves
> Shall have a voice and give him eloquent teachings.
> He shall so hear the solemn hymn that Death
> Has lifted up for all, that he shall go
> To his long resting-place without a tear."

We do not like to be ill-natured; but when one gentleman's purse is found in another gentleman's pocket, how did it come there?

---

[4]American poet William Cullen Bryant (1794–1878).

"Woods in Winter" is insipid, and totally thoughtless.

"The Hymn of the Moravian Nuns" is school-boyish in the extreme.

"Sunrise on the Hills" is only remarkable for another instance of palpable imitation:

> "I heard the distant waters dash
> I saw the current whirl and flash,
> And richly by the blue lake's silver beach," etc.

Every body must remember the lines of the "Prisoner of Chillon:"

> "——the wide long lake below
> And the blue Rhone in fullest flow,
> I heard the torrent leap and gush
> O'er channell'd rock and broken bush—
> I saw the white-wall 'd distant town," etc.

"The Spirit of Poetry" contains some fine thoughts—for example:

> "——where the silver brook
> From its full laver pours the white cascade,
> And, *babbling low amid the tangled woods*
> *Slips down through moss-grown stones with endless laughter.*"

And again:

> "Groves through whose broken roof the sky looks in—
> Mountain, and shattered cliff, and sunny vale,
> The distant lake, fountains—*and mighty trees*
> *In many a lazy syllable repeating*
> *Their old poetic legends to the wind.*"

Both of these examples, however, are disfigured with that vulgar poetic solecism—the endeavour to elevate objects of natural grandeur by likening them to the mere works of man. The grove has a "broken roof"; and the brook pours the cascade from a "laver."

"Burial of the Minnisink." There is nothing about it to distinguish it from a thousand other similar things.

The Translations commence with "Coplas de Manrique" from the Spanish—and this again with the line

> "O let the soul her slumbers break!
> Let thought be quickened and awake,
> Awake to see,
> How soon," &c.

And this, we presume, is what Mr. Longfellow calls original translation. We have at this moment, some verses ringing in our ears whose whereabouts we cannot call to memory—but no doubt there are many of our readers who can. They are nearly identical, however, with Mr. Longfellow's lines both in words, rhyme, metre and arrangement of stanza. They begin thus:

"O let the soul its slumber break

*   *   *   *   *   *   and awake

To see how soon,"

Etc. etc.

If we are not mistaken they are quoted in some of the Notes to Pope's:

"Arise my St. John, leave all meaner things."

"The Good Shepherd," from Lope de Vega, has "nothing in it." In the same category is "To-morrow," from the same—"The Native Land," from Francisco de Aldana—"The Image of God," from the same—and "The Brook," from the Spanish:—these pieces seem to have been translated with no other object than to show that Mr. Longfellow could translate. "The Celestial Pilot"—"The Terrestrial Paradise," and "Beatrice," from Dante, strike us as by no means equal to Cary.[5] These pieces abound also, in sheer affectations. Were Mr. Longfellow asked *why* he employed "withouten" and other words of that kind, what reasonable answer could he make?

"Spring," from the French of Charles D'Orleans, is utterly worthless as a poem:—of its merits as a translation we are not prepared to speak, never having seen the original. One thing, however, is quite certain, the versification is *not* translated. The French have no such metre or rhythm.

"The Child Asleep," from the French, is particularly French.

"The Grave," from the Anglo Saxon, is forcible—but the metre is mere prose, and, of course, should not have been retained.

"King Christian," from the Danish, has force.

"The Happiest Land," from the German, is mere common place.

"The Wave," from Tiedge, contains one thought, but that is scarcely worth the page it occupies.

"The Dead," from Klopstock, is nothing.

"The Bird and the Ship," from Müller, is pure inanity.

"Whither," from the same, is worse, if possible.

"Beware" is still worse—possible or not. We never saw a more sickening thing in a book.

"The Song of the Bell," has no business with a title which calls up the recollection of what is really meritorious.

"The Castle by the Sea," from Uhland, should have been rendered "The Castle *Over* the Sea." The whole dark suggestion of the poem is lost by the mis-translation. The force of the original throughout is greatly impaired by the milk and water of the version.

---

[5]Henry Francis Cary (1772–1844), English poet, known chiefly for his translations of Dante.

"The Black Knight," from the same is merely a German bugaboo story of the common kind, with no particular merit.

"The Song of the Silent Land," from Salis, has merely the merit of a suggestive title, the repetition of which at the close of each stanza is the one good point.

The volume ends with "L'Envoi," a most affected, far-fetched, and altogether contemptible imitation, or parody, of the worst mannerisms of the Germans.

The next volume we have is—"Ballads and other Poems," which we note in the order of their succession.

"The Skeleton in Armor" is one of the best poems of Longfellow; if not indeed his very best. It has the merits of directness and simplicity, and is besprinkled with vigorous thought tersely expressed. Its versification would be monotonous, did it not at points become so radically defective as to change into prose, as for example:

> "Mute did the minstrels stand
> *To* hear my story—"
> "Like birds within their nest
> *By* the hawk frighted—"
> "Many the hearts that bled
> *By* our stern orders—"
> "Came a dull voice of woe
> *For* this I sought thee."
> "Saw we old Hildebrand
> *With* twenty horsemen—"
> "Why did they leave that night
> *Her* nest unguarded?"
> etc. etc. etc.

These were meant to be Dactyls—but have degenerated into such a mixture of these, with Anapests, Trochees and Iambics, as to make quite decent prose, and nothing more.

"The Wreck of the Hesperus" has some remarkably spirited passages, but what can justify any man, to-day, in the use of daught*er,* and sail*or?*

"The Luck of Edenthall" is a capital translation of one of Uhland's best romances.

"The Elected Knight," from the Danish, is meant to prove, we presume, the Professor's acquaintance with the literature of Hardiknute.

"The Children of the Lord's Supper," from Tegner, is remarkable for nothing but its demonstration of the Professor's ignorance of the Greek and Roman Hexameters, which he here *professes* to imitate— the "inexorable hexameter," as he calls it. It is only inexorable to those who do not comprehend its elements. Here mere pedantry will carry a man very little way—and Professor Longfellow has no head for analysis. Most of his hexameters are pure prose, and, if written to the eye as such, would not be distinguished from prose by any human being. Some of them have a remarkable resemblance to the hexameters of Coleridge. For example: Coleridge says:

> "Young life lowed through the meadows, the woods, and the echoing mountains,
> Wandered bleating in valleys and warbled on blossoming branches."

Longfellow says:

> "Clear was the Heaven and blue, and May with her cap crowned with roses,
> Stood in her holiday dress in the fields, and the wind and the brooklet
> Murmured gladness and peace, God's peace, with lips rosy-tinted
> Whispered the race of the flowers, and merry on balancing branches,"

etc. etc. etc.

"The Village Blacksmith" is a mere Hood-ism[6]—nothing more.

"Endymion" has some well expressed common-places. For example:

> "No one is so accursed by Fate,
> No one so utterly desolate
>   But some heart, though unknown,
>   Responds unto his own."

When we speak of expression, here, we must not be understood as commending the versification, which is wretched. We should like to hear Professor Longfellow—or any one else—scan

> "But some heart, though unknown, etc."

"The Two Locks of Hair," from the German of Pfizer, should have remained in the original.

"It is not always May." The whole point of this effusion lies in the title.

"The Rainy Day." The whole point of this, lies in the repetition of "the day is dark and dreary."

"God's-Acre." Here we find one of those utterly insoluble knots of imagery which are Mr. Longfellow's forte. What is any man to make of

> "Comfort to those who in the grave have sown
> The seed that they had garnered in their hearts,
> Their bread of life, alas! no more their own?"

---

[6]Refers to the English poet Thomas Hood (1799–1845), a punster whose work was praised by Poe. Here, Poe may be suggesting that Longfellow's poem is little more than a Hood imitation.

Seeds (which are not seeds, but bread,) are garnered in a heart, and sown in a grave, by the persons who garnered it, and who having sown it (although it was as much bread as seed) lost possession of it thenceforward;—this is a literal rendition of the whole matter into prose—and a beautifully lucid thing it is.

"To the River Charles" is what its author calls it—"an idle song."

"Blind Bartimeus" is only *Zoe mou sas agapo*[7] over again.

"The Goblet of Life" is terse and well versified.

"Maidenhood" is a graceful little poem, spoilt by its didacticism, and by the awkward, monotonous and grossly artificial character of its versification.

"Excelsior" has one fine thought in its conclusion:

> And from the sky, serene and far,
> *A voice fell like a falling star.*

The third volume, is called "The Spanish Student." As a poem, it is meritorious at points—as a drama it is one of the most lamentable failures. It has several sparkling passages—but little vigor—and, as a matter almost of course, not a particle of originality. Indeed it professes to be taken, *in part,* from the "Gitanilla" of Cervantes. *In part,* also, it is taken from "Politian, a fragmentary Drama, by Edgar A. Poe," published in the second volume of the Southern Literary Messenger:—no acknowledgment, however, is made in the latter instance. The *imitation* is one of the most impudent ever known. In both cases a young and beautiful woman is sitting at table with books and flowers. In both cases there is a pert serving maid:—in both the lady reads aloud:—in both what she reads is poetry:—in both it is of a plaintive character in consonance with the sorrow of the reader:—in both the reader makes application of what is read to her own case:—in both she frequently calls on the maid:—who, in both, refuses to answer:—in both there is a quarrel about jewels:—in both a third person enters unseen behind: and lastly in both the lady reiterates the word "begone!" and draws a dagger. But the palpability of the plagiarism can be fully understood only by those who read and compare the two poems. The "Southern Literary Messenger," indeed, seems to have been the great store-house whence the Professor has derived most of his contraband goods.

The last volume to be noticed, is "The Waif." This is noticeable solely on the ground of the "Pröem," which is the only one of his acknowledged compositions it contains—but one which is, perhaps, upon the whole, the best which he has written. It is remarkably easy, graceful, and plaintive, while its versification seems to be

---

[7]"Zoe mine, I love you."

accidentally meritorious. Nothing is more clear indeed than that *all*
the merit of the Professor on this score is accidental. He knows less
than nothing of the principles of verse.

Since the issue of "Ballads and other Poems" he has written several things for "Graham's Magazine," and among others "The Belfry of
Bruges"—but let any person inquisitive as to Mr. Longfellow's pretensions to originality, merely take the trouble to compare the lines
in question with certain stanzas entitled "The Chimes of Antwerp,"[8]
published in "Graham's Magazine" for April, 1841. "The Belfry of
Bruges" is the number for January, 1843.

In the "New York Mirror," Mr. Poe concluded a notice of "The
Waif" in the following words:

> "There does appear in this little volume a very careful avoidance of
> all American poets who may be supposed especially to interfere with
> the claims of Mr. Longfellow. These men Mr. Longfellow can continu-
> ally *imitate* (*is* that the word?) and yet never even incidentally
> commend."

To which one of the Professor's Boston friends makes answer thus:

> "It has been asked, perhaps, why Lowell was neglected in this col-
> lection. Might it not as well be asked why Bryant, Dana, and Halleck
> were neglected! The answer is obvious to any one who candidly con-
> siders the object of the collection. It professed to be, according to the
> Pröem, from the humbler poets; and it was intended to embrace
> pieces that were anonymous or which were not easily accessible to the
> general reader—the *waifs* and *estrays* of literature."

The rejoinder to all this is obvious. If Lowell was omitted on these
grounds why was not Horace Smith, omitted on the same?—and
Browning—and Shelley—and A. C. Coxe—and Hood—and Mont-
gomery—and Emerson—and Marvel—and W. G. Clark—and Pierpont and five or six others? The fact is, none of these gentlemen
"interfered with Mr. Longfellow's claims"—but Lowell *did.* He was a
rising poet in Mr. Longfellow's own school—own manner—a
Bostonian—a neighbor.

It is possible, however, that Mr. Poe's allusions were not to Mr. Lowell,
but to himself; and, if so, who shall venture to blame him? He might
have thought it no more than justice on the part of Longfellow, to
give a place in "The Waif" to that "Haunted Palace," for example, of
which he had shown so flattering an admiration as to purloin everything that was worth purloining about it.

It is, indeed, for that whereas, Mr. Longfellow has stolen so much
from Mr. Poe, that we have alluded so much to the *exposé* of the

---

[8]A twelve-line poem whose author is identified only as "J.H."

latter; for it appeared to us, our course was but just. The latter, driven to it by a silly letter of Mr. Longfellow's friends, has exposed the knavery of the Professor, and any one who reads the "Broadway Journal," will acknowledge he has done it well.

There are other plagiarisms of Mr. Longfellow which we might easily expose; but we have said enough. There can be no reasonable doubt in the mind of any, out of the little clique, to which we at first alluded, that the author of "Outre Mer," is not only a servile imitator, but a most insolent literary thief. Commencing his literary life he began, struck with his quiet style, to imitate Bryant. As he pored over the pages of the Spanish, and then of the great Northern writers, his imitation took a new direction. Soon, to save labor, he began to filch a little here and a little there—some straw to make his bricks, something to temper his own heavy clay. Finding he was not detected, he stole with more confidence, until stealing became habit, and so second nature. At this time we doubt whether he could write without helping himself to the ideas and style of other people. Indeed, if he were by chance to perpetrate an original idea, he would be as much astonished as the world around; and would go about cackling and "making a fuss in general," like a little bantam hen, who by a strange freak of nature, had laid a second egg on the same day.

The Philosophy of Composition
[*Graham's Magazine*, April 1846]

This is perhaps Poe's most famous critical essay. Though interlaced with humor centering on his extended use of "The Raven" (which was popular in its own time, just as it is now) as a prototypical example of poetic beauty, Poe's demonstration of his own brand of formalism is also quite serious. In particular, Poe's argument opposes spontaneity in poetic creation, reserving a role for order and reason in concert with imagination.

Some critics have suggested that "The Philosophy of Composition" is Poe's answer to Emerson's "The Poet" (1844), an essay in which poets who rely on music boxes of rhymes and meters are mocked. This was a clear jab at Poe, whom Emerson elsewhere derided as a "jingle man." Two years later, in this essay, Poe in turn disparages the kind of poet Emerson was calling for, saying that those who wrote in the "fine frenzy" idealized by Emerson in fact were mere craftspeople. He takes a strong (and eccentric) formalist position against Emerson's organic theory of creativity.

Charles Dickens, in a note now lying before me, alluding to an examination I once made of the mechanism of "Barnaby Rudge," says—"By the way, are you aware that Godwin wrote his 'Caleb Williams' backwards? He first involved his hero in a web of difficulties, forming the second volume, and then, for the first, cast about him for some mode of accounting for what had been done."[1]

I cannot think this the *precise* mode of procedure on the part of Godwin—and indeed what he himself acknowledges, is not altogether in accordance with Mr. Dickens' idea—but the author of "Caleb Williams" was too good an artist not to perceive the advantage derivable from at least a somewhat similar process. Nothing is more clear than that every plot, worth the name, must be elaborated to its *dénouement* before any thing be attempted with the pen. It is only with the *dénouement* constantly in view that we can give a plot its indispensable air of consequence, or causation, by making the incidents, and especially the tone at all points, tend to the development of the intention.

There is a radical error, I think, in the usual mode of constructing a story. Either history affords a thesis—or one is suggested by an

---

[1]Dickens wrote to Poe regarding the latter's correct prediction, published in the midst of *Barnaby Rudge*'s serial publication, of who the novel's murderer would turn out to be. His statement about *Caleb Williams* (1794) and how it was constructed, is most probably based on the preface Godwin wrote to accompany an 1832 reissue of the novel.

incident of the day—or, at best, the author sets himself to work in the combination of striking events to form merely the basis of his narrative—designing, generally, to fill in with description, dialogue, or autorial comment, whatever crevices of fact, or action, may, from page to page, render themselves apparent.

I prefer commencing with the consideration of an *effect*. Keeping originality *always* in view—for he is false to himself who ventures to dispense with so obvious and so easily attainable a source of interest—I say to myself, in the first place, "Of the innumerable effects, or impressions, of which the heart, the intellect, or (more generally) the soul is susceptible, what one shall I, on the present occasion, select?" Having chosen a novel, first, and secondly a vivid effect, I consider whether it can best be wrought by incident or tone—whether by ordinary incidents and peculiar tone, or the converse, or by peculiarity both of incident and tone—afterward looking about me (or rather within) for such combinations of event, or tone, as shall best aid me in the construction of the effect.

I have often thought how interesting a magazine paper might be written by any author who would—that is to say, who could—detail, step by step, the processes by which any one of his compositions attained its ultimate point of completion. Why such a paper has never been given to the world, I am much at a loss to say—but, perhaps, the autorial vanity has had more to do with the omission than any one other cause. Most writers—poets in especial—prefer having it understood that they compose by a species of fine frenzy—an ecstatic intuition—and would positively shudder at letting the public take a peep behind the scenes, at the elaborate and vacillating crudities of thought—at the true purposes seized only at the last moment—at the innumerable glimpses of idea that arrived not at the maturity of full view—at the fully matured fancies discarded in despair as unmanageable—at the cautious selections and rejections—at the painful erasures and interpolations—in a word, at the wheels and pinions—the tackle for scene-shifting—the step-ladders and demon-traps—the cock's feathers, the red paint and the black patches, which, in ninety-nine cases out of the hundred, constitute the properties of the literary *histrio*.

I am aware, on the other hand, that the case is by no means common, in which an author is at all in condition to retrace the steps by which his conclusions have been attained. In general, suggestions, having arisen pell-mell, are pursued and forgotten in a similar manner.

For my own part, I have neither sympathy with the repugnance alluded to, nor, at any time, the least difficulty in recalling to mind the progressive steps of any of my compositions; and, since the interest of an analysis, or reconstruction, such as I have considered a *desideratum,* is quite independent of any real or fancied interest in the thing analyzed, it will not be regarded as a breach of decorum on my part to show the *modus operandi* by which some one of my own works was put together. I select "The Raven," as the most generally known. It is my design to render it manifest that no one point in its composition is referrible either to accident or intuition—that the work proceeded, step by step, to its completion with the precision and rigid consequence of a mathematical problem.

Let us dismiss, as irrelevant to the poem *per se,* the circumstance—or say the necessity—which, in the first place, gave rise to the intention of composing a poem that should suit at once the popular and the critical taste.

We commence, then, with this intention.

The initial consideration was that of extent. If any literary work is too long to be read at one sitting, we must be content to dispense with the immensely important effect derivable from unity of impression—for, if two sittings be required, the affairs of the world interfere, and every thing like totality is at once destroyed. But since, *ceteris paribus,* no poet can afford to dispense with *any thing* that may advance his design, it but remains to be seen whether there is, in extent, any advantage to counterbalance the loss of unity which attends it. Here I say no, at once. What we term a long poem is, in fact, merely a succession of brief ones—that is to say, of brief poetical effects. It is needless to demonstrate that a poem is such, only inasmuch as it intensely excites, by elevating, the soul; and all intense excitements are, through a psychal necessity, brief. For this reason, at least one half of the "Paradise Lost" is essentially prose—a succession of poetical excitements interspersed, *inevitably,* with corresponding depressions—the whole being deprived, through the extremeness of its length, of the vastly important artistic element, totality, or unity, of effect.

It appears evident, then, that there is a distinct limit, as regards length, to all works of literary art—the limit of a single sitting—and that, although in certain classes of prose composition, such as "Robinson Crusoe," (demanding no unity,) this limit may be advantageously overpassed, it can never properly be overpassed in a poem. Within this limit, the extent of a poem may be made to bear mathematical relation to its merit—in other words, to the excitement or elevation—again in other words, to the degree of the true poetical effect which it is capable of inducing; for it is clear that the brevity must be in direct ratio of the intensity of the intended effect:—this, with one proviso—that a certain degree of duration is absolutely requisite for the production of any effect at all.

Holding in view these considerations, as well as that degree of excitement which I deemed not above the popular, while not below the critical, taste, I reached at once what I conceived the proper *length* for my intended poem—a length of about one hundred lines. It is, in fact, a hundred and eight.

My next thought concerned the choice of an impression, or effect, to be conveyed: and here I may as well observe that, throughout the construction, I kept steadily in view the design of rendering the work *universally* appreciable. I should be carried too far out of my immediate topic were I to demonstrate a point upon which I have repeatedly insisted, and which, with the poetical, stands not in the slightest need of demonstration—the point, I mean, that Beauty is the sole legitimate province of the poem. A few words, however, in elucidation of my real meaning, which some of my friends have evinced a disposition to misrepresent. That pleasure which is at once the most intense, the most elevating, and the most pure, is, I believe, found in the contemplation of the beautiful. When, indeed, men speak of Beauty, they mean, precisely, not a quality, as is supposed, but an effect—they refer, in short, just to that intense and pure elevation of *soul*—*not* of intellect, or of heart—upon which I have commented, and which is experienced in consequence of contemplating "the beautiful." Now I designate Beauty as the province of the poem, merely because it is an obvious rule of Art that effects should be made to spring from direct causes—that objects should be attained through means best adapted for their attainment—no one as yet having been weak enough to deny that the peculiar elevation alluded to, is *most readily* attained in the poem. Now the object, Truth, or the satisfaction of the intellect, and the object Passion, or the excitement of the heart, are, although attainable, to a certain extent, in poetry, far more readily attainable in prose. Truth, in fact, demands a precision, and Passion, a *homeliness* (the truly passionate will comprehend me) which are absolutely antagonistic to that Beauty which, I maintain, is the excitement, or pleasurable elevation, of the soul. It by no means follows from any thing here said, that passion, or even truth, may not be introduced, and even profitably introduced, into a poem—for they may serve in elucidation, or aid the general effect, as do discords in music, by contrast—but the true artist will always contrive, first, to tone them into proper subservience to the predominant aim, and, secondly, to enveil them, as far as possible, in that Beauty which is the atmosphere and the essence of the poem.

Regarding, then, Beauty as my province, my next question referred to the *tone* of its highest manifestation—and all experience has shown that this tone is one of *sadness*. Beauty of whatever kind, in its supreme development, invariably excites the sensitive soul to tears. Melancholy is thus the most legitimate of all the poetical tones.

The length, the province, and the tone, being thus determined, I betook myself to ordinary induction, with the view of obtaining some artistic piquancy which might serve me as a key-note in the construction of the poem—some pivot upon which the whole structure might turn. In carefully thinking over all the usual artistic effects—or more properly *points*, in the theatrical sense—I did not fail to perceive immediately that no one had been so universally employed as that of the *refrain*. The universality of its employment sufficed to assure me of its intrinsic value, and spared me the necessity of submitting it to analysis. I considered it, however, with regard to its susceptibility of improvement, and soon saw it to be in a primitive condition. As commonly used, the *refrain*, or burden, not only is limited to lyric verse, but depends for its impression upon the force of monotone—both in sound and thought. The pleasure is deduced solely from the sense of identity—of repetition. I resolved to diversify, and so vastly heighten, the effect, by adhering, in general, to the monotone of sound, while I continually varied that of thought: that is to say, I determined to produce continuously novel effects, by the variation *of the application* of the *refrain*—the *refrain* itself remaining, for the most part, unvaried.

These points being settled, I next bethought me of the *nature* of my *refrain*. Since its application was to be repeatedly varied, it was clear that the *refrain* itself must be brief, for there would have been an insurmountable difficulty in frequent variations of application in any sentence of length. In proportion to the brevity of the sentence, would, of course, be the facility of the variation. This led me at once to a single word as the best *refrain*.

The question now arose as to the *character* of the word. Having made up my mind to a *refrain*, the division of the poem into stanzas was, of course, a corollary: the *refrain* forming the close to each stanza. That such a close, to have force, must be sonorous and susceptible of protracted emphasis, admitted no doubt: and these considerations inevitably led me to the long *o* as the most sonorous vowel, in connection with *r* as the most producible consonant.

The sound of the *refrain* being thus determined, it became necessary to select a word embodying this sound, and at the same time in the fullest possible keeping with that melancholy which I had predetermined as the tone of the poem. In such a search it would have been absolutely impossible to overlook the word "Nevermore." In fact, it was the very first which presented itself.

The next *desideratum* was a pretext for the continuous use of the one word "nevermore." In observing the difficulty which I at once found in inventing a sufficiently plausible reason for its continuous repetition, I did not fail to perceive that this difficulty arose solely from the pre-assumption that the word was to be so continuously or monotonously spoken by a *human* being—I did not fail to perceive, in short, that the difficulty lay in the reconciliation of this monotony with the exercise of reason on the part of the creature repeating the word. Here, then, immediately arose the idea of a *non*-reasoning creature capable of speech; and, very naturally, a parrot, in the first instance, suggested itself, but was superseded forthwith by a Raven, as equally capable of speech, and infinitely more in keeping with the intended *tone.*

I had now gone so far as the conception of a Raven—the bird of ill omen—monotonously repeating the one word, "Nevermore," at the conclusion of each stanza, in a poem of melancholy tone, and in length about one hundred lines. Now, never losing sight of the object *supremeness,* or perfection, at all points, I asked myself—"Of all melancholy topics, what, according to the *universal* understanding of mankind, is the *most* melancholy?" Death—was the obvious reply. "And when," I said, "is this most melancholy of topics most poetical?" From what I have already explained at some length, the answer, here also, is obvious—"When it most closely allies itself to *Beauty*: the death, then, of a beautiful woman is, unquestionably, the most poetical topic in the world—and equally is it beyond doubt that the lips best suited for such topic are those of a bereaved lover."

I had now to combine the two ideas, of a lover lamenting his deceased mistress and a Raven continuously repeating the word "Nevermore"—I had to combine these, bearing in mind my design of varying, at every turn, the *application* of the word repeated; but the only intelligible mode of such combination is that of imagining the Raven employing the word in answer to the queries of the lover. And here it was that I saw at once the opportunity afforded for the effect on which I had been depending—that is to say, the effect of the *variation of application.* I saw that I could make the first query propounded by the lover—the first query to which the Raven should reply "Nevermore"—that I could make this first query a commonplace one—the second less so—the third still less, and so on—until at length the lover, startled from his original *nonchalance* by the melancholy character of the word itself—by its frequent repetition—and by a consideration of the ominous reputation of the fowl that uttered it—is at length excited to superstition, and wildly propounds queries of a far different character—queries whose solution he has passionately at heart—propounds them half in superstition and half in that species of despair which delights in self-torture—propounds them not altogether because he believes in the prophetic or demoniac

character of the bird (which, reason assures him, is merely repeating
a lesson learned by rote) but because he experiences a phrenzied
pleasure in so modeling his questions as to receive from the *expected*
"Nevermore" the most delicious because the most intolerable of sorrow. Perceiving the opportunity thus afforded me—or, more strictly,
thus forced upon me in the progress of the construction—I first
established in mind the climax, or concluding query—that to which
"Nevermore" should be in the last place an answer—that in reply to
which this word "Nevermore" should involve the utmost conceivable
amount of sorrow and despair.

Here then the poem may be said to have its beginning—at the end,
where all works of art should begin—for it was here, at this point of
my preconsiderations, that I first put pen to paper in the composition of the stanza:

> "Prophet," said I, "thing of evil! prophet still if bird or devil!
> By that heaven that bends above us—by that God we both adore,
> Tell this soul with sorrow laden, if within the distant Aidenn,[2]
> It shall clasp a sainted maiden whom the angels name Lenore—
> Clasp a rare and radiant maiden whom the angels name Lenore."
>   Quoth the raven "Nevermore."

I composed this stanza, at this point, first that, by establishing the
climax, I might the better vary and graduate, as regards seriousness
and importance, the preceding queries of the lover—and, secondly,
that I might definitely settle the rhythm, the metre, and the length
and general arrangement of the stanza—as well as graduate the stanzas which were to precede, so that none of them might surpass this
in rhythmical effect. Had I been able, in the subsequent composition, to construct more vigorous stanzas, I should, without scruple,
have purposely enfeebled them, so as not to interfere with the cli-
macteric effect.

And here I may as well say a few words of the versification. My first
object (as usual) was originality. The extent to which this has been
neglected, in versification, is one of the most unaccountable things
in the world. Admitting that there is little possibility of variety in
mere *rhythm,* it is still clear that the possible varieties of metre and
stanza are absolutely infinite—and yet, *for centuries, no man, in verse,
has ever done, or ever seemed to think of doing, an original thing.* The fact
is, originality (unless in minds of very unusual force) is by no means
a matter, as some suppose, of impulse or intuition. In general, to be
found, it must be elaborately sought, and although a positive merit
of the highest class, demands in its attainment less of invention than
negation.

---

[2]Eden, or paradise.

Of course, I pretend to no originality in either the rhythm or metre of the "Raven." The former is trochaic—the latter is octameter acatalectic, alternating with heptameter catalectic repeated in the *refrain* of the fifth verse, and terminating with tetrameter catalectic. Less pedantically—the feet employed throughout (trochees) consist of a long syllable followed by a short: the first line of the stanza consists of eight of these feet—the second of seven and a half (in effect two-thirds)—the third of eight—the fourth of seven and a half—the fifth the same—the sixth three and a half. Now, each of these lines, taken individually, has been employed before, and what originality the "Raven" has, is in their *combination into stanza;* nothing even remotely approaching this combination has ever been attempted. The effect of this originality of combination is aided by other unusual, and some altogether novel effects, arising from an extension of the application of the principles of rhyme and alliteration.

The next point to be considered was the mode of bringing together the lover and the Raven—and the first branch of this consideration was the *locale.* For this the most natural suggestion might seem to be a forest, or the fields—but it has always appeared to me that a close *circumscription of space* is absolutely necessary to the effect of insulated incident:—it has the force of a frame to a picture. It has an indisputable moral power in keeping concentrated the attention, and, of course, must not be confounded with mere unity of place.

I determined, then, to place the lover in his chamber—in a chamber rendered sacred to him by memories of her who had frequented it. The room is represented as richly furnished—this in mere pursuance of the ideas I have already explained on the subject of Beauty, as the sole true poetical thesis.

The *locale* being thus determined, I had now to introduce the bird—and the thought of introducing him through the window, was inevitable. The idea of making the lover suppose, in the first instance, that the flapping of the wings of the bird against the shutter, is a "tapping" at the door, originated in a wish to increase, by prolonging, the reader's curiosity, and in a desire to admit the incidental effect arising from the lover's throwing open the door, finding all dark, and thence adopting the half-fancy that it was the spirit of his mistress that knocked.

I made the night tempestuous, first, to account for the Raven's seeking admission, and secondly, for the effect of contrast with the (physical) serenity within the chamber.

I made the bird alight on the bust of Pallas, also for the effect of contrast between the marble and the plumage—it being understood that the bust was absolutely *suggested* by the bird—the bust of *Pallas* being chosen, first, as most in keeping with the scholarship of the lover, and, secondly, for the sonorousness of the word, Pallas, itself.

About the middle of the poem, also, I have availed myself of the force of contrast, with a view of deepening the ultimate impression. For example, an air of the fantastic—approaching as nearly to the ludicrous as was admissible—is given to the Raven's entrance. He comes in "with many a flirt and flutter."

Not the *least obeisance made he*—not a moment stopped or stayed he,
But with mien of lord or lady, perched above my chamber door.

In the two stanzas which follow, the design is more obviously carried out:—

Then this ebony bird beguiling my sad fancy into smiling
By the *grave and stern decorum of the countenance it wore,*
"Though thy *crest be shorn and shaven* thou," I said, "art sure no craven,
Ghastly grim and ancient Raven wandering from the nightly shore—
Tell me what thy lordly name is on the Night's Plutonian Shore!"
                    Quoth the Raven "Nevermore."

Much I marvelled *this ungainly fowl* to hear discourse so plainly,
Though its answer little meaning—little relevancy bore;
For we cannot help agreeing that no living human being
Ever yet was blessed with seeing bird above his chamber door—
Bird or beast upon the sculptured bust above his chamber door,
                    With such name as "Nevermore."

The effect of the *dénouement* being thus provided for, I immediately drop the fantastic for a tone of the most profound seriousness:— this tone commencing in the stanza directly following the one last quoted, with the line,

But the Raven, sitting lonely on that placid bust, spoke only, etc.

From this epoch the lover no longer jests—no longer sees any thing even of the fantastic in the Raven's demeanor. He speaks of him as a "grim, ungainly, ghastly, gaunt, and ominous bird of yore," and feels the "fiery eyes" burning into his "bosom's core." This revolution of thought, or fancy, on the lover's part, is intended to induce a similar one on the part of the reader—to bring the mind into a proper frame for the *dénouement*—which is now brought about as rapidly and as *directly* as possible.

With the *dénouement* proper—with the Raven's reply, "Nevermore," to the lover's final demand if he shall meet his mistress in another world—the poem, in its obvious phase, that of a simple narrative, may be said to have its completion. So far, every thing is within the limits of the accountable—of the real. A raven, having learned by rote the single word "Nevermore," and having escaped from the custody of its owner, is driven, at midnight, through the violence of a storm, to seek admission at a window from which a light still gleams—the chamber-window of a student, occupied half in poring over a volume, half in dreaming of a beloved mistress deceased. The casement being thrown open at the fluttering of the bird's wings, the bird itself perches on the most convenient seat out of the immediate reach of the student, who, amused by the incident and the oddity of the visiter's demeanor, demands of it, in jest and without looking for a reply, its name. The raven addressed, answers with its customary word, "Nevermore"—a word which finds immediate echo in the melancholy heart of the student, who, giving utterance aloud to certain thoughts suggested by the occasion, is again startled by the fowl's repetition of "Nevermore." The student now guesses the state of the case, but is impelled, as I have before explained, by the human thirst for self-torture, and in part by superstition, to propound such queries to the bird as will bring him, the lover, the most of the luxury of sorrow, through the anticipated answer "Nevermore." With the indulgence, to the utmost extreme, of this self-torture, the narration, in what I have termed its first or obvious phase, has a natural termination, and so far there has been no overstepping of the limits of the real.

But in subjects so handled, however skilfully, or with however vivid an array of incident, there is always a certain hardness or nakedness, which repels the artistical eye. Two things are invariably required— first, some amount of complexity, or more properly, adaptation; and, secondly, some amount of suggestiveness—some under current, however indefinite of meaning. It is this latter, in especial, which imparts to a work of art so much of that *richness* (to borrow from colloquy a forcible term) which we are too fond of confounding with *the ideal*. It is the *excess* of the suggested meaning—it is the rendering this the upper instead of the under current of the theme—which turns into prose (and that of the very flattest kind) the so called poetry of the so called transcendentalists.

Holding these opinions, I added the two concluding stanzas of the poem—their suggestiveness being thus made to pervade all the narrative which has preceded them. The under current of meaning is rendered first apparent in the lines—

> "Take thy beak from out *my heart,* and take thy form from off my door!"
> Quoth the Raven "Nevermore!"

It will be observed that the words, "from out my heart," involve the first metaphorical expression in the poem. They, with the answer, "Nevermore," dispose the mind to seek a moral in all that has been previously narrated. The reader begins now to regard the Raven as

emblematical—but it is not until the very last line of the very last stanza, that the intention of making him emblematical of *Mournful and
Neverending Remembrance* is permitted distinctly to be seen:

> And the Raven, never flitting, still is sitting, still is sitting,
> On the pallid bust of Pallas just above my chamber door;
> And his eyes have all the seeming of a demon's that is dreaming,
> And the lamplight o'er him streaming throws his shadow on the floor;
> And my soul *from out that shadow* that lies floating on the floor
>   Shall be lifted—nevermore.

Excerpts from "The Literati of New York City"
[*Godey's Lady's Book*, 1846]

Some Honest Opinions at Random Respecting Their Autorial Merits, with Occasional Words of Personality
(May 1846)

*Louis A. Godey commissioned these verbal portraits from Poe for his epony-
mous magazine in the hope that they would "raise some commotion." He was
not disappointed. The "Literati" raised so much commotion, in fact, that
Godey turned his back on Poe and left him to face it alone. Poe's "Honest
Opinions" of his peers were advanced despite warnings from friends that he
had precious little margin for error should they be ill received. Reeling from the
Longfellow War, the Boston Atheneum scandal (which ensued when Poe
passed off one of his juvenile poems as a new one and then revealed the hoax
afterwards), and the flap over his versified flirtations with the poets Frances
Osgood and Elizabeth Ellet in the pages of the* Broadway Journal, *Poe nevertheless disdained caution and forged ahead into print. Given Poe's needling
tone of arch and ironic judgment in these portraits, the only surprise may be
that they resulted in just one lawsuit.*

In a criticism on Bryant published in the last number of this magazine, I was at some pains in pointing out the distinction between the
popular "opinion" of the merits of cotemporary authors and that
held and expressed of them in private literary society. The former
species of "opinion" can be called "opinion" only by courtesy. It is the
public's own, just as we consider a book our own when we have
bought it. In general, this opinion is adopted from the journals of the
day, and I have endeavoured to show that the cases are rare indeed
in which these journals express any other sentiment about books
than such as may be attributed directly or indirectly to the authors of
the books. The most "popular," the most "successful" writers among
us, (for a brief period, at least,) are, ninety-nine times out of a hundred, persons of mere address, perseverance, effrontery—in a word,
busy-bodies, toadies, quacks. These people easily succeed in *boring*
editors (whose attention is too often entirely engrossed by politics or
other "business" matter) into the admission of favourable notices
written or caused to be written by interested parties—or, at least, into
the admission of *some* notice where, under ordinary circumstances,
no notice would be given at all. In this way ephemeral "reputations"

are manufactured which, for the most part, serve all the purposes designed—that is to say, the putting money into the purse of the quack and the quack's publisher; for there never was a quack who could be brought to comprehend the value of mere fame. Now, men of genius will not resort to these manœuvres, because genius involves in its very essence a scorn of chicanery; and thus for a time the quacks always get the advantage of them, both in respect to pecuniary profit and what *appears* to be public esteem.

There is another point of view, too. Your literary quacks court, in especial, the personal acquaintance of those "connected with the press." Now these latter, even when penning a voluntary, that is to say, an uninstigated notice of the book of an acquaintance, feel as if writing not so much for the eye of the public as for the eye of the acquaintance, and the notice is fashioned accordingly. The bad points of the work are slurred over and the good ones brought out into the best light, all this through a feeling akin to that which makes it unpleasant to speak ill of one to one's face. In the case of men of genius, editors, as a general rule, have no such delicacy—for the simple reason that, as a general rule, they have no acquaintance with these men of genius, a class proverbial for shunning society.

But the very editors who hesitate at saying in print an ill word of an author personally known, are usually the most frank in speaking about him privately. In literary society, they seem bent upon avenging the wrongs self-inflicted upon their own consciences. Here, accordingly, the quack is treated as he deserves—even a little more harshly than he deserves—by way of striking a balance. True merit, on the same principle, is apt to be slightly overrated; but, upon the whole, there is a close approximation to absolute honesty of opinion; and this honesty is farther secured by the mere trouble to which it puts one in conversation to model one's countenance to a falsehood. We place on paper without hesitation a tissue of flatteries, to which in society we could not give utterance, for our lives, without either blushing or laughing outright.

For these reasons there exists a very remarkable discrepancy between the apparent public opinion of any given author's merits and the opinion which is expressed of him orally by those who are best qualified to judge. For example, Mr. Hawthorne, the author of "Twice-Told Tales," is scarcely recognized by the press or by the public, and when noticed at all, is noticed merely to be damned by faint praise. Now, my own opinion of him is, that although his walk is limited and he is fairly to be charged with mannerism, treating all subjects in a similar tone of dreamy *innuendo*, yet in this walk he evinces extraordinary genius, having no rival either in America or elsewhere—and this opinion I have never heard gainsaid by any one literary person in the country. That this opinion, however, is a spoken and not a written one, is referable to the facts, first, that Mr. Hawthorne *is* a poor man, and, second, that he *is not* an ubiquitous quack.

Again, of Mr. Longfellow, who, although little quacky *per se,* has, through his social and literary position as a man of property and a professor at Harvard, a whole legion of active quacks at his control— of *him* what is the apparent popular opinion? Of course, that he is a poetical phenomenon, as entirely without fault as is the luxurious paper upon which his poems are invariably borne to the public eye. In private society he is regarded with one voice as a poet of far more than usual ability, a skillful artist and a well-read man, but as less remarkable in either capacity than as a determined imitator and a dexterous adopter of the ideas of other people. For years I have conversed with no literary person who did not entertain precisely these ideas of Professor L.; and, in fact, on all literary topics there is in society a seemingly wonderful coincidence of opinion. The author accustomed to seclusion, and mingling for the first time with those who have been associated with him only through their works, is astonished and delighted at finding common to all whom he meets conclusions which he had blindly fancied were attained by himself alone and in opposition to the judgment of mankind.

In the series of papers which I now propose, my design is, in giving my own unbiased opinion of the *literati* (male and female) of New York, to give at the same time, very closely if not with absolute accuracy, that of conversational society in literary circles. It must be expected, of course, that, in innumerable particulars, I shall differ from the voice, that is to say, from what appears to be the voice of the public—but this is a matter of no consequence whatever.

New York literature may be taken as a fair representation of that of the country at large. The city itself is the focus of American letters. Its authors include, perhaps, one-fourth of all in America, and the influence they exert on their brethren, if seemingly silent, is not the less extensive and decisive. As I shall have to speak of many individuals, my limits will not permit me to speak of them otherwise than in brief; but this brevity will be merely consistent with the design, which is that of simple *opinion,* with little of either argument or detail. With one or two exceptions I am well acquainted with every author to be introduced, and I shall avail myself of the acquaintance to convey, generally, some idea of the personal appearance of all who, in this regard, would be likely to interest the readers of the magazine. As any precise order or arrangement seems unnecessary and may be inconvenient, I shall maintain none. It will be understood that, without reference to supposed merit or demerit, each individual is introduced absolutely at random.

Thomas Dunn English
(July 1846)

Understandably infuriated at being depicted here as an illiterate plagiarist, writer and editor Thomas Dunn English hit back hard, publicly accusing Poe of depravity, drunkenness, dishonesty, and quackery. A high profile exchange of insults ensued, climaxing in a libel suit which Poe won in 1847. The victory came at considerable cost, however, as English's charges (some of which were true) hung in the air long after the suit was concluded.

I have seen one or two brief poems of considerable merit with the signature of *Thomas Dunn English* appended. For example—

> "AZTHENE.
> "A sound melodious shook the breeze
>   When thy beloved name was heard:
>   Such was the music in the word
>   Its dainty rhythm the pulses stirred.
> But passed forever joys like these.
>   There is no joy, no light, no day;
>   But black despair and night alway,
>   And thickening gloom:
> And this, Azthene, is my doom.
>
> "Was it for this, for weary years,
>   I strove among the sons of men,
>   And by the magic of my pen—
>   Just sorcery—walked the lion's den
> Of slander void of tears and fears—
>   And all for thee? For thee!—alas,
>   As is the image on a glass
>   So baseless seems,
> Azthene, all my earthly dreams."

I must confess, however, that I do not appreciate the "dainty rhythm" of such a word as "Azthene," and, perhaps, there is a little taint of egotism in the passage about "the magic" of Mr. English's pen. Let us be charitable, however, and set all this down under the head of "pure imagination" or invention—one of the first of poetical requisites. The *inexcusable* sin of Mr. E. is imitation—if this be not too mild a term. Barry Cornwall and others of the *bizarre* school are his especial favorites. He has taken, too, most unwarrantable liberties, in the way of downright plagiarism, from a Philadelphian poet whose high merits have not been properly appreciated—*Mr. Henry B. Hirst.*

I place Mr. English, however, on my list of New York *literati,* not on account of his poetry, (which I presume he is not weak enough to estimate very highly,) but on the score of his having edited for several months, "with the aid of numerous collaborators," a monthly magazine called "The Aristidean." This work, although professedly a "monthly," was issued at irregular intervals, and was unfortunate, I fear, in not attaining at any period a very extensive circulation.

I learn that Mr. E. is not without talent; but the fate of "The Aristidean" should indicate to him the necessity of applying himself to study. No spectacle can be more pitiable than that of a man without the commonest school education busying himself in attempts to instruct mankind on topics of polite literature. The absurdity in such cases does not lie merely in the ignorance displayed by the would-be instructor, but in the transparency of the shifts by which he endeavours to keep this ignorance concealed. The editor of "The Aristidean," for example, was not laughed at so much on account of writing "lay" for "lie," etc. etc., and coupling nouns in the plural with verbs in the singular—as where he writes, above,

> "———so baseless *seems,*
> Azthene, all my earthly *dreams—*"

he was not, I say, laughed at *so much* for his excusable deficiencies in English grammar (although an editor should certainly be able to write *his own name*) as that, in the hope of disguising such deficiency, he was perpetually lamenting the "typographical blunders" that "in the most unaccountable manner" *would* creep into his work. Nobody was so stupid as to suppose for a moment that there existed in New York a single proof-reader—or even a single printer's devil—who would have permitted *such* errors to escape. By the excuses offered, therefore, the errors were only the more obviously nailed to the counter as Mr. English's own.

I make these remarks in no spirit of unkindness. Mr. E. is yet young—certainly not more than thirty-five—and might, with his talents, readily improve himself at points where he is most defective. No one of any generosity would think the worse of him for getting private instruction.

I do not personally know Mr. English. He is, I believe, from Philadelphia, where he was formerly a doctor of medicine, and subsequently took up the profession of law; more latterly he joined the Tyler party and devoted his attention to politics. About his personal appearance there is nothing very observable. I cannot say whether he is married or not.

Sarah Margaret Fuller
(September 1846)

Margaret Fuller's reputation in 1846 rested principally on her editorship of
The Dial, *the most important periodical of the Transcendentalist movement,
as well as her books, which included* Summer on the Lakes *(1843) and*
Woman in the Nineteenth Century *(1845). Poe duly cites these achievements, but seems chiefly grateful for Fuller's critical review of Longfellow, in
which she concurred with certain of Poe's criticisms of the poet.*

Miss Fuller was at one time editor, or one of the editors of "The Dial,"
to which she contributed many of the most forcible, and certainly
some of the most peculiar papers. She is known, too, by "Summer on
the Lakes," a remarkable assemblage of sketches, issued in 1844 by
Little & Brown, of Boston. More lately she has published "Woman in
the Nineteenth Century," a work which has occasioned much discussion, having had the good fortune to be warmly abused and chivalrously defended. At present, she is assistant editor of "The New York
Tribune," or rather a salaried contributor to that journal, for which
she has furnished a great variety of matter, chiefly critical notices of
new books, etc. etc., her articles being designated by an asterisk. Two
of the best of them were a review of Professor Longfellow's late magnificent edition of his own works, (with a portrait,) and an appeal to
the public in behalf of her friend Harro Harring. The review did her
infinite credit; it was frank, candid, independent—in even ludicrous
contrast to the usual mere glorifications of the day, giving honor *only*
where honor was due, yet evincing the most thorough capacity to
appreciate and the most sincere intention to place in the fairest light
the real and idiosyncratic merits of the poet.

In my opinion it is one of the very few reviews of Longfellow's
poems, ever published in America, of which the critics have not had
abundant reason to be ashamed. Mr. Longfellow is entitled to a certain and very distinguished rank among the poets of his country, but
that country is disgraced by the evident toadyism which would award
to his social position and influence, to his fine paper and large type,
to his morocco binding and gilt edges, to his flattering portrait of
himself, and to the illustrations of his poems by Huntingdon, that
amount of indiscriminate approbation which neither could nor
would have been given to the poems themselves.

The defence of Harro Harring, or rather the Philippic against
those who were doing him wrong, was one of the most eloquent and
well-*put* articles I have ever yet seen in a newspaper.

"Woman in the Nineteenth Century" is a book which few women in the country could have written, and no woman in the country would have published, with the exception of Miss Fuller. In the way of independence, of unmitigated radicalism, it is one of the "Curiosities of American Literature," and Doctor Griswold should include it in his book.[1] I need scarcely say that the essay is nervous, forcible, thoughtful, suggestive, brilliant, and to a certain extent scholar-like—for all that Miss Fuller produces is entitled to those epithets—but I must say that the conclusions reached are only in part my own. Not that they are too bold, by any means—too novel, too startling, or too dangerous in their consequences, but that in their attainment too many premises have been distorted and too many analogical inferences left altogether out of sight. I mean to say that the intention of the Deity as regards sexual differences—an intention which can be distinctly comprehended only by throwing the exterior (more sensitive) portions of the mental retina *casually* over the wide field of universal *analogy*—I mean to say that this *intention* has not been sufficiently considered. Miss Fuller has erred, too, through her own excessive objectiveness. She judges *woman* by the heart and intellect of Miss Fuller, but there are not more than one or two dozen Miss Fullers on the whole face of the earth. Holding these opinions in regard to "Woman in the Nineteenth Century," I still feel myself called upon to disavow the silly, condemnatory criticism of the work which appeared in one of the earlier numbers of "The Broadway Journal." That article was *not* written by myself, and *was* written by my associate Mr. Briggs.[2]

The most favorable estimate of Miss Fuller's genius (for high genius she unquestionably possesses) is to be obtained, perhaps, from her contributions to "The Dial," and from her "Summer on the Lakes." Many of the *descriptions* in this volume are unrivaled for *graphicality*, (why is there not such a word?) for the force with which they convey the true by the novel or unexpected, by the introduction of touches which other artists would be sure to omit as irrelevant to the subject. This faculty, too, springs from her subjectiveness, which leads her to paint a scene less by its features than by its effects.

Here, for example, is a portion of her account of Niagara:—

"Daily these proportions widened and towered more and more upon my sight, and I got at last a proper foreground for these sublime distances. Before coming away, I think I really saw the full wonder of the scene. After awhile it *so drew me into itself as to inspire an undefined*

---

[1] Rufus Griswold's *Curiosities of American Literature* was an American counterpart to Isaac D'Israeli's *Curiosities of Literature* (a 6-volume set published anonymously between 1791 and 1834), a work from which Poe borrowed a good deal in his own writing.
[2] Charles F. Briggs was Poe's co-editor on the *Broadway Journal* in 1845.

dread, such as I never knew before, such as may be felt when death is about to usher us into a new existence. The perpetual trampling of the waters seized my senses. *I felt that no other sound, however near, could be heard, and would start and look behind me for a foe.* I realized the identity of that mood of nature in which these waters were poured down with such absorbing force, with that in which the Indian was shaped on the same soil. For continually upon my mind came, unsought and unwelcome, *images, such as had never haunted it before, of naked savages stealing behind me with uplifted tomahawks.* Again and again this illusion recurred, and even *after I had thought it over and tried to shake it off, I could not help starting and looking behind me.* What I liked best was to sit on Table Rock close to the great fall; *there all power of observing details, all separate consciousness was quite lost.*"

The truthfulness of the passages italicized will be felt by all; the feelings described are, perhaps, experienced by every (imaginative) person who visits the fall; but most persons, through predominant subjectiveness, would scarcely be conscious of the feelings, or, at best, would never think of employing them in an attempt to convey to others an impression of the scene. Hence so many desperate failures to convey it on the part of ordinary tourists. Mr. William W. Lord, to be sure, in his poem "Niagara," is sufficiently objective; he describes not the fall, but very properly the effect of the fall upon *him.* He says that it made him think of his *own* greatness, of his *own* superiority, and so forth, and so forth; and it is only when we come to think that the thought of Mr. Lord's greatness is quite idiosyncratic, confined exclusively to Mr. Lord, that we are in condition to understand how, in despite of his objectiveness, he has failed to convey an idea of anything beyond one Mr. William W. Lord.

From the essay entitled "Philip Van Artevelde," I copy a paragraph which will serve at once to exemplify Miss Fuller's more earnest (declamatory) style, and to show the tenor of her prospective speculations:—

"At Chicago I read again 'Philip Van Artevelde,' and certain passages in it will always be in my mind associated with the deep sound of the lake, as heard in the night. I used to read a short time at night, and then open the blind to look out. The moon would be full upon the lake, and the calm breath, pure light, and the deep voice, harmonized well with the thought of the Flemish hero. When will this country have such a man? It is what she needs—no thin Idealist, no coarse Realist, but a man whose eye reads the heavens while his feet step firmly on the ground and his hands are strong and dextrous in the use of human instruments. A man, religious, virtuous and—sagacious; a man of universal sympathies, but self-possessed; a man who knows the region of emotion, though he is not its slave; a man to whom this world is no mere spectacle or fleeting shadow, but a great, solemn game, to be played with good heed, for its stakes are of eternal value, yet who, if his own play be true, heeds not what he loses by the falsehood of others. A man who lives from the past, yet knows that its honey can but moderately avail him; whose comprehensive eye scans the present, neither infatuated by its golden lures nor chilled by its many ventures; who possesses prescience, as the wise man must, but not so far as to be driven mad to-day by the gift which discerns to-morrow. When there is such a man for America, the thought which urges her on will be expressed."

From what I have quoted a *general* conception of the prose style of the authoress may be gathered. Her manner, however, is infinitely varied. It is always forcible—but I am not sure that it is always anything else, unless I say picturesque. It rather indicates than evinces scholarship. Perhaps only the scholastic, or, more properly, those accustomed to look narrowly at the structure of phrases, would be willing to acquit her of ignorance of grammar—would be willing to attribute her slovenliness to disregard of the shell in anxiety for the kernel; or to waywardness, or to affectation, or to blind reverence for Carlyle—would be able to detect, in her strange and continual inaccuracies, a capacity for the accurate.

> "I cannot sympathize with such an apprehension: the spectacle is *capable to* swallow *up* all such objects."
>
> "It is fearful, too, to know, as you look, that whatever has been swallowed by the cataract, is *like* to rise suddenly to light."
>
> "I took our *mutual* friends to see her."
>
> "It was always obvious that they had nothing in common *between them.*"
>
> "The Indian cannot be looked at truly *except* by a poetic eye."
>
> "McKenney's Tour to the Lakes gives some facts not to be met *with* elsewhere."
>
> "There is that mixture of culture and rudeness in the aspect of things *as* gives a feeling of freedom," etc. etc. etc.

These are merely a few, a very few instances, taken at random from among a multitude of *wilful* murders committed by Miss Fuller on the American of President Polk. She uses, too, the word "ignore," a vulgarity adopted only of late days (and to no good purpose, since there is no necessity for it) from the barbarisms of the law, and makes no scruple of giving the Yankee interpretation to the verbs "witness" and "realize" to say nothing of "use," as in the sentence, "I used to read a short time at night." It will not do to say, in defence of such words, that in such senses they may be found in certain dictionaries—in that of Bolles',[3] for instance;—*some* kind of "authority" may be found for *any* kind of vulgarity under the sun.

---

[3]The William Bolles work mentioned is *An Explanatory and Phonographic Pronouncing Dictionary* (1845).

In spite of these things, however, and of her frequent unjustifiable Carlyleisms,[4] (such as that of writing sentences which are no sentences, since, to be parsed, reference must be had to sentences preceding,) the style of Miss Fuller is one of the very best with which I am acquainted. In general effect, I know no style which surpasses it. It is singularly piquant, vivid, terse, bold, luminous—leaving details out of sight, it is everything that a style need be.

I believe that Miss Fuller has written much poetry, although she has published little. That little is tainted with the affectation of the *transcendentalists,* (I use this term, of course, in the sense which the public of late days seem resolved to give it,) but is brimful of the poetic *sentiment.* Here, for example, is something in Coleridge's manner, of which the author of "Genevieve" might have had no reason to be ashamed:—

> "A maiden sat beneath a tree;
> Tear-bedewed her pale cheeks be,
> And she sigheth heavily.
>
> "From forth the wood into the *light*
> A hunter strides with carol *light,*
> And a glance so bold and bright.
>
> "He careless stopped and eyed the maid:
> 'Why weepest thou?' he gently said;
> 'I love thee well, be not afraid.'
>
> "He takes her hand and leads her on—
> She should have waited there alone,
> For he was not her chosen one.
>
> "He *leans* her head upon his breast—
> She knew 'twas not her home of rest,
> But, ah, she had been sore distrest.
>
> "The sacred stars looked sadly down;
> The parting moon appeared to frown,
> To see thus dimmed the diamond crown.
>
> "Then from the thicket starts a deer—
> The huntsman, seizing *on* his spear
> Cries, 'Maiden, wait thou for me here.'
>
> "She sees him vanish into night—
> She starts from sleep in deep affright,
> For it was not her own true knight.

---

[4]The writings of Thomas Carlyle (1795–1887) were a major inspiration for Emerson, Fuller, and other members of the American Transcendentalist movement. See fn. 6 on p. 55.

"Though but in dream Gunhilda failed—
Though but a fancied ill assailed—
Though she but fancied fault bewailed—

"Yet thought of day makes dream of night;
She is not worthy of the knight;
The inmost altar burns not bright.

"If loneliness thou canst not bear—
Cannot the dragon's venom dare—
Of the pure meed thou shoulds't despair.

"Now sadder that lone maiden sighs;
Far bitterer tears profane her eyes;
Crushed in the dust her heart's flower lies."

To show the evident carelessness with which this poem was constructed, I have italicized an identical rhyme (of about the same force in versification as an identical proposition in logic) and two grammatical improprieties. *To lean* is a neuter verb, and "seizing *on*" is not properly to be called a pleonasm, merely because it is—nothing at all. The concluding line is difficult of pronunciation through excess of consonants. I should have preferred, indeed, the ante-penultimate tristich as the *finale* of the poem.

The supposition that the book of an author is a thing apart from the author's self, is, I think, ill-founded. The soul is a cypher, in the sense of a cryptograph; and the shorter a cryptograph is, the more difficulty there is in its comprehension—at a certain point of brevity it would bid defiance to an army of Champollions.[5] And thus he who has written very little, may in that little either conceal his spirit or convey quite an erroneous idea of it—of his acquirements, talents, temper, manner, tenor and depth (or shallowness) of thought—in a word, of his character, of himself. But this is impossible with him who has written much. Of such a person we get, from his books, not merely a just, but the most just representation. Bulwer, the individual, personal man, in a green velvet waistcoat and amber gloves, is not by any means the veritable Sir Edward Lytton, who is discoverable only in "Ernest Maltravers," where his soul is deliberately and nakedly set forth.[6] And who would ever know Dickens by looking at him or talking with him, or doing anything with him except reading his "Curiosity Shop?" What poet, in especial, but must feel at least the better portion of himself more fairly represented in even his commonest sonnet (earnestly written) than in his most elaborate or most intimate personalities?

---

[5]Jean François Champollion (1790–1832) was a major early figure in the first decipherings of Egyptian hieroglyphics.
[6]See fn. 2 on p. 38.

I put all this as a general proposition, to which Miss Fuller affords a marked exception—to this extent, that her personal character and her printed book are merely one and the same thing. We get access to her soul *as* directly from the one as from the other—no *more* readily from this than from that—easily from either. Her acts are bookish, and her books are less thoughts than acts. Her literary and her conversational manner are identical. Here is a passage from her "Summer on the Lakes:"—

> "The rapids enchanted me far beyond what I expected; they are so swift that they cease to *seem* so—you can think only of their *beauty*. The fountain beyond the Moss islands I discovered for myself, and thought it for some time an *accidental* beauty which it would not do to *leave*, lest I might never see it again. After I found it *permanent*, I returned many times to watch the play of its crest. In the little waterfall beyond, Nature seems, as she often does, to have made a *study* for some larger design. She delights in this—a sketch within a sketch—a dream with *a dream*. Whatever we see it, the lines of the great buttress in the fragment of stone, the hues of the waterfall, copied in the flowers that *star* its bordering mosses, we are *delighted*; for all the lineaments become *fluent*, and we mould the scene in congenial thought with its *genius*."

Now all this is precisely as Miss Fuller would *speak* it. She is perpetually saying just such things in just such words. To get the *conversational* woman in the mind's eye, all that is needed is to imagine her reciting the paragraph just quoted: but first let us have the *personal* woman. She is of the medium height; nothing remarkable about the figure; a profusion of lustrous light hair; eyes a bluish gray, full of fire; capacious forehead; the mouth when in repose indicates profound sensibility, capacity for affection, for love—when moved by a slight smile, it becomes even beautiful in the intensity of this expression; but the upper lip, as if impelled by the action of involuntary muscles, habitually uplifts itself, conveying the impression of a sneer. Imagine, now, a person of this description looking you at one moment earnestly in the face, at the next seeming to look only within her own spirit or at the wall; moving nervously every now and then in her chair; speaking in a high key, but musically, deliberately, (not hurriedly or loudly,) with a delicious distinctness of enunciation—speaking, I say, the paragraph in question, and emphasizing the words which I have italicized, not by impulsion of the breath, (as is usual,) but by drawing them out as long as possible, nearly closing her eyes the while—imagine all this, and we have both the woman and the authoress before us.

Lydia M. Child
(September 1846)

Lydia Maria Child was a prominent and influential social reformer, a crusader for the rights of Native Americans and slaves, and the author of many books, including the controversial An Appeal for that Class of Americans Called Africans *(1833). Poe's brief sketch of Child is most notable for what it leaves out; he refuses to acknowledge her concern with racial injustice, focusing instead on her prose style and personal appearance.*

Mrs. Child has acquired a just celebrity by many compositions of high merit, the most noticeable of which are "Hobomok," "Philothea," and a "History of the Condition of Women." "Philothea," in especial, is written with great vigor, and, as a classical romance, is not far inferior to the "Anacharsis" of Barthelemi;—its style is a model for purity, chastity and ease. Some of her magazine papers are distinguished for graceful and brilliant *imagination*—a quality rarely noticed in our countrywomen. She continues to write a great deal for the monthlies and other journals, and invariably writes well. Poetry she has not often attempted, but I make no doubt that in this she would excel. It seems, indeed, the legitimate province for her fervid and fanciful nature. I quote one of her shorter compositions, as well to instance (from the subject) her intense appreciation of genius in others as to exemplify the force of her poetic expression:—

"MARIUS AMID THE RUINS OF CARTHAGE.

"Pillars are fallen at thy feet,
  Fanes quiver in the air,
A prostrate city in thy seat,
  And thou alone art there.

"No change comes o'er thy noble brow,
  Though ruin is around thee;
Thine eyebeam burns as proudly now
  As when the laurel crowned thee.

"It cannot bend thy lofty soul
  Though friends and fame depart—
The car of Fate may o'er thee roll
  Nor crush thy Roman heart.

"And genius hath electric power
  Which earth can never tame;
Bright suns may scorch and dark clouds lower,
  Its flash is still the same.

"The dreams we loved in early life
    May melt like mist away;
High thoughts may seem, 'mid passion's strife,
    Like Carthage in decay;

"And proud hopes in the human heart
    May be to ruin hurled,
Like mouldering monuments of art
    Heaped on a sleeping world:

"Yet there is something will not die
    Where life hath once been fair;
Some towering thoughts still rear on high,
    Some Roman lingers there."

Mrs. Child, casually observed, has nothing particularly striking in her personal appearance. One would pass her in the street a dozen times without notice. She is low in stature and slightly framed. Her complexion is florid; eyes and hair are dark; features in general diminutive. The expression of her countenance, when animated, is highly intellectual. Her dress is usually plain, not even neat—anything but fashionable. Her bearing needs excitement to impress it with life and dignity. She is of that order of beings who are themselves only on "great occasions." Her husband is still living. She has no children. I need scarcely add that she has always been distinguished for her energetic and active philanthropy.

The Rationale of Verse*
[*Southern Literary Messenger,* October–November 1848]

In "The Rationale of Verse" Poe works out at length his "mathematical" approach to poetic composition. This comprehensive statement of his formalist aesthetics is the longest and most detailed of his critical treatises. Poe's elaborate treatment of prosody highlights his view of creativity as the intertwined application of reason and imagination to create harmonious unity.

The word "Verse" is here used not in its strict or primitive sense, but as the term most convenient for expressing generally and without pedantry all that is involved in the consideration of rhythm, rhyme, metre, and versification.

There is, perhaps, no topic in polite literature which has been more pertinaciously discussed, and there is certainly not one about which so much inaccuracy, confusion, misconception, misrepresentation, mystification, and downright ignorance on all sides, can be fairly said to exist. Were the topic really difficult, or did it lie, even, in the cloud-land of metaphysics, where the doubt-vapors may be made to assume any and every shape at the will or at the fancy of the gazer, we should have less reason to wonder at all this contradiction and perplexity; but in fact the subject is exceedingly simple; one tenth of it, possibly, may be called ethical; nine tenths, however, appertain to the mathematics; and the whole is included within the limits of the commonest common sense.

"But, if this is the case, how," it will be asked, "can so much misunderstanding have arisen? Is it conceivable that a thousand profound scholars, investigating so very simple a matter for centuries, have not been able to place it in the fullest light, at least, of which it is susceptible?" These queries, I confess, are not easily answered:— at all events a satisfactory reply to them might cost more trouble than would, if properly considered, the whole *vexata quæstio* to which they have reference. Nevertheless, there is little difficulty or danger in suggesting that the "thousand profound scholars" *may* have failed, first because they were scholars, secondly because they were profound, and thirdly because they were a thousand—the impotency of the scholarship and profundity having been thus multiplied a thousand fold. I am serious in these suggestions; for, first again, there is something in "scholarship" which seduces us into blind worship of

---

*Some few passages of this article appeared, about four years ago, in "The Pioneer," a monthly Magazine published by J. R. Lowell and R. Carter. Although an excellent work it had a *very* limited circulation.

Bacon's Idol of the Theatre—into irrational deference to antiquity; secondly, the proper "profundity" is rarely profound—it is the nature of Truth in general, as of some ores in particular, to be richest when most superficial; thirdly, the clearest subject may be overclouded by mere superabundance of talk. In chemistry, the best way of separating two bodies is to add a third; in speculation, fact often agrees with fact and argument with argument, until an additional well-meaning fact or argument sets every thing by the ears. In one case out of a hundred a point is excessively discussed because it is obscure; in the ninety-nine remaining it is obscure because excessively discussed. When a topic is thus circumstanced, the readiest mode of investigating it is to forget that any previous investigation has been attempted.

But, in fact, while much has been written on the Greek and Latin rhythms, and even on the Hebrew, little effort has been made at examining that of any of the modern tongues. As regards the English, comparatively nothing has been done. It may be said, indeed, that we are without a treatise on our own verse. In our ordinary grammars and in our works on rhetoric or prosody in general, may be found occasional chapters, it is true, which have the heading, "Versification," but these are, in all instances, exceedingly meagre. They pretend to no analysis; they propose nothing like system; they make no attempt at even rule; every thing depends upon "authority." They are confined, in fact, to mere exemplification of the supposed varieties of English feet and English lines;—although in no work with which I am acquainted are these feet correctly given or these lines detailed in anything like their full extent. Yet what has been mentioned is all—if we except the occasional introduction of some pedagogue-ism, such as this, borrowed from the Greek Prosodies:— "When a syllable is wanting, the verse is said to be catalectic; when the measure is exact, the line is acatalectic; when there is a redundant syllable it forms hypermeter."[1] Now whether a line be termed catalectic or acatalectic is, perhaps, a point of no vital importance;—it is even possible that the student may be able to decide, promptly, when the *a* should be employed and when omitted, yet be incognizant, at the same time, of *all* that is worth knowing in regard to the structure of verse.

A leading defect in each of our treatises, (if treatises they can be called,) is the confining the subject to mere *Versification*, while Verse in general, with the understanding given to the term in the heading of this paper, is the real question at issue. Nor am I aware of even one of our Grammars which so much as properly defines the word

---

[1] This quotation is from Goold Brown's *The Institutes of English Grammar* (1833).

versification itself. "Versification," says a work now before me, of which the accuracy is far more than usual—the "English Grammar" of Goold Brown—"Versification is the art of arranging words into lines of correspondent length, so as to produce harmony by the regular alternation of syllables differing in quantity." The commencement of this definition might apply, indeed, to the *art* of versification, but not to versification itself. Versification is not the art of arranging &c., but the actual arranging—a distinction too obvious to need comment. The error here is identical with one which has been too long permitted to disgrace the initial page of every one of our school grammars. I allude to the definitions of English Grammar itself. "English Grammar," it is said, "is the art of speaking and writing the English language correctly." This phraseology, or something essentially similar, is employed, I believe, by Bacon, Miller, Fisk, Greenleaf, Ingersoll, Kirkland, Cooper, Flint, Pue, Comly, and many others.[2] These gentlemen, it is presumed, adopted it without examination from Murray, who derived it from Lily, (whose work was *"quam solam Regia Majestas in omnibus scholis docendam præcipit,"*)[3] and who appropriated it without acknowledgment, but with some unimportant modification, from the Latin Grammar of Leonicenus.[4] It may be shown, however, that this definition, so complacently received, is not, and cannot be, a proper definition of English Grammar. A definition is that which so describes its object as to distinguish it from all others:—it is no definition of any one thing if its terms are applicable to any one other. But if it be asked—"What is the design—the end—the aim of English Grammar?" our obvious answer is, "The art of speaking and writing the English language correctly:"—that is to say, we must use the precise words employed as the definition of English Grammar itself. But the object to be obtained by any means is, assuredly, not the means. English Grammar and the end contemplated by English Grammar, are two matters sufficiently distinct; nor can the one be more reasonably regarded as the other than a fishing-hook as a fish. The definition, therefore, which is applicable in the latter instance, *cannot,* in the former, be true. Grammar in general is the analysis of language; English Grammar of the English.

But to return to Versification as defined in our extract above. "It is the art," says this extract, "of arranging words into lines *of correspondent length.*" Not so:—a correspondence in the length of lines is by no means essential. Pindaric odes are, surely, instances of versification,

---

[2]The names listed are all of authors of English grammar texts of Poe's day.
[3]"a thing which royal majesty alone perceives should be taught in all the schools."
[4]Omnibonus Leonicenus, *De octo partibus orationis* (1473).

yet these compositions are noted for extreme diversity in the length of their lines.

The arrangement is moreover said to be for the purpose of producing "*harmony* by the regular alternation," &c. But *harmony* is not the sole aim—not even the principal one. In the construction of verse, *melody* should never be left out of view; yet this is a point which all our Prosodies have most unaccountably forborne to touch. Reasoned rules on this topic should form a portion of all systems of rhythm.

"So as to produce harmony," says the definition, "by the *regular alternation*," &c. A *regular* alternation, as described, forms no part of any principle of versification. The arrangement of spondees and dactyls, for example, in the Greek hexameter, is an arrangement which may be termed *at random*. At least it is arbitrary. Without interference with the line as a whole, a dactyl may be substituted for a spondee, or the converse, at any point other than the ultimate and penultimate feet, of which the former is always a spondee, the latter nearly always a dactyl. Here, it is clear, we have no "*regular* alternation of syllables differing in quantity."

"So as to produce harmony," proceeds the definition, "by the regular alternation of *syllables differing in quantity*,"—in other words by the alternation of long and short syllables; for in rhythm all syllables are necessarily either short or long. But not only do I deny the necessity of any *regularity* in the succession of feet and, by consequence, of syllables, but dispute the essentiality of any *alternation*, regular or irregular, of syllables long and short. Our author, observe, is now engaged in a definition of versification in general, not of English versification in particular. But the Greek and Latin metres abound in the spondee and pyrrhic—the former consisting of two long syllables; the latter of two short; and there are innumerable instances of the immediate succession of many spondees and many pyrrhics.

Here is a passage from Silius Italicus:

> Fallis te mensas inter quod credis inermem
> Tot bellis quæsita viro, tot cædibus armat
> Majestas eterna ducem: si admoveris ora
> Cannas et Trebium ante oculos Trasymenaque busta,
> Et Pauli stare ingentem miraberis umbram.[5]

Making the elisions demanded by the classic Prosodies, we should scan these Hexameters thus:

---

[5]"You deceive yourself if you believe he sits at table unarmed. An eternal majesty gained in so many wars and by so much bloodshed arms him: If you but look more closely you will be astonished to see standing before you Cannae, Trebia, the graves of Lake Trasimene, and the mighty shade [soul] of Paulus." *Punica*, II, 342–346 (transl. George Shea).

Fāllĭs | tē mēn | sās ĭn | tēr qūod | crēdĭs ĭn | ērmēm |
Tōt bēl | lĭs qūæ | sītă vĭ | rō tōt | cædĭbŭs | ārmāt |
Mājēs | tās ē | tērnă dŭ | cēm s'ād | mōvĕrĭs | ōrā |
Cānnās | ēt Trĕbĭ' | ānt'ŏcŭ | lōs Trăsy | mēnăquĕ | būstā
ēt Pāu | lī stā | r'īngēn | tēm mī | rābĕrĭs | ūmbrām |

It will be seen that, in the first and last of these lines, we have only two short syllables in thirteen, with an uninterrupted succession of no less than *nine* long syllables. But how are we to reconcile all this with a definition of versification which describes it as "the art of arranging words into lines of correspondent length so as to produce harmony by the *regular alternation of syllables differing in quantity?*"

It may be urged, however, that our prosodist's *intention* was to speak of the English metres alone, and that, by omitting all mention of the spondee and pyrrhic, he has virtually avowed their exclusion from our rhythms. A grammarian is never excusable on the ground of good intentions. We demand from him, if from any one, rigorous precision of style. But grant the design. Let us admit that our author, following the example of all authors on English Prosody, has, in defining versification at large, intended a definition merely of the English. All these prosodists, we will say, reject the spondee and pyrrhic. Still all admit the iambus, which consists of a short syllable followed by a long; the trochee, which is the converse of the iambus; the dactyl, formed of one long syllable followed by two short; and the anapæst—two short succeeded by a long. The spondee is improperly rejected, as I shall presently show. The pyrrhic is rightfully dismissed. Its existence in either ancient or modern rhythm is purely chimerical, and the insisting on so perplexing a nonentity as a foot of *two short* syllables, affords, perhaps, the best evidence of the gross irrationality and subservience to authority which characterize our Prosody. In the meantime the acknowledged dactyl and anapæst are enough to sustain my proposition about the "alternation," &c., without reference to feet which are assumed to exist in the Greek and Latin metres alone: for an anapæst and a dactyl may meet in the same line; when of course we shall have an uninterrupted succession of four short syllables. The meeting of these two feet, to be sure, is an accident not contemplated in the definition now discussed; for this definition, in demanding a "regular alternation of syllables differing in quantity," insists on a regular succession of similar *feet*. But here is an example:

Sīng tŏ mē | Isăbēlle.[6]

---

[6]Henry B. Hirst, a contemporary whose work Poe reviewed favorably, is the author of this ballad.

This is the opening line of a little ballad now before me, which proceeds in the same rhythm—a peculiarly beautiful one. More than all
this:—English lines are often well composed, entirely, of a regular
succession of syllables *all of the same quantity*:—the first lines, for
instance, of the following quatrain by Arthur C. Coxe:

> *March! march! march!*
> Making sounds as they tread,
> Ho! ho! how they step,
> Going down to the dead!

The line italicized is formed of three cæsuras. The cæsura, of
which I have much to say hereafter, is rejected by the English
Prosodies and grossly misrepresented in the classic. It is a perfect
foot—the most important in all verse—and consists of a single *long*
syllable; *but the length of this syllable varies.*

It has thus been made evident that there is *not one* point of the definition in question which does not involve an error. And for anything
more satisfactory or more intelligible we shall look in vain to any published treatise on the topic.

So general and so total a failure can be referred only to radical misconception. In fact the English Prosodists have blindly followed the
pedants. These latter, like *les moutons de Panurge*,[7] have been occupied
in incessant tumbling into ditches, for the excellent reason that their
leaders have so tumbled before. The Iliad, being taken as a starting
point, was made to stand in stead of Nature and common sense.
Upon this poem, in place of facts and deduction form fact, or from
natural law, were built systems of feet, metres, rhythms, rules,—rules
that contradict each other every five minutes, and for nearly all of
which there may be found twice as many exceptions as examples. If
any one has a fancy to be thoroughly confounded—to see how far the
infatuation of what is termed "classical scholarship" can lead a bookworm in the manufacture of darkness out of sunshine, let him turn
over, for a few moments, any one of the German Greek Prosodies.
The only thing clearly made out in them is a very magnificent contempt for Liebnitz's principle of "a sufficient reason."[8]

To divert attention from the real matter in hand by any farther reference to these works, is unnecessary, and would be weak. I cannot
call to mind, at this moment, one essential particular of information
that is to be gleaned from them; and I will drop them here with merely this one observation: that, employing from among the numerous

---

[7]"The sheep of Panurge"—Panurge was the roguish companion of Pantagruel in
Rabelais' *La Farce de Maître Pierre Pantelin*—creatures which follow their leader blindly into the water and then drown.
[8]Leibnitz's principle: Whatever is, must have a sufficient or adequate cause for being.

"*ancient*" feet the spondee, the trochee, the iambus, the anapæst, the dactyl, and the cæsura alone, I will engage to scan *correctly* any of the Horatian rhythms, or any true rhythm that human ingenuity can conceive. And this excess of chimerical feet is, perhaps, the very least of the scholastic supererogations. *Ex uno disce omnia.*[9] The fact is that *Quantity* is a point in whose investigation the lumber of mere learning may be dispensed with, if ever in any. Its appreciation is universal. It appertains to no region, nor race, nor æra in especial. To melody and to harmony the Greeks hearkened with ears precisely similar to those which we employ for similar purposes at present; and I should not be condemned for heresy in asserting that a pendulum at Athens would have vibrated much after the same fashion as does a pendulum in the city of Penn.

Verse originates in the human enjoyment of equality, fitness. To this enjoyment, also, all the moods of verse—rhythm, metre, stanza, rhyme, alliteration, the *refrain,* and other analogous effects—are to be referred. As there are some readers who habitually confound rhythm and metre, it may be as well here to say that the former concerns the *character* of feet (that is, the arrangements of syllables) while the latter has to do with the *number* of these feet. Thus by "a dactylic *rhythm*" we express a sequence of dactyls. By "a dactylic hexa*meter*" we imply a line or measure consisting of six of these dactyls.

To return to *equality.* Its idea embraces those of similarity, proportion, identity, repetition, and adaptation or fitness. It might not be very difficult to go even behind the idea of equality, and show both how and why it is that the human nature takes pleasure in it, but such an investigation would, for any purpose now in view, be supererogatory. It is sufficient that the *fact* is undeniable—the fact that man derives enjoyment from his perception of equality. Let us examine a crystal. We are at once interested by the equality between the sides and between the angles of one of its faces: the equality of the sides pleases us; that of the angles doubles the pleasure. On bringing to view a second face in all respects similar to the first, this pleasure seems to be squared; on bringing to view a third it appears to be cubed, and so on. I have no doubt, indeed, that the delight experienced, if measurable, would be found to have exact mathematical relations such as I suggest; that is to say, as far as a certain point, beyond which there would be a decrease in similar relations.

The perception of pleasure in the equality of *sounds* is the principle of *Music.* Unpractised ears can appreciate only simple equalities,

---

[9]A slight misquotation on Poe's part. It is from Virgil (*Aeneid,* II, 65) and reads *ab uno disce omnes,* "from one learn about them all." In rhetorical discourse, the phrase often refers to a faulty induction.

such as are found in ballad airs. While comparing one simple sound with another they are too much occupied to be capable of comparing the equality subsisting between these two simple sounds, taken conjointly, and two other similar simple sounds taken conjointly. Practised ears, on the other hand, appreciate both equalities at the same instant—although it is absurd to suppose that both are *heard* at the same instant. One is heard and appreciated from itself: the other is heard by the memory; and the instant glides into and is confounded with the secondary, appreciation. Highly cultivated musical taste in this manner enjoys not only these double equalities, all appreciated at once, but takes pleasurable cognizance, through memory, of equalities the members of which occur at intervals so great that the uncultivated taste loses them altogether. That this latter can properly estimate or decide on the merits of what is called scientific music, is of course impossible. But scientific music has no claim to intrinsic excellence—it is fit for scientific ears alone. In its excess it is the triumph of the *physique* over the *morale* of music. The sentiment is overwhelmed by the sense. On the whole, the advocates of the simpler melody and harmony have infinitely the best of the argument;—although there has been very little of real argument on the subject.

In *verse*, which cannot be better designated than as an inferior or less capable Music, there is, happily, little chance for complexity. Its rigidly simple character not even Science—not even Pedantry can greatly pervert.

The rudiment of verse may, possibly, be found in the *spondee*. The very germ of a thought seeking satisfaction in equality of sound, would result in the construction of words of two syllables, equally accented. In corroboration of this idea we find that spondees most abound in the most ancient tongues. The second step we can easily suppose to be the comparison, that is to say, the collocation, of two spondees—of two words composed each of a spondee. The third step would be the juxta-position of three of these words. By this time the perception of monotone would induce farther consideration: and thus arises what Leigh Hunt so flounders in discussing under the title of "The *Principle* of Variety in Uniformity." Of course there is no principle in the case—nor in maintaining it. The "Uniformity" is the principle:—the "Variety" is but the principle's natural safeguard from self-destruction by excess of self. "Uniformity," besides, is the very worst word that could have been chosen for the expression of the *general* idea at which it aims.

The perception of monotone having given rise to an attempt at its relief, the first thought in this new direction would be that of collating two or more words formed each of two syllables differently accented (that is to say, short and long) but having the same order in each word:—in other terms, of collating two or more iambuses, or two or more trochees. And here let me pause to assert that more pitiable nonsense has been written on the topic of *long* and *short* syllables than on any other subject under the sun. In general, a syllable is long or short, just as it is difficult or easy of enunciation. The *natural* long syllables are those encumbered—the *natural* short ones are those *un*encumbered, with consonants; all the rest is mere artificiality and jargon. The Latin Prosodies have a rule that "a vowel before two consonants is long." This rule is deduced from "authority"—that is, from the observation that vowels so circumstanced, in the ancient poems, are always in syllables long by the laws of scansion. The philosophy of the rule is untouched, and lies simply in the physical difficulty of giving voice to such syllables—of performing the lingual evolutions necessary for their utterance. Of course, it is not the *vowel* that is long (although the rule says so) but the syllable of which the vowel is a part. It will be seen that the length of a syllable, depending on the facility or difficulty of its enunciation, must have great variation in various syllables; but for the purposes of verse we suppose a long syllable equal to two short ones:—and the natural deviation from this relativeness we correct in perusal. The more closely our long syllables approach this relation with our short ones, the better, *ceteris paribus,* will be our verse: but if the relation does not exist of itself, we force it by emphasis, which can, of course, make any syllable as long as desired;—or, by an effort we can pronounce with unnatural brevity a syllable that is naturally too long. *Accented* syllables are of course always long—but, where *un*encumbered with consonants, must be classed among the *unnaturally* long. Mere custom has declared that we shall accent them—that is to say, dwell upon them; but no inevitable lingual difficulty forces us to do so. In fine, every long syllable must of its own accord occupy in its utterance, or must be *made* to occupy, precisely the time demanded for two short ones. The only exception to this rule is found in the cæsura—of which more anon.

The success of the experiment with the trochees or iambuses (the one would have suggested the other) must have led to a trial of dactyls or anapæsts—natural dactyls or anapæsts—dactylic or anapæstic *words*. And now some degree of complexity has been attained. There is an appreciation, first, of the equality between the several dactyls, or anapæsts, and, secondly, of that between the long syllable and the two short conjointly. But here it may be said that step after step would have been taken, in continuation of this routine, until all the feet of the Greek Prosodies became exhausted. Not so:— these remaining feet have no existence except in the brains of the scholiasts. It is needless to imagine men inventing these things, and

folly to explain how and why they invented them, until it shall be first
shown that they are actually invented. All other "feet" than those
which I have specified, are, if not impossible at first view, merely combinations of the specified; and, although this assertion is rigidly true,
I will, to avoid misunderstanding, put it in a somewhat different
shape. I will say, then, that at present I am aware of no *rhythm*—nor
do I believe that any one can be constructed—which, in its last analysis, will not be found to consist altogether of the feet I have mentioned, either existing in their individual and obvious condition, or
interwoven with each other in accordance with simple natural laws
which I will endeavor to point out hereafter.

We have now gone so far as to suppose men constructing indefinite
sequences of spondaic, iambic, trochaic, dactylic, or anapæstic words.
In *extending* these sequences, they would be again arrested by the
sense of monotone. A succession of spondees would *immediately* have
displeased; one of iambuses or of trochees, on account of the variety
included within the foot itself, would have taken longer to displease;
one of dactyls or anapæsts still longer: but even the last if extended
very far, must have become wearisome. The idea, first, of curtailing,
and, secondly, of defining the length of a sequence, would thus at
once have arisen. Here then is the *line,* or verse proper.* The principle of equality being constantly at the bottom of the whole process,
lines would naturally be made, in the first instance, equal in the number of their feet; in the second instance there would be variation in
the mere number; one line would be twice as long as another; then
one would be some less obvious multiple of another; then still less
obvious proportions would be adopted:—nevertheless there would
be *proportion,* that is to say a phase of equality, still.

Lines being once introduced, the necessity of distinctly defining
these lines *to the ear,* (as yet written verse does not exist,) would lead
to a scrutiny of their capabilities *at their terminations:*—and now would
spring up the idea of equality in sound between the final syllables—
in other words, of *rhyme.* First, it would be used only in the iambic,
anapæstic, and spondaic rhythms, (granting that the latter had not
been thrown aside, long since, on account of its tameness;) because
in these rhythms the concluding syllable, being long, could best sustain the necessary protraction of the voice. No great while could
elapse, however, before the effort, found pleasant as well as useful,
would be applied to the two remaining rhythms. But as the chief
force of rhyme must lie in the accented syllable, the attempt to
create rhyme at all in these two remaining rhythms, the trochaic and

---

*Verse, from the Latin *vertere,* to turn, is so called on account of the turning or recom-
mencement of the series of feet. Thus a verse, strictly speaking, is a line. In this sense,
however, I have preferred using the latter word alone; employing the former in the
general acceptation given it in the heading of this paper.

dactylic, would necessarily result in double and triple rhymes, such as *beauty* with *duty* (trochaic) and *beautiful* with *dutiful* (dactylic.)

It must be observed that in suggesting these processes I assign them no date; nor do I even insist upon their order. Rhyme is supposed to be of modern origin, and were this proved, my positions remain untouched. I may say, however, in passing, that several instances of rhyme occur in the "Clouds" of Aristophanes, and that the Roman poets occasionally employ it. There is an effective species of ancient rhyming which has never descended to the moderns; that in which the ultimate and penultimate syllables rhyme with each other. For example:

> Parturiunt montes et nascitur ridicu*lus mus*.[10]

and again—

> Litoreis ingens inventa sub ilici*bus sus*.[11]

The terminations of Hebrew verse, (as far as understood,) show no signs of rhyme; but what thinking person can doubt that it did actually exist? That men have so obstinately and blindly insisted, *in general,* even up to the present day, in confining rhyme to the *ends* of lines, when its effect is even better applicable elsewhere, intimates, in my opinion, the sense of some *necessity* in the connexion of the end with the rhyme—hints that the origin of rhyme lay in a necessity which connected it with the end—shows that neither mere accident nor mere fancy gave rise to the connexion—points, in a word, at the very necessity which I have suggested, (that of some mode of defining lines *to the ear,*) as the true origin of rhyme. Admit this and we throw the origin far back in the night of Time—beyond the origin of written verse.

But to resume. The amount of complexity I have now supposed to be attained is very considerable. Various systems of equalization are appreciated at once (or nearly so) in their respective values and in the value of each system with reference to all the others. As our present *ultimatum* of complexity we have arrived at triple-rhymed, natural-dactylic lines, existing proportionally as well as equally with regard to other triple-rhymed, natural-dactylic lines. For example:

> Virginal Lilian, rigidly, humblily dutiful;
> Saintlily, lowlily,
> Thrillingly, holily
> Beautiful![12]

Here we appreciate, first, the absolute equality between the long syllable of each dactyl and the two short conjointly; secondly, the

---

[10]"The mountains are in labor and a ridiculous mouse is born." Horace, *Ars Poetica,* V, 139.

[11]"A huge sow found beneath the oaks along the shore." Virgil, *Aeneid,* III, 390.

[12]These lines are by Poe.

absolute equality between each dactyl and any other dactyl—in other words, among all the dactyls; thirdly, the absolute equality between the two middle lines; fourthly, the absolute equality between the first line and all the others taken conjointly; fifthly, the absolute equality between the two last syllables of the respective words "dutiful" and "beautiful;" sixthly, the absolute equality between the two last syllables of the respective words "lowlily" and "holily;" seventhly, the proximate equality between the first syllable of "dutiful" and the first syllable of "beautiful;" eighthly, the proximate equality between the first syllable of "lowlily" and that of "holily;" ninthly, the proportional equality, (that of five to one,) between the first line and each of its members, the dactyls; tenthly, the proportional equality, (that of two to one,) between each of the middle lines and its members, the dactyls; eleventhly, the proportional equality between the first line and each of the two middle—that of five to two; twelfthly, the proportional equality between the first line and the last—that of five to one; thirteenthly, the proportional equality between each of the middle lines and the last—that of two to one; lastly, the proportional equality, as concerns number, between all the lines, taken collectively, and any individual line—that of four to one.

The consideration of this last equality would give birth immediately to the idea of *stanza**—that is to say, the insulation of lines into equal or obviously proportional masses. In its primitive, (which was also its best,) form, the stanza would most probably have had absolute unity. In other words, the removal of any one of its lines would have rendered it imperfect; as in the case above, where if the last line, for example, be taken away, there is left no rhyme to the "dutiful" of the first. Modern stanza is excessively loose, and where so, ineffective as a matter of course.

Now, although in the deliberate written statement which I have here given of these various systems of equalities, there seems to be an infinity of complexity—so much that it is hard to conceive the mind taking cognizance of them all in the brief period occupied by the perusal or recital of the stanza—yet the difficulty is in fact apparent only when we will it to become so. Any one fond of mental experiment may satisfy himself, by trial, that, in listening to the lines, he does actually, (although with a seeming unconsciousness, on account of the rapid evolutions of sensation,) recognize and instantaneously appreciate, (more or less intensely as his ear is cultivated,) each and all of the equalizations detailed. The pleasure received, or receivable, has very much such progressive increase, and in very nearly such mathematical relations, as those which I have suggested in the case of the crystal.

---

*A stanza is often vulgarly, and with gross impropriety, called a *verse*.

It will be observed that I speak of merely a proximate equality between the first syllable of "dutiful" and that of "beautiful;" and it may be asked why we cannot imagine the earliest rhymes to have had absolute instead of proximate equality of sound. But absolute equality would have involved the use of identical words; and it is the duplicate sameness or monotony—that of sense as well as that of sound—which would have caused these rhymes to be rejected in the very first instance.

The narrowness of the limits within which verse composed of natural feet alone, must necessarily have been confined, would have led, after a *very* brief interval, to the trial and immediate adoption of artificial feet—that is to say of feet *not* constituted each of a single word, but two or even three words; or of parts of words. These feet would be intermingled with natural ones. For example:

ă brēath | căn māke | thĕm ās | ă brēath | hăs māde.[13]

This is an iambic line in which each iambus is formed of two words. Again:

Thĕ ūn | īmā | gīnā | blĕ mīght | ŏf Jōve. |

This is an iambic line in which the first foot is formed of a word and a part of a word; the second and third of parts taken from the body or interior of a word; the fourth of a part and a whole; the fifth of two complete words. There are no *natural* feet in either lines. Again:

Cān ĭt bĕ | fāncĭĕd thăt | Dēĭty | ēvĕr vĭn | dīctĭvely |
Māde ĭn hĭs | īmagĕ ă | mānnĭkĭn | mĕrely tŏ | māddĕn ĭt? |

These are two dactylic lines in which we find natural feet, ("Deity," "mannikin;") feet composed of two words ("fancied that," "image a," "merely to," "madden it;") feet composed of three words ("can it be," "made in his;") a foot composed of a part of a word ("dictively;") and a foot composed of a word and a part of a word ("ever vin.")

And now, in our supposititious progress, we have gone so far as to exhaust all the *essentialities* of verse. What follows may, strictly speaking, be recorded as embellishment merely—but even in this embellishment, the rudimental sense of *equality* would have been the never-ceasing impulse. It would, for example, be simply in seeking farther administration to this sense that men would come, in time, to think of the *refrain*, or burden, where, at the closes of the several stanzas of a poem, one word or phrase is *repeated*; and of alliteration, in whose simplest form a consonant is *repeated* in the commencements of various words. This effect would be extended so as to embrace repetitions both of vowels and of consonants, in the bodies as well as in the beginnings of words; and, at a later period, would be made to infringe on

---

[13]This and the next three quotations are by Poe.

the province of rhyme, by the introduction of general similarity of sound between whole feet occurring in the body of a line:—all of which modifications I have exemplified in the line above,

Made in his image a *mannikin* merely to *madden it.*

Farther cultivation would improve also the *refrain* by relieving its monotone in slightly varying the phrase at each repetition, or, (as I have attempted to do in "The Raven,") in retaining the phrase and varying its application—although this latter point is not strictly a rhythmical effect *alone.* Finally, poets when fairly wearied with following precedent—following it the more closely the less they perceived it in company with Reason—would adventure so far as to indulge in positive rhyme at other points than the ends of lines. First, they would put it in the middle of the line; then at some point where the multiple would be less obvious; then alarmed at their own audacity, they would undo all their work by cutting these lines in two. And here is the fruitful source of the infinity of "short metre," by which modern poetry, if not distinguished, is at least disgraced. It would require a high degree, indeed, both of cultivation and of courage, on the part of any versifier, to enable him to place his rhymes—and let them remain—at unquestionably their best position, that of unusual and *unanticipated* intervals.

On account of the stupidity of some people, or, (if talent be a more respectable word,) on account of their talent for misconception—I think it necessary to add here, first, that I believe the "processes" above detailed to be nearly if not accurately those which *did* occur in the gradual creation of what we now call verse; secondly, that, although I so believe, I yet urge neither the assumed fact nor my belief in it, as a part of the true proposition of this paper; thirdly, that in regard to the aim of this paper, it is of no consequence whether these processes did occur either in the order I have assigned them, or at all; my design being simply, in presenting a general type of what such processes *might* have been and *must* have resembled, to help *them,* the "some people," to an easy understanding of what I have farther to say on the topic of Verse.

There is one point which, in my summary of the processes, I have purposely forborne to touch; because this point, being the most important of all, on account of the immensity of error usually involved in its consideration, would have led me into a series of detail inconsistent with the object of a summary.

Every reader of verse must have observed how seldom it happens that even any one line proceeds uniformly with a succession, such as I have supposed, of absolutely equal feet; that is to say, with a succession of iambuses only, or of trochees only, or of dactyls only, or of anapæsts only, or of spondees only. Even in the most musical lines we find the succession interrupted. The iambic pentameters of Pope, for example, will be found on examination, frequently varied by trochees in the beginning, or by (what seem to be) anapæsts in the body, of the line.

> ŏh thōu | whătē | vĕr tī | tlĕ pleāse | thīne eār |
> Dĕan Drā | piĕr Bĭck | ĕrstäff | ŏr Gūl | ĭvēr |
> Whēthĕr | thŏu choōse | Cĕrvān | tĕs' sē | rĭoŭs äir |
> ŏr laūgh | ănd shāke | ĭn Rāb | ĕlaĭs' eā | sy chaīr. |[14]

Were any one weak enough to refer to the Prosodies for a solution of the difficulty here, he would find it *solved* as usual by a *rule*, stating the fact, (or what it, the rule, supposes to be the fact,) but without the slightest attempt at the *rationale*. "By a *synæresis* of the two short syllables," say the books, "an anapæst may sometimes be employed for an iambus, or a dactyl for a trochee. . . . In the beginning of a line a trochee is often used for an iambus."

Blending is the plain English for *synæresis*—but there should be *no* blending; neither is an anapæst *ever* employed for an iambus, or a dactyl for a trochee. These feet differ in time; and *no* feet so differing can ever be legitimately used in the same line. An anapæst is equal to four short syllables—an iambus only to three. Dactyls and trochees hold the same relation. The principle of *equality*, in verse, admits, it is true, of variation at certain points, for the relief of monotone, as I have already shown, but the point of *time* is that point which, being the rudimental one, must never be tampered with at all.

To explain:—In farther efforts for the relief of monotone than those to which I have alluded in the summary, men soon came to see that there was no absolute necessity for adhering to the precise number of syllables, provided the time required for the whole foot was preserved inviolate. They saw, for instance, that in such a line as

> ŏr laūgh | ănd shāke | ĭn Rāb | ĕlaĭs' eā | sy chaīr, |

the equalization of the three syllables *elais ea* with the two syllables composing any of the other feet, could be readily effected by pronouncing the two syllable *elais* in double quick time. By pronouncing each of the syllables *e* and *lais* twice as rapidly as the syllable *sy*, or the syllable *in*, or any other short syllable, they could bring the two of them, taken together, to the length, that is to say to the time, of any one short syllable. This consideration enabled them to effect the agreeable variation of three syllables in place of the uniform two. And variation was the object—variation to the ear. What sense is there, then, in supposing this object rendered null by the *blending* of the two syllables so as to render them, in absolute effect, one? Of course, there must be *no* blending. Each syllable must be

---

[14]from Alexander Pope's first *Dunciad* (1728), II, 19–22.

pronounced as distinctly as possible, (or the variation is lost,) but
with twice the rapidity in which the ordinary short syllable is enunciated. That the syllables *elais ea* do not compose an *anapæst* is evident,
and the signs (˘ ˘ ¯) of their accentuation are erroneous. The foot
might be written thus (˄ ˄ ¯) the inverted crescents expressing double
quick time; and might be called a bastard iambus.

Here is a trochaic line:

Sēe thĕ | dēlĭcăte | fōotĕd | rēin-deĕr. |[15]

The prosodies—that is to say the most considerate of them—would
here decide that "*delicate*" is a dactyl used in place of a trochee, and
would refer to what they call their "rule," for justification. Others,
varying the stupidity, would insist upon a Procrustean adjustment
thus (del'cate)—an adjustment recommended to all such words as
silvery, murmuring, etc., which, it is said, should be not only pronounced, but written *silv'ry, murm'ring*, and so on, whenever they find
themselves in trochaic predicament. I have only to say that "delicate,"
when circumstanced as above, is neither a dactyl nor a dactyl's equivalent; that I would suggest for it this (- ˄ ˄) accentuation; that I think
it as well to call it a bastard trochee; and that all words, at all events,
should be written and pronounced *in full*, and as nearly as possible
as nature intended them.

About eleven years ago, there appeared in "The American
Monthly Magazine," (then edited, I believe, by Mess. Hoffman and
Benjamin,) a review of Mr. Willis' Poems; the critic putting forth his
strength, or his weakness, in an endeavor to show that the poet was
either absurdly affected, or grossly ignorant of the laws of verse; the
accusation being based altogether on the fact that Mr. W. made occasional use of this very word "delicate," and other similar words, in
"the Heroic measure which every one knew consisted of feet of two
syllables." Mr. W. has often, for example, such lines as

That binds him to a woman's *delicate* love—
In the gay sunshine, *reverent* in the storm—
With its *invisible* fingers my loose hair.

Here, of course, the feet *licate love, verent in*, and *sible fin*, are bastard
iambuses; are *not* anapæsts; and are *not* improperly used. Their employment, on the contrary, by Mr. Willis is but one of the innumerable
instances he has given of keen sensibility in all those matters of taste
which may be classed under the general head of *fanciful embellishment*.

It is also about eleven years ago, if I am not mistaken, since Mr.
Horne, (of England,) the author of "Orion," one of the noblest epics
in any language, thought it necessary to preface his "Chaucer

---

[15]Another line of Poe's composition.

Modernized" by a very long and evidently a very elaborate essay, of which the greater portion was occupied in a discussion of the seemingly anomalous foot of which we have been speaking. Mr. Horne upholds Chaucer in its frequent use; maintains his superiority, *on account* of his so frequently using it, over all English versifiers; and, indignantly repelling the common idea of those who make verse on their fingers—that the superfluous syllable is a roughness and an error—very chivalrously makes battle for it as "a grace." That a grace it *is*, there can be no doubt; and what I complain of is, that the author of the most happily versified long poem in existence, should have been under the necessity of discussing this grace merely *as* a grace, through forty or fifty vague pages, solely because of his inability to show *how* and *why* it is a grace—by which showing the question would have been settled in an instant.

About the trochee used for an iambus, as we see it in the beginning of the line,

> Whĕthĕr thou choose Cervantes' serious air,

there is little that need be said. It brings me to the general proposition that, in all rhythms, the prevalent or distinctive feet may be varied at will, and nearly at random, by the *occasional* introduction of equivalent feet—that is to say, feet the sum of whose syllabic times is equal to the sum of the syllabic times of the distinctive feet. Thus the trochee, *whĕthĕr*, is equal, in the sum of the times of its syllables, to the iambus, *thŏu choōse*, in the sum of the times of *its* syllables; each foot being, in time, equal to three short syllables. Good versifiers who happen to be, also, good poets, contrive to relieve the monotone of a series of feet, by the use of equivalent feet only at rare intervals, and at such points of their subject as seem in accordance with the *startling* character of the variation. Nothing of this care is seen in the line quoted above—although Pope has some fine instances of the duplicate effect. Where vehemence is to be strongly expressed, I am not sure that we should be wrong in venturing on *two consecutive* equivalent feet—although I cannot say that I have ever known the adventure made, except in the following passage, which occurs in "Al Aaraaf," a boyish poem, written by myself when a boy. I am referring to the sudden and rapid advent of a star:

> Dim was its little disk, and angel eyes
> Alone could see the phantom in the skies,
> Whĕn first thĕ phāntŏm's coūrse wăs foūnd tŏ bē
> Hēadlŏng hīthĕrward o'er the starry sea.

In the "general proposition" above, I speak of the *occasional* introduction of equivalent feet. It sometimes happens that unskilful versifiers, without knowing what they do, or why they do it, introduce so

many "variations" as to exceed in number the "distinctive" feet; when
the ear becomes at once baulked by the *bouleversement* of the rhythm.
Too many trochees, for example, inserted in an iambic rhythm,
would convert the latter to a trochaic. I may note here, that, in all
cases, the rhythm designed should be commenced and continued,
without variation, until the ear has had full time to comprehend what
is the rhythm. In violation of a rule so obviously founded in common
sense, many even of our best poets, do not scruple to begin an iambic
rhythm with a trochee, or the converse; or a dactylic with an anapæst,
or the converse; and so on.

A somewhat less objectionable error, although still a decided one,
is that of commencing a rhythm, not with a different equivalent foot,
but with a "bastard" foot of the rhythm intended. For example:

Mān̄y ă | thoūght wĭll | cōme tŏ | mēmŏry. |

Here *many a* is what I have explained to be a bastard trochee, and to
be understood should be accented with inverted crescents. It is objectionable solely on account of its position as the *opening* foot of a
trochaic rhythm. *Memory,* similarly accented, is also a bastard trochee,
but *un*objectionable, although by no means demanded.

The farther illustration of this point will enable me to take an
important step.

One of our finest poets, Mr. Christopher Pease Cranch,[16] begins a
very beautiful poem thus:

> Many are the thoughts that come to me
>   In my lonely musing;
> And they drift so strange and swift
>   There's no time for choosing
> Which to follow; for to leave
>   Any, seems a losing.[17]

"A losing" to Mr. Cranch, of course—but this *en passant.* It will be
seen here that the intention is trochaic;—although we do *not* see this
intention by the opening foot, as we should do—or even by the opening line. Reading the whole stanza, however, we perceive the trochaic rhythm as the general design, and so, after some reflection, we
divide the first line thus:

Many are the | thōughts thăt | cōme tō | me. |

Thus scanned, the line will seem musical. It *is*—highly so. And it is
because there is no end to instances of just such lines of apparently

---

[16]Christopher Pearse Cranch (1830–1890), one of Poe's poetic contemporaries. Poe
    misspells his middle name here.
[17]This poem, "My Thoughts," was published both in Rufus Wilmot Griswold's *Poets and
    Poetry of America* (1842) and in Cranch's *Poems* (1844). See Poe's review of Griswold's
    volume elsewhere in this collection.

incomprehensible music, that Coleridge thought proper to invent his nonsensical *system* of what he calls "scanning by accents"—as if "scanning by accents" were anything more than a phrase.[18] Whenever "Christabel" is really *not rough,* it can be as readily scanned by the true *laws* (not the supposititious *rules*) of verse, as can the simplest pentameter of Pope; and where it *is* rough (*passim*) these same laws will enable any one of common sense to show *why* it is rough and to point out, instantaneously, the remedy for the roughness.

A reads and re-reads a certain line, and pronounces it false in rhythm—unmusical. *B,* however, reads it *to A,* and *A* is at once struck with the perfection of the rhythm, and wonders at his dulness in not "catching" it before. Henceforward he admits the line to be musical. *B,* triumphant, asserts that, to be sure, the line is musical—for it is the work of Coleridge—and that it is *A* who is *not;* the fault being in *A*'s false reading. Now here *A* is right and *B* wrong. *That* rhythm is erroneous, (at some point or other more or less obvious,) which *any* ordinary reader *can,* without design, read improperly. It is the business of the poet so to construct his line that the intention *must* be caught *at once.* Even when men have precisely the same understanding of a sentence, they differ and often widely, in their modes of enunciating it. Any one who has taken the trouble to examine the topic of emphasis, (by which I here mean not *accent* of particular syllables, but the dwelling on entire words,) must have seen that men emphasize in the most singularly arbitrary manner. There are certain large classes of people, for example, who persist in emphasizing their monosyllables. Little uniformity of emphasis prevails; because the thing itself—the idea, emphasis,—is referable to no natural—at least to no well comprehended and therefore uniform law. Beyond a very narrow and vague limit, the whole matter is conventionality. And if we differ in emphasis even when we agree in comprehension, how much more so in the former when in the latter too! Apart, however, from the consideration of natural disagreement, is it not clear that, by tripping here and mouthing there, any sequence of words may be twisted into any species of rhythm? But are we thence to deduce that all sequences of words are rhythmical in a rational understanding of the term?—for this is the deduction, precisely to which the *reductio ad absurdum* will, in the end, bring all the propositions of Coleridge. Out of a hundred readers of "Christabel," fifty will be able to make nothing of its rhythm, while forty-nine of the remaining fifty will, with some ado, fancy they

---

[18]The metrical system Coleridge presented in his preface to "Christabel" (1816) focused on counting the accented or stressed syllables in a line of verse. Thus a line should contain four accented syllables, for instance, but the number of unaccented ones could vary—from seven to twelve. Because Coleridge considered accent or stress the critical element in metre, precisely the view that Poe is disputing here, it is no wonder Poe calls Coleridge's system "nonsensical."

comprehend it, after the fourth or fifth perusal. The one out of the whole hundred who shall both comprehend and admire it at first sight—must be an unaccountably clever person—and I am by far too modest to assume, for a moment, that that very clever person is myself.

In illustration of what is here advanced I cannot do better than quote a poem:

> Pease porridge hot—pease porridge cold—
> Pease porridge in the pot—nine days old.

Now those of my readers who have never *heard* this poem pronounced according to the nursery conventionality, will find its rhythm as obscure as an explanatory note; while those who *have* heard it, will divide it thus, declare it musical, and wonder how there can be any doubt about it.

> Pease | porridge | hot | pease | porridge | cold |
> Pease | porridge | in the | pot | nine | days | old. |

The chief thing in the way of this species of rhythm, is the necessity which it imposes upon the poet of travelling in constant company with his compositions, so as to be ready at a moment's notice, to avail himself of a well understood poetical license—that of reading aloud one's own doggrel.

In Mr. Cranch's line,

> Many are the | thoughts that | come to | me, |

the general error of which I speak is, of course, very partially exemplified, and the purpose for which, chiefly, I cite it, lies yet further on in our topic.

The two divisions (*thoughts that*) and (*come to*) are ordinary trochees. Of the last division (*me*) we will talk hereafter. The first division (many are the) would be thus accented by the Greek Prosodies (mány ăre thĕ) and would be called by them αστρολογος.[19] The Latin books would style the foot *Pæon Primus,* and both Greek and Latin would swear that it was composed of a trochee and what they term a pyrrhic—that is to say a foot of two *short* syllables—a thing that *cannot be,* as I shall presently show.

But now, there is an obvious difficulty. The *astrologos,* according to the Prosodies' own showing, is equal to *five* short syllables, and the trochee to *three*—yet, in the line quoted, these two feet are equal. They occupy *precisely* the same time. In fact, the whole music of the line depends upon their being *made* to occupy the same time. The

---

[19] *astrologos,* which means "astrologer," (Poe seems to have misunderstood the term's use in one of the prosodies to which he refers) is an example of a *Paeon Primus* ("first foot"): a metrical foot comprising one long or stressed syllable, followed by three short ones.

Prosodies then, have demonstrated what all mathematicians have stu-
pidly failed in demonstrating—that three and five are one and the
same thing.

After what I have already said, however, about the bastard trochee
and the bastard iambus, no one can have any trouble in understanding
that *many are the* is of similar character. It is merely a bolder variation
than usual from the routine of trochees, and introduces to the bastard
trochee one additional syllable. But this syllable is not *short*. That is, it is
not short in the sense of "*short*" as applied to the final syllable of the
ordinary trochee, where the word means merely *the half of long*.

In this case (that of the additional syllable) "short," if used at all,
must be used in the sense of *the sixth of long*. And all the three final
syllables can be called *short* only with the same understanding of the
term. The three together are equal only to the one short syllable
(whose place they supply) of the ordinary trochee. It follows that
there is no sense in thus (˘) accenting these syllables. We must devise
for them some new character which shall denote the sixth of long.
Let it be (ɩ)—the crescent placed with the curve to the left. The
whole foot (mānȳ arė thė) might be called a *quick trochee*.

We come now to the final division (*me*) of Mr. Cranch's line. It is
clear that this foot, short as it appears, is fully equal in time to each
of the preceding. It is in fact the cæsura—the foot which, in the
beginning of this paper, I called the most important in all verse. Its
chief office is that of pause or termination; and here—at the end of
a line—its use is easy, because there is no danger of misapprehend-
ing its value. We pause on it, by a seeming necessity, just so long as it
has taken us to pronounce the preceding feet, whether iambus,
trochees, dactyls or anapæsts. It is thus a *variable foot*, and, with some
care, may be well introduced into the body of a line, as in a little
poem of great beauty by Mrs. Welby:[20]

> I have | a lit | tle step | sŏn | of on | ly three | years old. | .

Here we dwell on the cæsura, *son*, just as long as it requires us to pronounce either of the preceding or succeeding iambusses. Its value,
therefore, in this line, is that of three short syllables. In the following
dactylic line its value is that of four short syllables.

> Pale as a | lily was | Emily | G͡r͡ay.

I have accented the cæsura with a (͡͡͡) by way of expressing this variability of value.

I observed, just now, that there could be no such foot as one of two
short syllables. What we start from in the very beginning of all idea on the
topic of verse, is quantity, *length*. Thus when we enunciate an independent syllable it is long, as a matter of course. If we enunciate two, dwelling

---

[20]Amelia Welby (1819–1852), popular magazine poet admired by Poe.

on both equally, we express equality in the enumeration, or length, and have a right to call them two long syllables. If we dwell on one more than the other, we have also a right to call one short, because it is short in relation to the other. But if we dwell on both equally and with a tripping voice, saying to ourselves here are two short syllables, the query might well be asked of us—"in relation to what are they short?" Shortness is but the negation of length. To say, then, that two syllables, placed independently of any other syllable, are short, is merely to say that they have no positive length, or enunciation—in other words that they are no syllables—that they do not exist at all. And if, persisting, we add anything about their equality, we are merely floundering in the idea of an identical equation, where, x being equal to x, nothing is shown to be equal to zero. In a word we can form no conception of a pyrrhic as of an independent foot. It is a mere chimera bred in the mad fancy of a pedant.

From what I have said about the equalization of the several feet of a *line,* it must not be deduced that any *necessity* for equality in time exists between the rhythm of *several* lines. A poem, or even a stanza, may begin with iambuses, in the first line, and proceed with anapæsts in the second, or even with the less accordant dactyls, as in the opening of quite a pretty specimen of verse by Miss Mary A. S. Aldrich:[21]

> The wa | ter li | ly sleeps | in pride |
> Dōwn ĭn thĕ | dĕpths ŏf thĕ | āzūre | la͡ke. |

Here *azure* is a spondee, equivalent to a dactyl; *lake* a cæsura.

I shall now best proceed in quoting the initial lines of Byron's "Bride of Abydos:"

> Know ye the land where the cypress and myrtle
>   Are emblems of deeds that are done in their clime—
> Where the rage of the vulture, the love of the turtle
>   Now melt into softness, now madden to crime?
> Know ye the land of the cedar and vine,
> Where the flowers ever blossom, the beams ever shine,
> And the light wings of Zephyr, oppressed with perfume,
> Wax faint o'er the gardens of Gul in their bloom?
> Where the citron and olive are fairest of fruit
> And the voice of the nightingale never is mute—
> Where the virgins are soft as the roses they twine,
> And all save the spirit of man is divine?
> 'Tis the land of the East—'tis the land of the Sun—
> Can he smile on such deeds as his children have done?
> Oh, wild as the accents of lovers' farewell
> Are the hearts that they bear and the tales that they tell.

---

[21]Known only as the author of the poem "Water Lily," printed in the December 1846 issue of *Godey's Lady's Book.*

Now the flow of these lines, (as times go,) is very sweet and musical. They have been often admired, and justly—as times go—that is to say, it is a rare thing to find better versification of its kind. And where verse is pleasant to the ear, it is silly to find fault with it because it refuses to be scanned. Yet I have heard men, professing to be scholars, who made no scruple of abusing these lines of Byron's on the ground that they were musical in spite of *all law*. Other gentlemen, *not* scholars, abused "all law" for the same reason:—and it occurred neither to the one party nor to the other that the law about which they were disputing might possibly be no law at all—an ass of a law in the skin of a lion.

The Grammars said something about dactylic lines, and it was easily seen that *these* lines were at least meant for dactylic. The first one was, therefore, thus divided:

Knōw yĕ thĕ | lānd whĕre thĕ | cyprĕss ănd | myrtle. |

The concluding foot was a mystery; but the Prosodies said something about the dactylic "measure" calling now and then for a double rhyme; and the court of enquiry were content to rest in the double rhyme, without exactly perceiving what a double rhyme had to do with the question of an irregular foot. Quitting the first line, the second was thus scanned:

Arē ĕmblĕms | ōf deĕds thăt | āre dŏne ĭn | thēir clīme. |

It was immediately seen, however, that *this* would not do:—it was at war with the whole emphasis of the reading. It could not be supposed that Byron, or any one in his senses, intended to place stress upon such monosyllables as "are," "of," and "their," nor could "their clime," collated with "to crime," in the corresponding line below, be fairly twisted into anything like a "double rhyme," so as to bring everything within the category of the Grammars. But farther these Grammars spoke not. The inquirers, therefore, in spite of their sense of harmony in the lines, when considered without reference to scansion, fell back upon the idea that the "Are" was a blunder—an excess for which the poet should be sent to Coventry—and, striking it out, they scanned the remainder of the line as follows:

—ēmblĕms ŏf | deēds thăt āre | dōne ĭn thēir | clīme. |

This answered pretty well; but the Grammars admitted no such foot as a foot of one syllable; and besides the rhythm was dactylic. In despair, the books are well searched, however, and at last the investigators are gratified by a full solution of the riddle in the profound "Observation" quoted in the beginning of this article:—"When a syllable is wanting, the verse is said to be catalectic; when the measure is exact, the line is acatalectic; when there is a redundant syllable it

forms hypermeter." This is enough. The anomalous line is pronounced to be catalectic at the head and to form hypermeter at the
tail:—and so on, and so on; it being soon discovered that nearly all
the remaining lines are in a similar predicament, and that what flows
so smoothly to the ear, although so roughly to the eye, is, after all, a
mere jumble of catalecticism, acatalecticism, and hypermeter—not
to say worse.

Now, had this court of inquiry been in possession of even the shadow of the *philosophy* of Verse, they would have had no trouble in reconciling this oil and water of the eye and ear, by merely scanning the
passage without reference to lines, and, continuously, thus:

> Know ye the | land where the | cypress and | myrtle Are | emblems of |
> deeds that are | done in their | clime Where the | rage of the | vulture
> the | love of the | turtle Now | melt into | softness now | madden to |
> *crime* | Know ye the | land of the | cedar and | vine Where the | flowers
> ever | blossom the | beams ever | shine Where the | light wings of |
> Zephyr op | pressed by per | *fume Wax* | faint o'er the | gardens of | Gul
> in their | bloom Where the | citron and | olive are | fairest of | fruit And
> the | voice of the | nightingale | never is | mute Where the | virgins are
> | soft as the | roses they | *twine And* | all save the | spirit of | man is di |
> vine 'Tis the | land of the | East 'tis the | clime of the | Sun Can he |
> smile on such | deeds as his | children have | *done Oh* | wild as the |
> accents of | lovers' fare | well Are the | hearts that they | bear and the |
> tales that they | *tell.*

Here "crime" and "tell" (italicized) are cæsuras, each having the value
of a dactyl, four short syllables; while "fume Wax," "twine and," and
"done Oh," are spondees which, of course, being composed of two
long syllables, are also equal to four short, and are the dactyl's natural equivalent. The nicety of Byron's ear has led him into a succession
of feet which, with two trivial exceptions as regards melody, are
absolutely accurate—a very rare occurrence this in dactylic or anapæstic rhythms. The exceptions are found in the spondee "*twine And*" and
the dactyl, "*smile on such.*" Both feet are false in point of melody. In
"*twine And,*" to make out the rhythm, we must force "*And*" into a
length which it will not naturally bear. We are called on to sacrifice
either the proper length of the syllable as demanded by its position as
a member of a spondee, or the customary accentuation of the word in
conversation. There is no hesitation, and should be none. We at once
give up the sound for the sense; and the rhythm is imperfect. In this
instance it is *very* slightly so;—not one person in ten thousand could,
by ear, detect the inaccuracy. But the *perfection* of verse, as regards
melody, consists in its *never* demanding any such sacrifice as is here
demanded. The rhythmical must agree, *thoroughly,* with the reading
flow. This perfection has in no instance been attained—but is unquestionably attainable. "*Smile on such,*" the dactyl, is incorrect, because

"*such*," from the character of the two consonants *ch*, cannot *easily* be enunciated in the ordinary time of a short syllable, which its position declares that it is. Almost every reader will be able to appreciate the slight difficulty here; and yet the error is by no means so important as that of the "*And*" in the spondee. By dexterity we *may* pronounce "*such*" in the true time; but the attempt to remedy the rhythmical deficiency of the *And* by drawing it out, merely aggravates the offence against natural enunciation, by directing attention to the offence.

My main object, however, in quoting these lines, is to show that, in spite of the Prosodies, the length of a line is entirely an arbitrary matter. We might divide the commencement of Byron's poem thus:

Know ye the | land where the. |

or thus:

Know ye the | land where the | cypress and. |

or thus:

Know ye the | land where the | cypress and | myrtle are. |

or thus:

Know ye the | land where the | cypress and | myrtle are | emblems of. |

In short we may give it any division we please, and the lines will be good—provided we have at least *two* feet in a line. As in mathematics two units are required to form number, so rhythm, (from the Greek αριθμος, number,) demands for its formation at least two feet. Beyond doubt, we often see such lines as

Know ye the—
Land where the—

lines of one foot; and our Prosodies admit such; but with impropriety; for common sense would dictate that every so obvious division of a poem as is made by a line, should include within itself all that is necessary for its own comprehension; but in a line of one foot we can have no appreciation of *rhythm,* which depends upon the equality between *two* or more pulsations. The false lines, consisting sometimes of a single cæsura, which are seen in mock Pindaric odes, are of course "rhythmical" only in connection with some other line; and it is this want of independent rhythm which adapts them to the purposes of burlesque alone. Their effect is that of incongruity (the principle of mirth;) for they intrude the blankness of prose amid the harmony of verse.

My second object in quoting Byron's lines, was that of showing how absurd it often is to cite a single line from amid the body of a poem, for the purpose of instancing the perfection or imperfection of the line's rhythm. Were we to see by itself

> Know ye the land where the cypress and myrtle,

we might justly condemn it as defective in the final foot, which is equal to only three, instead of being equal to four, short syllables.

In the foot (*flowers ever*) we shall find a further exemplification of the principle in the bastard iambus, bastard trochee, and quick trochee, as I have been at some pains in describing these feet above. All the Prosodies on English verse would insist upon making an elision in "flowers," thus (flow'rs,) but this is nonsense. In the quick trochee (mānу are the) occurring in Mr. Cranch's *trochaic* line, we had to equalize the time of the three syllables (*ny, are, the,*) to that of the one *short* syllable whose position they usurp. Accordingly each of these syllables is equal to the third of a short syllable, that is to say, the *sixth of a long*. But in Byron's *dactylic* rhythm, we have to equalize the time of the three syllables (*ers, ev, er,*) to that of the one *long* syllable whose position they usurp or, (which is the same thing,) of the *two short*. Therefore the value of each of the syllables (*ers, ev,* and *er*) is the *third of a long*. We enunciate them with only half the rapidity we employ in enunciating the three final syllables of the quick trochee— which latter is a rare foot. The "*flowers ever,*" on the contrary, is as common in the dactylic rhythm as is the *bastard* trochee in the trochaic, or the bastard iambus in the iambic. We may as well accent it with the curve of the crescent to the right, and call it a *bastard dactyl*. A *bastard anapæst,* whose nature I now need be at no trouble in explaining, will of course occur, now and then, in an anapæstic rhythm.

In order to avoid any chance of that confusion which is apt to be introduced in an essay of this kind by too sudden and radical an alteration of the conventionalities to which the reader has been accustomed, I have thought it right to suggest for the accent marks of the bastard trochee, bastard iambus, etc., etc., certain characters which, in merely varying the direction of the ordinary short accent (˘) should imply, what is the fact, that the feet themselves are not *new* feet, in any proper sense, but simply modifications of the feet, respectively, from which they derive their names. Thus a bastard iambus is, in its essentiality, that is to say, in its time, an iambus. The variation lies only in the *distribution* of this time. The time, for example, occupied by the one short (or *half of long*) syllable, in the ordinary iambus, is, in the bastard, spread equally over two syllables, which are accordingly the *fourth of long*.

But this fact—the fact of the essentiality, or while time, of the foot being unchanged, is now so fully before the reader, that I may venture to propose, finally, an accentuation which shall answer the real purpose—that is to say what should be the real purpose of all accentuation—the purpose of expressing to the eye the exact relative value of every syllable employed in Verse.

I have already shown that enunciation, or *length,* is the point from which we start. In other words, we begin with *a long syllable.* This then is our unit; and there will be no need of accenting it at all. An unaccented syllable, in a system of accentuation, is to be regarded always as a long syllable. Thus a spondee would be without accent. In an iambus, the first syllable being "short," or the *half* of long, should be accented with a small 2, placed *beneath* the syllable; the last syllable, being long, should be unaccented;—the whole would be thus (control.) In a trochee, these accents would be merely conversed, thus (man$\underset{2}{\text{ly}}$.) In a dactyl, each of the two final syllables, being the half of long, should, also, be accented with a small 2 beneath the syllable; and the first syllable left unaccented, the whole would be thus (hap$\underset{2}{\text{pi}}$$\underset{2}{\text{ness}}$.) In an anapæst we should converse the dactyl thus, (in $\underset{2}{\text{the}}$ $\underset{2}{\text{land}}$.) In the bastard dactyl, each of the three concluding syllables being the *third* of long, should be accented with a small 3 beneath the syllable, and the whole foot would stand thus, (flow$\underset{3}{\text{ers}}$ $\underset{3}{\text{ev}}$er.) In the bastard anapæst we should converse the bastard dactyl thus, (in $\underset{3}{\text{the}}$ $\underset{3}{\text{re}}$bound.) In the bastard iambus, each of the two initial syllables, being the fourth of long, should be accented, below, with a small 4; the whole foot would be thus, (in $\underset{4}{\text{the}}$ $\underset{4}{\text{rain}}$.) In the bastard trochee, we should converse the bastard iambus thus, (ma$\underset{4}{\text{ny}}$ $\underset{4}{\text{a}}$.) In the quick trochee, each of the three concluding syllables, being the *sixth* of long, should be accented, below, with a small 6; the whole foot would be thus, (ma$\underset{6}{\text{ny}}$ $\underset{6}{\text{are}}$ $\underset{6}{\text{the}}$.) The quick iambus is not yet created, and most probably never will be; for it would be excessively useless, awkward, and liable to misconception—as I have already shown that even the quick trochee is:—but, should it appear, we must accent it by conversing the quick trochee. The cæsura, being variable in length, but always *longer than "long,"* should be accented, *above,* with a number expressing the length, or value, of the distinctive foot of the rhythm in which it occurs. Thus a cæsura, occurring in a spondaic rhythm, would be accented with a small 2 above the syllable, or, rather, foot. Occurring in a dactylic or anapæstic rhythm, we also accent it with the 2, above the foot. Occurring in an iambic rhythm, however, it must be accented, above, with 1½; for this is the relative value of the iambus. Occurring in the trochaic rhythm, we give it, of course, the same accentuation. For the complex 1½, however, it would be advisable to substitute the simpler expression $\frac{3}{2}$ which amounts to the same thing.

In this system of accentuation Mr. Cranch's lines, quoted above, would thus be written:

Many are the | thoughts that | come to | me $\frac{3}{2}$
　6　6　6　　　　　　　2　　　　2
In my | lonely | musing, |
　2　　　2　　　　2

And they | drift so | strange and | swift $\frac{3}{2}$
　2　　　2　　　　　　　2
There's no | time for | choosing |
　2　　　2　　　　2

Which to | follow, | for to | leave $\frac{3}{2}$
　2　　　2　　　　2
Any, | seems a | losing. |
　2　　　2　　　2

In the ordinary system the accentuation would be thus:

Mãny arĕ thĕ | thōughts thăt | cōme tŏ | mē
In my | lōnely | mūsing, |
ānd thĕy | drīft sŏ | strānge ănd | swīft
Therē's nŏ | timē fŏr | choōsing |
Whīch tŏ | fōllŏw, | fōr tŏ | lēave
āny, | seēms ă | lōsing. |

It must first be observed, here, that I do not grant this to be the "ordinary" *scansion*. On the contrary, I never yet met the man who had the faintest comprehension of the true scanning of these lines, or of such as these. But granting this to be the mode in which our Prosodies would divide the feet, they would accentuate the syllables as just above.

Now, let any reasonable person compare the two modes. The first advantage seen in my mode is that of simplicity—of time, labor, and ink saved. Counting the fractions as *two* accents, even, there will be found only *twenty-six* accents to the stanza. In the common accentuation there are *forty-one*. But admit that all this is a trifle, which it is *not*, and let us proceed to points of importance. Does the common accentuation express the truth, in particular, in general, or in any regard? Is it consistent with itself? Does it convey either to the ignorant or to the scholar a just conception of the rhythm of the lines? Each of these questions must be answered in the negative. The crescents, being precisely similar, must be understood as expressing, all of them, one and the same thing; and so all prosodies have always understood them and wished them to be understood. They express, indeed, "short"—but this word has all kinds of meanings. It serves to represent (the reader is left to guess *when*) sometimes the half, sometimes the third, sometimes the fourth, and sometimes the sixth, of "long"—while "long" itself, in the books, is left undefined and undescribed. On the other hand, the horizontal accent, it may be said, expresses sufficiently well, and unvaryingly, the syllables which are meant to be long. It does nothing of the kind. This horizontal accent is placed over the cæsura (wherever, as in the Latin Prosodies, the cæsura is recognized) as well as over the ordinary long syllable, and implies anything and everything, just as the crescent. But grant that it does express the ordinary long syllables, (leaving the cæsura out of question,) have I not given the identical expression, by not employing any expression at all? In a word, while the Prosodies, with a certain number of accents, express *precisely nothing whatever*, I, with scarcely half the number, have expressed everything which, in a system of accentuation, demands expression. In glancing at my mode in the lines of Mr. Cranch, it will be seen that it conveys not only the exact relation of the syllables and feet, among themselves, in those particular lines, but their precise value in relation to any other existing or conceivable feet or syllables, in any existing or conceivable system of rhythm.

The object of what we call *scansion* is the distinct making of the rhythmical flow. Scansion without accents or perpendicular lines between the feet—that is to say scansion *by* the voice only—is scansion *to* the ear only; and all very good in its way. The written scansion addresses the ear through the eye. In either case the object is the distinct making of the rhythmical, musical, or reading flow. There *can* be no other object and there is none. Of course, then, the scansion and the reading flow should go hand in hand. The former must agree with the latter. The former represents and expresses the latter; and is good or bad as it truly or falsely represents and expresses it. If by the written scansion of a line we are not enabled to perceive any rhythm or music in the line, then either the line is unrhythmical or the scansion false. Apply all this to the English lines which we have quoted, at various points, in the course of this article. It will be found that the scansion exactly conveys the rhythm, and thus thoroughly fulfils the only purpose for which scansion is required.

But let the scansion *of the schools* be applied to the Greek and Latin verse, and what result do we find?—that the verse is one thing and the scansion quite another. The ancient verse, *read* aloud, is in general musical, and occasionally *very* musical. *Scanned* by the Prosodial rules we can, for the most part, make nothing of it whatever. In the case of the English verse, the more emphatically we dwell on the divisions between the feet, the more distinct is our perception of the kind of rhythm intended. In the case of the Greek and Latin, the more we dwell the *less* distinct is this perception. To make this clear by an example:

> Mæcenas, atavis edite regibus,
> O, et præsidium et dulce decus meum,
> Sunt quos curriculo pulverem Olympicum
> Collegisse juvat, metaque fervidis
> Evitata rotis, palmaque nobilis
> Terrarum dominos evehit ad Deos.[22]

Now in *reading* these lines, there is scarcely one person in a thousand who, if even ignorant of Latin, will not immediately feel and appreciate their flow—their music. A prosodist, however, informs the public that the *scansion* runs thus:

> Mæce | nas ata | vis | edite | regibus |
> O, et | præsidi' | et | dulce de | cus meum |
> Sunt quos | curricu | lo | pulver' O | lympicum |
> Colle | gisse ju | vat | metaque | fervidis |
> Evi | tata ro | tis | palmaque | nobilis |
> Terra | rum domi | nos | evehit | ad Deos. |

Now I do not deny that we get a *certain sort* of music from the lines if we read them according to this scansion, but I wish to call attention to the fact that this scansion and the certain sort of music which grows out of it, are entirely at war not only with the reading flow which any ordinary person would naturally give the lines, but with the reading flow universally given them, and never denied them, by even the most obstinate and stolid of scholars.

And now these questions are forced upon us—"Why exists this discrepancy between the modern verse with its scansion, and the ancient verse with its scansion?"—"Why, in the former case, are there agreement and representation, while in the latter there is neither the one nor the other?" or, to come to the point,—"How are we to reconcile the ancient verse with the scholastic scansion of it?" This absolutely necessary conciliation—shall we bring it about by supposing the scholastic scansion wrong because the ancient verse is right, or by maintaining that the ancient verse is wrong because the scholastic scansion is not to be gainsaid?

Were we to adopt the latter mode of arranging the difficulty, we might, in some measure, at least simplify the expression of the arrangement by putting it thus—Because the pedants have no eyes, therefore the old poets had no ears.

"But," say the gentlemen without the eyes, "the scholastic scansion,

---

[22]Maecenas, sprung from an ancient line of kings,
  My stronghold, my pride and my delight,
  Some like to collect Olympic dust
  On their chariots, and if their scorching wheels
  Graze the turning post and they win the palm of glory
  They become lords of the earth and rise to the gods.
          Horace, *Odes*, I, 1. (transl. David West).

although certainly not handed down to us in form from the old poets themselves (the gentlemen without the ears,) is nevertheless deduced, Baconially, from certain facts which are supplied us by careful observation of the old poems."

And let us illustrate this strong position by an example from an American poet—who must be a poet of some eminence, or he will not answer the purpose. Let us take Mr. Alfred B. Street. I remember these two lines of his:

> His sinuous path, by blazes, wound
> Among trunks grouped in myriads round.[23]

With the *sense* of these lines I have nothing to do. When a poet is in a "fine phrensy" he may as well imagine a large forest as a small one—and "by blazes!" is *not* intended for an oath. My concern is with the rhythm, which is iambic.

Now let us suppose that, a thousand years hence, when the "American language" is dead, a learned prosodist should be deducing from "careful observation" of our best poets, a system of scansion for our poetry. And let us suppose that this prosodist had so little dependence in the generality and immutability of the laws of Nature, as to assume in the outset, that, because we lived a thousand years before his time and made use of steam-engines instead of mesmeric balloons, we must therefore have had a *very* singular fashion of mouthing our vowels, and altogether of hudsonizing[24] our verse. And let us suppose that with these and other fundamental propositions carefully put away in his brain, he should arrive at the line,

> Among | trunks grouped | in my | riads round.

Finding it in an obviously iambic rhythm, he would divide it as above, and observing that "trunks" made the first member of an iambus, he would call it short, as Mr. Street intended it to be. Now farther:—if instead of admitting the possibility that Mr. Street, (who by that time would be called Street simply, just as we say Homer)—that Mr. Street might have been in the habit of writing carelessly, as the poets of the prosodist's own era did, and as all poets will do (on account of being geniuses)—instead of admitting this, suppose the learned scholar should make a "rule" and put it in a book, to the effect that, in the American verse, the vowel *u, when found embedded among nine consonants,* was *short.* What, under such circumstances, would the sensible people of the scholar's day have a right not only to think, but to say of that scholar?—why, that he was "a fool,—by blazes!"

I have put an extreme case, but it strikes at the root of the error.

---

[23]From "The Lost Hunter," printed in Griswold's *Poets and Poetry of America.*
[24]Hudson was Henry Norman Hudson, author of *Lectures on Shakespeare* (2nd edition, 1848).

The "rules" are grounded in "authority"—and this "authority"—can any one tell us what it means? or can any one suggest anything that it may *not* mean? Is it not clear that the "scholar" above referred to, might as readily have deduced from authority a totally false system as a partially true one? To deduce from authority a consistent prosody of the ancient metres would indeed have been within the limits of the barest possibility; and the task has *not* been accomplished, for the reason that it demands a species of ratiocination altogether out of keeping with the brain of a bookworm. A rigid scrutiny will show that the very few "rules" which have not as many exceptions as examples, are those which have, by accident, their true bases not in authority, but in the omniprevalent laws of syllabification; such, for example, as the rule which declares a vowel before two consonants to be long.

In a word, the gross confusion and antagonism of the scholastic prosody, as well as its marked inapplicability to the reading flow of the rhythms it pretends to illustrate, are attributable, first to the utter absence of natural principle as a guide in the investigations which have been undertaken by inadequate men; and secondly to the neglect of the obvious consideration that the ancient poems, which have been the *criteria* throughout, were the work of men who must have written as loosely, and with as little definitive system, as ourselves.

Were Horace alive to day, he would divide for us his first Ode thus, and "make great eyes" when assured by the prosodists that he had no business to make any such division:

> Mæcenas | atavis | edite | regibus |
> O et præ | sidium et | dulce de | cus meum |
> Sunt quos cur | riculo | pulverem O | lympicum |
> Collegisse | juvat | metaque | fervidis |
> Evitata | rotis | palmaque | nobilis |
> Terrarum | dominos | evehit | ad Deos. |

Read by this scansion, the flow is preserved; and the more we dwell on the divisions, the more the intended rhythm becomes apparent. Moreover, the feet have all the same time; while, in the scholastic scansion, trochees—admitted trochees—are absurdly employed as equivalents to spondees and dactyls. The books declare, for instance, that *Colle,* which begins the fourth line, is a trochee, and seem to be gloriously unconscious that to put a trochee in apposition with a longer foot, is to violate the inviolable principle of all music, *time.*

It will be said, however, by "some people" that I have no business to make a dactyl out of such obviously long syllables as *sunt, quos, cur.* Certainly I have no business to do so. I *never* do so. And Horace should not have done so. But he did. Mr. Bryant and Mr. Longfellow do the same thing every day. And merely because these gentlemen, now and then, forget themselves in this way, it would be hard if some future prosodist should insist upon twisting the "Thanatopsis," or the "Spanish Student," into a jumble of trochees, spondees, and dactyls.

It may be said, also, by some other people that in the word *decus*, I have succeeded no better than the books, in making the scansional agree with the reading flow; and that *decus* was not pronounced de*cus*. I reply that there can be no doubt of the word having been pronounced, in this case, de*cus*. It must be observed that the Latin *case*, or variation of a noun in its terminating syllables, caused the Romans—*must* have caused them to pay greater attention to the termination of a noun than to its commencement, or than we do to the terminations of our nouns. The end of the Latin word established that relation of the word with other words, which we establish by prepositions. Therefore, it would seem infinitely less odd to them than it does to us, to dwell at any time, for any slight purpose, abnormally, on a terminating syllable. In verse this license, scarcely a license, would be frequently admitted. These ideas unlock the secret of such lines as the

Litoreis ingens inventa sub ilici*bus sus*,

and the

Parturiunt montes nascetur ridicu*lus mus*,

which I quoted, some time ago, while speaking of rhyme.

As regards the prosodial elisions, such as that of *rem* before *O*, in *pulverem Olympicum*, it is really difficult to understand how so dismally silly a notion could have entered the brain even of a pedant. Were it demanded of me why the books cut off one *vowel* before another, I might say—it is, perhaps, because the books think that, since a bad reader is so apt to slide the one vowel into the other at any rate, it is just as well to print them *ready-slided*. But in the case of the terminating *m*, which is the most readily pronounced of all consonants, (as the infantile *mama* will testify,) and the most impossible to cheat the ear of by any system of sliding—in the case of the *m*, I should be driven to reply that, to the best of my belief, the prosodists did the thing, because they had a fancy for doing it, and wished to see how funny it would look after it was done. The thinking reader will perceive that, from the great facility with which *em* may be enunciated, it is admirably suited to form one of the rapid short syllables in the bastard dactyl (pulverem O)[25]—but because the books had no conception of a bastard dactyl, they knocked it in the head at once—by cutting off its tail.

_{3 3   3}

---

[25]Probably taken from the phrase *Pulverem Olympicum*, "Olympic dust," from Horace, *Odes*, I, 1.

Let me now give a specimen of the true scansion of another Horatian measure; embodying an instance of proper elision.

> Integer | vitæ | scelerisque | purus |
>   2   2   3 3   3
> Non eget | Mauri | jaculis ne | que arcu |
>   2 2   3   3   3
> Nec vene | natis | gravida sa | gittis,
>   2   2   3   3   3
>   Fusce, pha | retra.[26]
>   2   2

Here the regular recurrence of the bastard iambus,[27] gives great animation to the rhythm. The *e* before the *a* in *que arcu* is, almost of sheer necessity, cut off—that is to say, run into the *a* so as to preserve the spondee. But even this license it would have been better not to take.

Had I space, nothing would afford me greater pleasure than to proceed with the scansion of *all* the ancient rhythms, and to show how easily, by the help of common sense, the intended music of each and all can be rendered instantaneously apparent. But I have already overstepped my limits, and must bring this paper to an end.

It will never do, however, to omit all mention of the heroic hexameter.

I began the "processes" by a suggestion of the spondee as the first step towards verse. But the innate monotony of the spondee has caused its disappearance, as the basis of rhythm, from all modern poetry. We *may* say, indeed, that the French heroic—the most wretchedly monotonous verse in existence—is, to all intents and purposes, spondaic. But it is not designedly spondaic—and if the French were ever to examine it at all, they would no doubt pronounce it iambic. It must be observed that the French language is strangely peculiar in this point—*that it is without accentuation and consequently without verse.* The genius of the people, rather than the structure of the tongue, declares that their words are, for the most part, enunciated with an uniform dwelling on each syllable. For example, *we* say "syl*labi*fi*ca*tion." A Frenchman would say syl-la-bi-fi-ca-ti-on; dwelling on no one of the syllables with any noticeable particularity. Here again I put an extreme case, in order to be well understood; but the general fact is as I give it—that comparatively, the French have *no* accentuation. And there can be nothing worth the name of verse, without. Therefore, the French have no verse worth the name— which is the fact, put in sufficiently plain terms. Their iambic rhythm

---

[26]The man who is pure of heart and innocent of evil
Needs no Moorish spears, Fuscus,
Nor bow, nor quiver heavy
    With poison arrows.
        Horace, *Odes,* I, 21. (transl. David West).
[27]Poe probably meant to say "bastard dactyl."

so superabounds in absolute spondees as to warrant me in calling its basis spondaic; but French is the *only* modern tongue which has any rhythm with such basis; and even in the French, it is, as I have said, unintentional.

Admitting, however, the validity of my suggestion that the spondee was the first approach to verse, we should expect to find, first, natural spondees, (words each forming just a spondee,) most abundant in the most ancient languages, and, secondly, we should expect to find spondees forming the basis of the most ancient rhythms. These expectations are in both cases confirmed.

Of the Greek hexameter, the intentional basis is spondaic. The dactyls are the *variation* of the theme. It will be observed that there is no absolute certainty about *their* points of interposition. The penultimate foot, it is true, is usually a dactyl; but not uniformly so; while the ultimate, on which the ear *lingers* is always a spondee. Even that the penultimate is usually a dactyl may be clearly referred to the necessity of winding up with the *distinctive* spondee. In corroboration of this idea, again, we should look to find the penultimate spondee most usual in the most ancient verse; and, accordingly, we find it more frequent in the Greek than in the Latin hexameter.

But besides all this, spondees are not only more prevalent in the heroic hexameter than dactyls, but occur to such an extent as is even unpleasant to modern ears, on account of monotony. What the modern chiefly appreciates and admires in the Greek hexameter is the *melody of the abundant vowel sounds*. The Latin hexameters *really* please very few moderns—although so many pretend to fall into ecstasies about them. In the hexameters quoted, several pages ago, from Silius Italicus, the preponderance of the spondee is strikingly manifest. Besides the natural spondees of the Greek and Latin, numerous artificial ones arise in the verse of these tongues on account of the tendency which *case* has to throw full accentuation on terminal syllables; and the preponderance of the spondee is farther ensured by the comparative infrequency of the small prepositions which *we* have to serve us *instead* of case, and also the absence of the diminutive auxiliary verbs with which *we* have to eke out the expression of our primary ones. These are the monosyllables whose abundance serve to stamp the poetic genius of a language as tripping or dactylic.

Now paying no attention to these facts, Sir Philip Sidney, Professor Longfellow, and innumerable other persons more or less modern, have busied themselves in constructing what they supposed to be "English hexameters on the model of the Greek." The only difficulty was that (even leaving out of question the melodious masses of vowel,) these gentlemen never could get their English hexameters to *sound* Greek. Did they *look* Greek?—that should have been the query;

and the reply might have led to a solution of the riddle. In placing a copy of ancient hexameters side by side with a copy (in similar type) of such hexameters as Professor Longfellow, or Professor Felton, or the Frogpondian[28] Professors collectively, are in the shameful practice of composing "on the model of the Greek," it will be seen that the latter (hexameters, not professors) are about one third longer *to the eye*, on an average, than the former. The more abundant dactyls make the difference. And it is the greater number of spondees in the Greek than in the English—in the ancient than in the modern tongue—which has caused it to fall out that while these eminent scholars were groping about in the dark for a Greek hexameter, which is a spondaic rhythm varied now and then by dactyls, they merely stumbled, to the lasting scandal of scholarship, over something which, on account of its long-leggedness, we may as well term a Feltonian hexameter, and which is a dactylic rhythm, interrupted, rarely, by artificial spondees which are no spondees at all, and which are curiously thrown in by the heels at all kinds of improper and impertinent points.

Here is a specimen of the Longfellownian hexameter.

Also the | church with | in was a | dorned for | this was the | season |
In which the | young their | parents' | hope and the | loved ones of |
    Heaven |
Should at the | foot of the | altar re | new the | vows of their | baptism |
Therefore each | nook and | corner was | swept and | cleaned and the | dust
    was |
Blown from the | walls and | ceiling and | from the | oil-painted benches. |[29]

Mr. Longfellow is a man of imagination—but *can* he imagine that any individual, with a proper understanding of the danger of lock-jaw, would make the attempt of twisting his mouth into the shape necessary for the emission of such spondees as "par*ents*," or such dactyls as "cleaned and the" and "loved ones of?" "Baptism" is by no means a bad spondee—perhaps because it happens to be a dactyl;—of all the rest, however, I am dreadfully ashamed.

But these feet—dactyls and spondees, all together,—should thus be put at once into their proper position:

> "Also, the church within was adorned; for this was the season in which
> the young, their parents' hope, and the loved ones of Heaven, should,
> at the feet of the altar, renew the vows of their baptism. Therefore,
> each nook and corner was swept and cleaned; and the dust was blown
> from the walls and ceiling, and from the oil-painted benches."

---

[28]Cornelius Conway Felton had positively reviewed the Longfellow works Poe derides here. "Frogpondians" was Poe's epitaph for the scholars and intellectuals of Boston—the reference being to the frog pond on Boston Common.
[29]From "Children of The Lord's Supper," by Tegner, translated by Longfellow in 1842.

There!—that is respectable prose; and it will incur no danger of ever getting its character ruined by any body's mistaking it for verse.

But even when we let these modern hexameters go, as Greek, and merely hold them fast in their proper character of Longfellownian, or Feltonian, or Frogpondian, we must still condemn them as having been committed in a radical misconception of the philosophy of verse. The spondee, as I observed, is the *theme* of the Greek line. Most of the ancient hexameters *begin* with spondees, for the reason that the spondee *is* the theme; and the ear is filled with it as with a burden. Now the Feltonian dactylics have, in the same way, dactyls for the theme, and most of them begin with dactyls—which is all very proper if not very Greek—but, unhappily, the one point at which they *are* very Greek is that point, precisely, at which they should be nothing but Feltonian. They always *close* with what is meant for a spondee. To be consistently silly, they should die off in a dactyl.

That a truly Greek hexameter *cannot,* however, be readily composed in English, is a proposition which I am by no means inclined to admit. I think I could manage the point myself. For example:

Do tell! | when may we | hope to make | men of sense | out of the | Pundits |
Born and brought | up with their | snouts deep | down in the | mud of the |
    Frog-pond?
Why ask? | who ever | yet saw | money made | out of a | fat old—
Jew, or | downright | upright | nutmegs | out of a | pine-knot? |

The proper spondee predominance is here preserved. Some of the dactyls are not so good as I could wish—but, upon the whole, the rhythm is very decent—to say nothing of its excellent sense.

Review

[*Southern Literary Messenger,* March 1849]

James Russell Lowell, *A Fable for the Critics*
(New York: George P. Putnam)

Poet, critic, and Harvard professor, James Russell Lowell (1819–1891) was also one of Poe's most reliable defenders among the New England literary establishment. He described Poe at one point as "the most discriminating, philosophical, and fearless critic . . . in America" (albeit one who "seems sometimes to mistake his phial of prussic-acid for his inkstand"). But when Poe mounted his one-man campaign against Longfellow, Lowell bailed out and Poe lost a valuable ally. Lowell's A Fable for the Critics *is a topical satire that ridicules Poe and other figures of the day. Ever welcoming of attention of any kind, Poe actually quotes the passage that lampoons him in the following review of the poem. His criticism of the work is sectional in nature; the focus on Lowell's omission of Southern writers shows where Poe's own allegiance lies.*

What have we Americans accomplished in the way of Satire? "The Vision of Rubeta," by Laughton Osborn,[1] is probably our best composition of the kind: but, in saying this, we intend no excessive commendation. Trumbull's clumsy and imitative work is scarcely worth mention—and then we have Halleck's "Croakers," local and ephemeral—but what is there besides? Park Benjamin has written a clever address, with the title "Infatuation," and Holmes has an occasional scrap, piquant enough in its way—but we can think of nothing more that can be fairly called "satire." Some matters we have produced, to be sure, which were excellent in the way of burlesque— (the Poems of William Ellery Channing, for example)—without meaning a syllable that was not utterly solemn and serious. Odes, ballads, songs, sonnets, epics and epigrams, possessed of this unintentional excellence, we should have no difficulty in designating by the dozen; but in the particular of direct and obvious satire, it cannot be denied that we are unaccountably deficient.

It has been suggested that this deficiency arises from the want of a suitable field for satirical display. In England, it is said, satire abounds, because the people there find a proper target in the

---

[1]Laughton Osborn (1809–1878), New York author. The work Poe mentions, published in 1838, includes criticism of several authors of the day.

aristocracy, whom they (the people) regard as a distinct race with whom they have little in common; relishing even the most virulent abuse of the upper classes with a gusto undiminished by any feeling that they (the people) have any concern in it. In Russia, or Austria, on the other hand, it is urged, satire is unknown; because there is danger in touching the aristocracy, and self-satire would be odious to the mass. In America, also, the people who write are, it is maintained, the people who read:—thus in satirizing the people we satirize only ourselves and are never in condition to sympathize with the satire.

All this is more verisimilar than true. It is forgotten that no individual considers himself as one of the mass. Each person, in his own estimate, is the pivot on which all the rest of the world spins round. We may abuse *the people* by wholesale, and yet with a clear conscience so far as regards any compunction for offending any one from among the multitude of which that "people" is composed. Every one of the crowd will cry "*Encore!*—give it to them, the vagabonds!—it serves them right." It seems to us that, in America, we have refused to encourage satire—not because what we have had touches us too nearly—but because it has been too pointless to touch us at all. Its namby-pambyism has arisen, in part, from the general want, among our men of letters, of that minute *polish*—of that skill in details—which, in combination with natural sarcastic power, satire, more than any other form of literature, so imperatively demands. In part, also, we may attribute our failure to the colonial sin of imitation. We content ourselves—at this point not less supinely than at all others—with doing what not only has been done before, but what, however well done, has yet been done *ad nauseam*. We should not be able to endure infinite repetitions of even absolute excellence; but what is "McFingal" more than a faint echo from "Hudibras"?—and what is "The Vision of Rubeta" more than a vast gilded swill-trough overflowing with Dunciad and water? Although we are not all Archilochuses, however—although we have few pretensions to the ηχεηντες ιαμβοι²—although, in short, we are no satirists ourselves—there can be no question that we answer sufficiently well as subjects for satire.

"The Vision" is bold enough—if we leave out of sight its anonymous issue—and bitter enough, and witty enough, if we forget its pitiable punning on names—and long enough (Heaven knows) and well constructed and decently versified; but it fails in the principal element of all satire—*sarcasm*—because the *intention* to be sarcastic (as in the "English Bards and Scotch Reviewers," and in all the more classical satires) is permitted to render itself manifest. The malevolence *appears*. The author is never very severe, because he is at no

²See fn. 1 on p. 42.

time particularly cool. We laugh not so much at his victims as at himself for letting them put him in such a passion. And where a deeper sentiment than mirth is excited—where it is pity or contempt that we are made to feel—the feeling is too often reflected, in its object, from the satirized to the satirist—with whom we sympathize in the discomfort of his animosity. Mr. Osborn has not many superiors in downright invective; but this is the awkward left arm of the satiric Muse. *That* satire alone is worth talking about which at least *appears* to be the genial, good humored outpouring of irrepressible merriment.

"The Fable for the Critics," just issued, has not the name of its author on the title-page; and but for some slight foreknowledge of the literary opinions, likes, dislikes, whims, prejudices and crotchets of Mr. *James Russell Lowell,* we should have had much difficulty in attributing so very *loose* a brochure to *him*. The "Fable" is essentially "loose"—ill conceived and feebly executed, as well in detail as in general. Some good hits and some sparkling witticisms do not serve to compensate us for its rambling plot (if plot it can be called) and for the want of artistic finish so particularly noticeable throughout the work—especially in its versification. In Mr. Lowell's prose efforts we have before observed a certain *disjointedness,* but never, until now, in his verse—and we confess some surprise at his putting forth so unpolished a performance. The author of "The Legend of Brittany" (which is decidedly the noblest poem, of the same length, written by an American) could not do a better thing than to take the advice of those who mean him well, in spite of his fanaticism, and leave prose, with satiric verse, to those who are better able to manage them; while he contents himself with that class of poetry for which, and for which alone, he seems to have an especial vocation—the poetry of *sentiment*. This, to be sure, is *not* the very loftiest order of verse; for it is far inferior to either that of the imagination or that of the passions—but it is the loftiest region in which Mr. Lowell can get his breath without difficulty.

Our primary objection to this "Fable for the Critics" has reference to a point which we have already touched in a general way. "The malevolence appears." We laugh not so much at the author's victims as at himself for letting them put him in such a passion. The very title of the book shows the want of a due sense in respect to the satiric essence, *sarcasm.* This "fable"—this severe lesson—is meant *"for the Critics."* "Ah!" we say to ourselves at once—"we see how it is. Mr. L. is a poor-devil poet, and some critic has been reviewing him, and making him feel very uncomfortable; whereupon, bearing in mind that Lord Byron, when similarly assailed, avenged his wrongs in a satire which he called 'English Bards and Scotch Reviewers,' he

(Mr. Lowell) imitative as usual has been endeavoring to get redress in a parallel manner—by a satire with a parallel title—'A Fable for the Critics.' "

All this the reader says to himself; and all this tells *against* Mr. L. in two ways—first, by suggesting unlucky comparisons between Byron and Lowell, and, secondly, by reminding us for the various criticisms, in which we have been amused (rather ill-naturedly) at seeing Mr. Lowell "used up."

The title starts us on this train of thought and the satire sustains us in it. Every reader versed in our literary gossip, is at once put *dessous des cartes*[3] as to the particular provocation which engendered the "Fable." Miss Margaret Fuller, some time ago, in a silly and conceited piece of Transcendentalism which she called an "Essay on American Literature," or something of that kind, had the consummate pleasantry, after *selecting* from the list of American poets, *Cornelius Mathews* and *William Ellery Channing*,[4] for especial commendation, to speak of *Longfellow* as a booby and of *Lowell* as so wretched a poetaster "as to be disgusting even to his best friends." All this Miss Fuller *said*, if not in our precise words, still in words quite as much to the purpose. *Why* she said it, Heaven only knows—unless it was because she was Margaret Fuller, and wished to be taken for nobody else. Messrs. Longfellow and Lowell, so pointedly picked out for abuse as the *worst* of our poets, are, upon the whole, perhaps, our best—although Bryant, and one or two others are scarcely inferior. As for the two favorites, selected just as pointedly for laudation, by Miss F.—it is really difficult to think of them, in connexion with poetry, without laughing. Mr. Mathews once wrote some sonnets "On Man," and Mr. Channing some lines on "A Tin Can," or something of that kind—and if the former gentleman be not the very worst poet that ever existed on the face of the earth, it is only because he is not quite so bad as the latter. To speak algebraically:—Mr. M. is *ex*ecrable, but Mr. C. is x plus ı-ecrable.

Mr. Lowell has obviously aimed his "Fable" at Miss Fuller's head, in the first instance, with an eye to its ricochêt-ing so as to knock down Mr. Mathews in the second. Miss F. is first introduced as Miss F——, rhyming to "cooler," and afterwards as "Miranda;" while poor Mr. M.

---

[3]"in on the secret."
[4]Cornelius Mathews (1817–1889), New York author and editor (at *Arcturus,* for instance—see fn. 4 on p. 54) who published in many genres. William Ellery Channing (1818–1901), poet, essayist, brother-in-law of Margaret Fuller and nephew of a clergyman by the same name who published several important books in support of abolition. Thoreau was Channing's walking companion, but not always his admirer—he once called Channing's style "sublimo-slipshod." Poe reviewed his work very unfavorably.

is brought in upon all occasions, head and shoulders; and now and then a sharp thing, although never very original, is said *of* them or *at* them; but all the true satiric *effect* wrought, is that produced by the satirist against himself. The reader is all the time smiling to think that so unsurpassable a—(*what* shall we call her?—we wish to be civil,) a transcendentalist as Miss Fuller, should, by *such* a criticism, have had the power to put a respectable poet in *such* a passion.

As for the plot or conduct of this Fable, the less we say of it the better. It is so weak—so flimsy—so ill put together—as to be not worth the trouble of understanding:—something, as usual, about Apollo and Daphne. Is there *no* originality on the face of the earth? Mr. Lowell's total want of it is shown at all points—very especially in his Preface of rhyming verse written without distinction by lines or initial capitals, (a hackneyed matter, originating, we believe, with Frazer's Magazine:)[5]—very especially also, in his long continuations of some particular rhyme—a fashion introduced, if we remember aright, by Leigh Hunt, more than twenty-five years ago, in his "Feast of the Poets"—which, by the way, has been Mr. L's model in many respects.

Although ill-temper has evidently engendered this "Fable," it is by no means a satire throughout. Much of it is devoted to panegyric—but our readers would be quite puzzled to know the grounds of the author's laudations, in many cases, unless made acquainted with a fact which we think it as well they should be informed of at once. Mr. Lowell is one of the most rabid of the Abolition fanatics; and no Southerner who does not wish to be insulted, and at the same time revolted by a bigotry the most obstinately blind and deaf, should ever touch a volume by this author.* His fanaticism about slavery is a mere local outbreak of the same innate wrong-headedness which, if he owned slaves, would manifest itself in atrocious ill-treatment of them, with murder of any abolitionist who should endeavor to set them free. A fanatic of Mr. L's species, is simply a fanatic for the sake of fanaticism, and *must* be a fanatic in whatever circumstances you place him.

His prejudices on the topic of slavery break out every where in his present book. Mr. L. has not the common honesty to speak well, even in a literary sense, of any man who is not a ranting abolitionist. With the exception of Mr. Poe, (who has written some commendatory criticisms on his poems,) no Southerner is mentioned *at all* in this "Fable." It is a fashion among Mr. Lowell's set to affect a belief that

---

[5]*Frazer's* was a high-toned British literary magazine.
*This "Fable *for the Critics*"—this *literary* satire—this benevolent *jeu d'esprit* is disgraced by such passages as the following:
> Forty fathers of Freedom, of whom twenty bred
> Their sons for the rice swamps at so much a head,
> And their daughters for—faugh!

there is *no such thing* as Southern Literature. Northerners—people who have really nothing to speak of as men of letters,—are cited by the dozen and lauded by this candid critic without stint, while Legaré, Simms, Longstreet,[6] and others of equal note are passed by in contemptuous silence. Mr. L. cannot carry his frail honesty of opinion even so far South as New York. All whom he praises are Bostonians. Other writers are barbarians and satirized accordingly— if mentioned at all.

To show the general *manner* of the Fable, we quote a portion of what he says about Mr. Poe:

> Here comes Poe with his Raven, like Barnaby Rudge—
> Three-fifths of him genius, and two-fifths sheer fudge;
> Who talks like a book of iambs and pentameters,
> In a way to make all men of common sense d—n metres;
> Who has written some things far the best of their kind;
> But somehow the heart seems squeezed out by the mind.*

We may observe here that *profound* ignorance on any particular topic is always sure to manifest itself by some allusion to "common sense" as an all-sufficient instructor. So far from Mr. P's talking "like a book" on the topic at issue, his chief purpose has been to demonstrate that there exists *no* book on the subject worth talking *about*; and "common sense," after all, has been the basis on which *he* relied, in contradistinction from the *un*common nonsense of Mr. L. and the small pedants.

And now let us see how far the unusual "common sense" of our satirist has availed him in the structure of his verse. First, by way of showing what his *intention* was, we quote three accidentally accurate lines:

> But a boy | he could ne | ver be right | ly defined.
> As I said | he was ne | ver precise | ly unkind.
> But as Ci | cero says | he won't say | this or that.

Here it is clearly seen that Mr. L. intends a line of four anapæsts. (An anapæst is a foot composed of two short syllables followed by a long.) With this observation, we will now simply copy a few of the

---

[6]James Mathewes Legaré (1823–1859), a Charleston-born poet; William Gilmore Simms (1806–1870), proslavery intellectual and novelist of the society, history and politics of South Carolina. As fellow Southern writers, Poe and Simms promoted each other. In 1844, Poe called Simms "the best writer of fiction in America." Augustus Baldwin Longstreet (1790–1870) was a Georgian lawyer, clergyman and author. His classic *Georgia Scenes, Characters, Incidents &c. in the First Half Century of the Republic,* was warmly reviewed by Poe, who hailed it as "a sure omen of better days for the literature of the South."

*We must do Mr. L. the justice to say that his book was in press before he could have seen Mr. Poe's "*Rationale of Verse*" published in this Magazine for November and December last.

lines which constitute the body of the poem; asking any of our readers to *read them if they can*; that is to say, we place the question, without argument, on the broad basis of the very commonest "common
sense."

> They're all from one source, monthly, weekly, diurnal . . .
> Disperse all one's good and condense all one's poor traits . . .
> The one's two-thirds Norseman, the other half Greek . . .
> He has imitators in scores who omit . . .
> Should suck milk, strong will-giving brave, such as runs . . .
> Along the far rail-road the steam-snake glide white . . .
> From the same runic type-fount and alphabet . . .
> Earth has six truest patriots, four discoverers of ether . . .
> Every cockboat that swims clears its fierce (pop) gundeck at him . . .
> Is some of it pr—— no, 'tis not even prose . . .
> O'er his principles when something else turns up trumps . . .
> But a few silly (syllo I mean) gisms that squat 'em . . .
> *Nos,* we don't want extra freezing in winter . . .
> Plough, dig, sail, forge, build, carve, paint, make all things new . . .

But enough:—we have given a fair specimen of the *general* versification. It might have been better—but we are quite sure that it *could
not have been worse.* So much for "common sense," in Mr. Lowell's
understanding of the term. Mr. L. should not have meddled with the
anapæstic rhythm: it is exceedingly awkward in the hands of one who
knows nothing about it and who *will* persist in fancying that he can
write it by ear. Very especially, he should have avoided this rhythm in
satire, which, more than any other branch of Letters, is dependent
upon seeming trifles for its effect. Two-thirds of the force of the
"Dunciad" may be referred to its exquisite finish; and had "The Fable
for the Critics" been, (what it is *not,*) the quintessence of the satiric
spirit itself, it would nevertheless, in so slovenly a form, have failed.
As it is, no failure was ever more complete or more pitiable. By the
publication of a book at once so ambitious and so feeble—so malev-
olent in design and so harmless in execution—a work so roughly and
clumsily yet so weakly constructed—so very different, in body and
spirit, from anything that he has written before—Mr. Lowell has committed an irrevocable *faux pas* and lowered himself at least fifty per
cent in the literary public opinion.

Marginalia
[*Southern Literary Messenger,* April 1849]

Poe continued to write for the Southern Literary Messenger *from time to time, even after he moved on to edit other publications. The* Marginalia, *which Poe published in several magazines over the last five years of his life, contain his jottings on issues of topical and continuing interest to him. They are sometimes repetitive, and often draw on previously published writing by himself and others. Poe was alone among his contemporaries in publishing his marginalia. He presents them as if they were, literally, idle thoughts he's pencilled into the margins of books, yet there is in fact no evidence to suggest that Poe wrote in his books at all. Polished for publication, the* Marginalia *are not so much spontaneous as representative of spontaneity; this emphasis on craft to create the* effect *of spontaneity is entirely consistent with Poe's creative values. The following selections, excerpted from those published in April 1849, show how Southern in his sentiments Poe remained even long after his peregrinations took him Northward.*

Had the "George Balcombe" of Professor Beverley Tucker been the work of any one born North of Mason and Dixon's line, it would have been long ago recognized as one of the very noblest fictions ever written by an American. It is almost as good as "Caleb Williams." The manner in which the cabal of the "North American Review" first write all our books and then review them, puts me in mind of the fable about the Lion and the Painter.[1] It is high time that the literary South took its own interests into its own charge.

———

Here is a good idea for a Magazine paper:—let somebody "work it up:"—A flippant pretender to universal acquirement—a would-be Crichton[2]—engrosses, for an hour or two perhaps, the attention of a large company—most of whom are profoundly impressed by his knowledge. He is very witty, in especial, at the expense of a modest young gentleman, who ventures to make no reply, and who, finally, leaves the room as if overwhelmed with confusion;—the Crichton greeting his exit with a laugh. Presently he returns, followed by a footman carrying an armfull of books. These are deposited on the

---

[1]Poe is referring to Aesop's Fable "The Man and the Lion," in which a man points to a sculpture depicting a man strangling a lion as evidence that men are superior to lions. In response, his companion—a lion—points out that had a lion been the sculptor, the work would have shown the *lion* prevailing. Poe turns Aesop's sculptor into a painter, but the moral remains: *Consider the source of the evidence before you believe it.*
[2]See fn. 6 on p. 47.

table. The young gentleman, now, referring to some pencilled notes which he had been secretly taking during the Crichton's display of erudition, pins the latter to his statements, each by each, and refutes them all in turn, by reference to the very authorities cited by the egotist himself—whose ignorance at all points is thus made apparent.

———

A long time ago—twenty-three or four years at least—*Edward C. Pinckney,* of Baltimore, published an exquisite poem entitled "A Health." It was profoundly admired by the critical few, but had little circulation:—this for no better reason than that the author was born *too far South.* I quote a few lines:

> Affections are as *thoughts* to her,
>   *The measures of her hours*—
> Her feelings have the fragrancy,
>   The freshness of young *flowers.*
> To her the better elements
>   And kindlier stars have given
> *A form so fair, that, like the air,*
>   *'Tis less of Earth than Heaven.*

Now, in 1842, *Mr. George Hill* published "The Ruins of Athens and Other Poems"—and from one of the "Other Poems" I quote what follows:

> And thoughts go sporting through her mind
>   Like children among *flowers;*
> And deeds of gentle goodness are
>   *The measures of her hours.*
> In soul or face she bears no trace
>   Of one from Eden driven,
> *But like the rainbow seems, though born*
>   *Of Earth, a part of Heaven.*

Is this plagiarism or is it *not?*—I merely ask for information.

———

"Grace," says Horace Walpole, "will save any book, and without it none can live long." I can never read Mrs. Osgood's[3] poetry without a strong propensity to ring the changes upon this indefinite word "grace" and its derivatives. About every thing she writes we perceive this indescribable charm; of which, perhaps, the elements are a vivid fancy and a quick sense of the proportionate. "Grace," however, may be most satisfactorily defined, at least for the present, as "a term

---

[3]Frances Sargent Osgood (1811–1850), American. Author of several books of poetry and a frequent contributor to the *Broadway Journal,* where Poe was her editor. Poe flirted with her in the pages of that same magazine, to the detriment of his reputation.

applied, in despair, to that class of the impressions of Beauty which admit of no analysis." Mrs. O. has lately evinced a *true* imagination, with a *"movement"* (as Schlegel has it) or energy, of which I have been considering her incapable. *Beyond all question the first of American poetesses:*—and yet we must judge her less by what she has done than by what she shows ability to do. A happy refinement—an instinctive sense of the pure and delicate—is one of her most noticeable merits. She *could* accomplish much—*very* much.

One of our truest poets is *Thomas Buchanan Read.* His most distinctive features are, first, "tenderness," or subdued passion, and secondly, fancy. His sin is imitativeness. *At present,* although evincing high capacity, he is but a copyist of Longfellow—that is to say, but the echo of an echo. Here is a beautiful thought which is *not* the property of Mr. Read:

> And, where the spring-time sun had longest shone,
> *A violet looked up and found itself alone.*

Here again: a Spirit

> Slowly through the lake descended,
> Till from her hidden form below
> The waters took a golden glow,
> *As if the star which made her forehead bright*
> *Had burst and filled the lake with light.*

Lowell has some lines very similar, ending with

> As if a star had burst within his brain.

I cannot say that I ever fairly comprehended the force of the term *"insult,"* until I was given to understand, one day, by a member of the *"North American Review"* clique, that this journal was "not only willing but anxious to render me that justice which had been already rendered me by the *'Revue Francaise'* and the *'Revue des Deux Mondes'"*— but was "restrained from so doing" by my "invincible spirit of antagonism." I wish the "North American Review" to express *no* opinion of me whatever—for I have none of it. In the meantime, as I see no motto on its title-page, let me recommend it one from Sterne's "Letter from France." Here it is:—"As we rode along the valley we saw a heard of asses on the top of one of the mountains—how they viewed and *reviewed* us!"

I blush to see, in the——, an invidious notice of Bayard Taylor's *"Rhymes of Travel."* What makes the matter *worse,* the *critique* is from the pen of one who, although undeservedly, holds, himself, some position as a poet:—and what makes the matter *worst,* the attack is

anonymous, and (while ostensibly commending) most zealously
endeavors to damn the young writer "with faint praise." In his whole
life, the author of the criticism never published a poem, long or
short, which could compare, either in the higher merits, or in the
minor morals of the Muse, with *the worst* of Mr. Taylor's compositions.
Observe the generalizing, disingenuous, patronizing tone:—

> "It is the empty charlatan, to whom all things are alike impossible,
> who attempts every thing. He can do one thing as well as another; for
> he can really do nothing. . . . Mr. Taylor's volume, as we have intimat-
> ed, is an advance upon his previous publication. We could have
> wished, indeed, something more of restraint in the rhetoric, but," &c.,
> &c., &c.

The concluding sentence, here, is an excellent example of one of
the most ingeniously malignant of critical *ruses*—that of condemning
an author, in especial, for what the world, in general, *feel* to be his
principal merit. In fact, the "rhetoric" of Mr. Taylor, in the sense
intended by the critic, is Mr. Taylor's *distinguishing excellence.* He is,
unquestionably, the most terse, glowing, and vigorous of all our
poets, young or old—in point, I mean, of *expression.* His sonorous,
well-balanced rhythm puts me often in mind of Campbell (in spite of
our anonymous friend's *implied* sneer at "mere jingling of rhymes,
brilliant and successful for the moment,") and his rhetoric in general is of the highest order:—By "rhetoric" I intend the *mode generally* in
which Thought is presented. Where shall we find more magnificent
passages than these?

First queenly Asia, from the fallen thrones
  Of twice three thousand years,
Came *with the woe a grieving Goddess owns*
  Who longs for mortal tears.
The dust of ruin to her mantle clung
  And dimmed her crown of gold,
While *the majestic sorrows of her tongue*
  From Tyre to Indus rolled.

Mourn with me, sisters, in my realm of woe
  Whose only glory streams
From its lost childhood like the Arctic glow
  Which sunless winter dreams.
In the red desert moulders Babylon
  And the wild serpent's hiss
Echoes in Petra's palaces of stone
  And waste Persepolis.

Then from her seat, *amid the palms embowered*
  That shade the Lion-land,

Swart Africa in dusky aspect towered,
　The fetters on her hand.
Backward she saw, from out the drear eclipse,
　The mighty Theban years,
And the deep anguish of her mournful lips
Interpreted her tears.

I copy these passages first, because the critic in question has copied them, without the slightest appreciation of their grandeur—for they *are* grand; and secondly, to put the question of "rhetoric" at rest. No artist who reads them will deny that they are the perfection of *skill* in their way. But thirdly, I wish to call attention to the glowing *imagination* evinced in the lines italicized. My very soul revolts at *such* efforts, (as the one I refer to,) to depreciate *such* poems as Mr. Taylor's. *Is* there *no* honor—no chivalry left in the land? Are our most deserving writers to be *forever* sneered down, or hooted down, or damned down with faint praise, by a set of men who possess little other ability than that which assures temporary success to *them,* in common with Swaim's Panacea or Morrison's pills? The fact is, some person should write, at once, a Magazine paper exposing—*ruthlessly* exposing, the *dessous de cartes*[4] of our literary affairs. He should show how and why it is that the ubiquitous quack in letters can always "succeed," while *genius,* (which implies self-respect, with a scorn of creeping and crawling,) must inevitably succumb. He should point out the "easy arts" by which any one, base enough to do it, can get himself placed at the very head of American Letters by an article in that magnanimous journal, "The —— Review." He should explain, too, how readily the same work can be induced (as in the case of Simms,) to villify, and villify *personally,* any one not a Northerner, for a trifling "consideration." In fact, our criticism needs a thorough regeneration, *and must have it.*

---

[4]"secrets."

The Poetic Principle

[*Sartain's Union Magazine*, October 1850]

"The Poetic Principle" stands as Poe's critical valedictory. In it he revisits many of the ideas he had been developing over the years about poetic form and the creation of beauty. In particular, he harkens back to the points made in his two-part review of Longfellow's Ballads and Other Poems *(Graham's Magazine, March 1842, April 1842), which constituted a major engagement in the "Longfellow War." In the present skirmish, Poe takes aim at Longfellow's "obtrusive" didacticism. Poe's final definition of poetry focuses on the "sense of the Beautiful" by which humans struggle for a glimpse of the "supernal Loveliness" that poetry can provide. In rejecting the singer of the world around him—one who describes "the sights, and sounds, and odours, and colors, and sentiments, which greet* him *in common with all mankind"—as no poet at all, Poe explicitly disdains the visionary Emersonian aesthetic that found its most famous expression in the free verse of Walt Whitman. For Poe, poetry was more magnificent artifice than natural freedom, more crafted and disciplined than organic and spontaneous. As "The Rhythmical Creation of Beauty," such art touches the "Poetic Sentiment" and "elevate[s] the soul."*

In speaking of the Poetic Principle, I have no design to be either thorough or profound. While discussing, very much at random, the essentiality of what we call Poetry, my principal purpose will be to cite for consideration, some few of those minor English or American poems which best suit my own taste, or which, upon my own fancy, have left the most definite impression. By "minor poems" I mean, of course, poems of little length. And here, in the beginning, permit me to say a few words in regard to a somewhat peculiar principle, which, whether rightfully or wrongfully, has always had its influence in my own critical estimate of the poem. I hold that a long poem does not exist. I maintain that the phrase, "a long poem," is simply a flat contradiction in terms.

I need scarcely observe that a poem deserves its title only inasmuch as it excites, by elevating the soul. The value of the poem is in the ratio of this elevating excitement. But all excitements are, through a psychal necessity, transient. That degree of excitement which would entitle a poem to be so called at all, cannot be sustained throughout a composition of any great length. After the lapse of half an hour, at the very utmost, it flags—fails—a revulsion ensues—and then the poem is, in effect, and in fact, no longer such.

There are, no doubt, many who have found difficulty in

reconciling the critical dictum that the "Paradise Lost" is to be devoutly admired throughout, with the absolute impossibility of maintaining for it, during perusal, the amount of enthusiasm which that critical dictum would demand. This great work, in fact, is to be regarded as poetical, only when, losing sight of that vital requisite in all works of Art, Unity, we view it merely as a series of minor poems. If, to preserve its Unity—its totality of effect or impression—we read it (as would be necessary) at a single sitting, the result is but a constant alternation of excitement and depression. After a passage of what we feel to be true poetry, there follows, inevitably, a passage of platitude which no critical pre-judgment can force us to admire; but if, upon completing the work, we read it again, omitting the first book—that is to say, commencing with the second—we shall be surprised at now finding that admirable which we before condemned— that damnable which we had previously so much admired. It follows from all this that the ultimate, aggregate, or absolute effect of even the best epic under the sun, is a nullity:—and this is precisely the fact.

In regard to the Iliad, we have, if not positive proof, at least very good reason for believing it intended as a series of lyrics; but, granting the epic intention, I can say only that the work is based in an imperfect sense of art. The modern epic is, of the supposititious ancient model, but an inconsiderate and blindfold imitation. But the day of these artistic anomalies is over. If, at any time, any very long poem *were* popular in reality, which I doubt, it is at least clear that no very long poem will ever be popular again.

That the extent of a poetical work is, *cæteris paribus,* the measure of its merit, seems undoubtedly, when we thus state it, a proposition sufficiently absurd—yet we are indebted for it to the Quarterly Reviews. Surely there can be nothing in mere *size,* abstractly considered— there can be nothing in mere *bulk,* so far as a volume is concerned, which has so continuously elicited admiration from these saturnine pamphlets! A mountain, to be sure, by the mere sentiment of physical magnitude which it conveys, *does* impress us with a sense of the sublime—but no man is impressed after *this* fashion by the material grandeur of even "The Columbiad."[1] Even the Quarterlies have not instructed us to be so impressed by it. *As yet,* they have not *insisted* on our estimating Lamartine by the cubic foot, or Pollock by the pound[2]—but what else are we to *infer* from their continual prating about "sustained effort?" If, by "sustained effort," any little gentleman has accomplished an epic, let us frankly commend him for the

---

[1] An 1807 patriotic epic by Joel Barlow (1754–1812).
[2] The French politician and poet Alphonse de Lamartine (1790–1869) was notoriously long-winded. Robert Pollock of Scotland was known for a long, didactic, religious poem, *The Course of Time* (1827).

effort—if this indeed be a thing commendable—but let us forbear praising the epic on the effort's account. It is to be hoped that common sense, in the time to come, will prefer deciding upon a work of art, rather by the impression it makes, by the effect it produces, than by the time it took to impress the effect, or by the amount of "sustained effort" which had been found necessary in effecting the impression. The fact is, that perseverance is one thing, and genius quite another; nor can all the Quarterlies in Christendom confound them. By and by, this proposition, with many which I have been just urging, will be received as self-evident. In the mean time, by being generally condemned as falsities, they will not be essentially damaged as truths.

On the other hand, it is clear that a poem may be improperly brief. Undue brevity degenerates into mere epigrammatism. A *very* short poem, while now and then producing a brilliant or vivid, never produces a profound or enduring effect. There must be the steady pressing down of the stamp upon the wax. De Béranger[3] has wrought innumerable things, pungent and spirit-stirring; but, in general, they have been too imponderous to stamp themselves deeply into the public attention; and thus, as so many feathers of fancy, have been blown aloft only to be whistled down the wind.

A remarkable instance of the effect of undue brevity in depressing a poem—in keeping it out of the popular view—is afforded by the following exquisite little Serenade.

> I arise from dreams of thee,
>   In the first sweet sleep of night,
> When the winds are breathing low,
>   And the stars are shining bright.
> I arise from dreams of thee,
>   And a spirit in my feet
> Has led me—who knows how?—
>   To thy chamber-window, sweet!
>
> The wandering airs they faint
>   On the dark, the silent stream—
> The champak odours fail
>   Like sweet thoughts in a dream;
> The nightingale's complaint,
>   It dies upon her heart
> As I must die on thine,
>   O, beloved as thou art!
>
> O, lift me from the grass!
>   I die, I faint, I fail!

---

[3]See fn. 1 on p. 59.

> Let thy love in kisses rain
> On my lips and eyelids pale.
> My cheek is cold and white, alas!
> My heart beats loud and fast:
> Oh! press it close to thine again,
> Where it will break at last!

Very few, perhaps, are familiar with these lines—yet no less a poet than Shelley is their author. Their warm, yet delicate and ethereal imagination will be appreciated by all—but by none so thoroughly as by him who has himself arisen from sweet dreams of one beloved, to bathe in the aromatic air of a southern mid-summer night.

One of the finest poems by Willis[4]—the very best, in my opinion, which he has ever written—has, no doubt, through this same defect of undue brevity, been kept back from its proper position, not less in the critical than in the popular view.

> The shadows lay along Broadway,
> 'Twas near the twilight-tide—
> And slowly there a lady fair
> Was walking in her pride.
> Alone walked she; but, viewlessly,
> Walked spirits at her side.
>
> Peace charmed the street beneath her feet,
> And Honour charmed the air;
> And all astir looked kind on her,
> And called her good as fair—
> For all God ever gave to her
> She kept with chary care.
>
> She kept with care her beauties rare
> From lovers warm and true—
> For her heart was cold to all but gold,
> And the rich came not to woo—
> But honoured well are charms to sell
> If priests the selling do.
>
> Now walking there was one more fair—
> A slight girl, lily-pale;
> And she had unseen company
> To make the spirit quail—
> 'Twixt Want and Scorn she walked forlorn,
> And nothing could avail.
>
> No mercy now can clear her brow
> For this world's peace to pray;

---

[4]Nathaniel Parker Willis (1806–1867), American poet, foreign correspondent and editor of the New York *Mirror*, where he worked with Poe for a time.

> For, as love's wild prayer dissolved in air,
> Her woman's heart gave way!—
> But the sin forgiven by Christ in Heaven
> By man is cursed alway!

In this composition we find it difficult to recognise the Willis who has written so many mere "verses of society." The lines are not only richly ideal, but full of energy; while they breathe an earnestness—an evident sincerity of sentiment—for which we look in vain throughout all the other works of this author.

While the epic mania—while the idea that, to merit in poetry, prolixity is indispensable—has, for some years past, been gradually dying out of the public mind, by mere dint of its own absurdity—we find it succeeded by a heresy too palpably false to be long tolerated, but one which, in the brief period it has already endured, may be said to have accomplished more in the corruption of our Poetical Literature than all its other enemies combined. I allude to the heresy of *The Didactic.* It has been assumed, tacitly and avowedly, directly and indirectly, that the ultimate object of all Poetry is Truth. Every poem, it is said, should inculcate a moral; and by this moral is the poetical merit of the work to be adjudged. We Americans, especially, have patronised this happy idea; and we Bostonians, very especially, have developed it in full. We have taken it into our heads that to write a poem simply for the poem's sake, and to acknowledge such to have been our design, would be to confess ourselves radically wanting in the true Poetic dignity and force:—but the simple fact is, that, would we but permit ourselves to look into our own souls, we should immediately there discover that under the sun there neither exists nor *can* exist any work more thoroughly dignified—more supremely noble than this very poem—this poem *per se*—this poem which is a poem and nothing more—this poem written solely for the poem's sake.

With as deep a reverence for the True as ever inspired the bosom of man, I would, nevertheless, limit, in some measure, its modes of inculcation. I would limit to enforce them. I would not enfeeble them by dissipation. The demands of Truth are severe. She has no sympathy with the myrtles.[5] All *that* which is so indispensable in Song, is precisely all *that* with which *she* has nothing whatever to do. It is but making her a flaunting paradox, to wreathe her in gems and flowers. In enforcing a truth, we need severity rather than efflorescence of

---

[5]The myrtle was a sacred emblem to the ancient Greeks, particularly to Venus, the goddess of Love, who was known for her supreme beauty. Also, this may be a reference to the first line of Byron's "Bride of Abydos," which Poe quotes and discusses at some length in "The Rationale of Verse." In both allusions, the myrtle seems to serve as an emblem for poetry that is meant primarily to express beauty—in Poe's view, a higher goal than the expression of truth.

language. We must be simple, precise, terse. We must be cool, calm, unimpassioned. In a word, we must be in that mood which, as nearly as possible, is the exact converse of the poetical. *He* must be blind, indeed, who does not perceive the radical and chasmal differences between the truthful and the poetical modes of inculcation. He must be theory-mad beyond redemption who, in spite of these differences, shall still persist in attempting to reconcile the obstinate oils and waters of Poetry and Truth.

Dividing the world of mind into its three most immediately obvious distinctions, we have the Pure Intellect, Taste, and the Moral Sense.[6] I place Taste in the middle, because it is just this position, which, in the mind, it occupies. It holds intimate relations with either extreme; but from the Moral Sense is separated by so faint a difference that Aristotle has not hesitated to place some of its operations among the virtues themselves. Nevertheless, we find the *offices* of the trio marked with a sufficient distinction. Just as the Intellect concerns itself with Truth, so Taste informs us of the Beautiful while the Moral Sense is regardful of Duty. Of this latter, while Conscience teaches the obligation, and Reason the expediency, Taste contents herself with displaying the charms:—waging war upon Vice solely on the ground of her deformity—her disproportion—her animosity to the fitting, to the appropriate, to the harmonious—in a word, to Beauty.

An immortal instinct, deep within the spirit of man, is thus, plainly, a sense of the Beautiful. This it is which administers to his delight in the manifold forms, and sounds, and odours, and sentiments amid which he exists. And just as the lily is repeated in the lake, or the eyes of Amaryllis in the mirror, so is the mere oral or written repetition of these forms, and sounds, and colours, and odours, and sentiments, a duplicate source of delight. But this mere repetition is not poetry. He who shall simply sing, with however glowing enthusiasm, or with however vivid a truth of description, of the sights, and sounds, and odours, and colours, and sentiments, which greet *him* in common with all mankind—he, I say, has yet failed to prove his divine title. There is still a something in the distance which he has been unable to attain. We have still a thirst unquenchable, to allay which he has not shown us the crystal springs. This thirst belongs to the immortality of Man. It is at once a consequence and an indication of his perennial existence. It is the desire of the moth for the star. It is no mere appreciation of the Beauty before us—but a wild effort to reach the Beauty above. Inspired by an ecstatic prescience of the glories beyond the grave, we struggle, by multiform combinations among

---

[6]Here, Poe is making use of ideas Immanuel Kant presented in *The Critique of Judgment* (1793).

the things and thoughts of Time, to attain a portion of that
Loveliness whose very elements, perhaps, appertain to eternity alone.
And thus when by Poetry—or when by Music, the most entrancing of
the Poetic moods—we find ourselves melted into tears—we weep
then—not as the Abbaté Gravina supposes—through excess of pleasure, but through a certain, petulant, impatient sorrow at our inability to grasp *now,* wholly, here on earth, at once and for ever, those
divine and rapturous joys, of which *through* the poem, or *through* the
music, we attain to but brief and indeterminate glimpses.

The struggle to apprehend the supernal Loveliness—this struggle,
on the part of souls fittingly constituted—has given to the world all
that which it (the world) has ever been enabled at once to understand and *to feel* as poetic.

The Poetic Sentiment, of course, may develope itself in various
modes—in Painting, in Sculpture, in Architecture, in the Dance—
very especially in Music—and very peculiarly, and with a wide field,
in the composition of the Landscape Garden. Our present theme,
however, has regard only to its manifestation in words. And here let
me speak briefly on the topic of rhythm. Contenting myself with the
certainty that Music, in its various modes of metre, rhythm, and
rhyme, is of so vast a moment in Poetry as never to be wisely rejected—is so vitally important an adjunct, that he is simply silly who
declines its assistance. I will not now pause to maintain its absolute
essentiality. It is in Music, perhaps, that the soul most nearly attains
the great end for which, when inspired with the Poetic Sentiment, it
struggles—the creation of supernal Beauty. It *may* be, indeed, that
here this sublime end is, now and then, attained *in fact.* We are often
made to feel, with a shivering delight, that from an earthly harp are
stricken notes which *cannot* have been unfamiliar to the angels. And
thus there can be little doubt that in the union of Poetry with Music
in its popular sense, we shall find the widest field for the Poetic development. The old Bards and Minnesingers had advantages which we
do not possess—and Thomas Moore, singing his own songs, was, in
the most legitimate manner, perfecting them as poems.

To recapitulate, then:—I would define, in brief, the Poetry of
words as *The Rhythmical Creation of Beauty.* Its sole arbiter is Taste. With
the Intellect or with the Conscience, it has only collateral relations.
Unless incidentally, it has no concern whatever either with Duty or
with Truth.

A few words, however, in explanation. *That* pleasure which is at
once the most pure, the most elevating, and the most intense, is
derived, I maintain, from the contemplation of the Beautiful. In the
contemplation of Beauty we alone find it possible to attain that pleasurable elevation, or excitement, *of the soul,* which we recognise as the

Poetic Sentiment, and which is so easily distinguished from Truth, which is the satisfaction of the Reason, or from Passion, which is the excitement of the heart. I make Beauty, therefore—using the word as inclusive of the sublime—I make Beauty the province of the poem, simply because it is an obvious rule of Art that effects should be made to spring as directly as possible from their causes:—no one as yet having been weak enough to deny that the peculiar elevation in question is at least *most readily* attainable in the poem. It by no means follows, however, that the incitements of Passion, or the precepts of Duty, or even the lessons of Truth, may not be introduced into a poem, and with advantage; for they may subserve, incidentally, in various ways, the general purposes of the work:—but the true artist will always contrive to tone them down in proper subjection to that *Beauty* which is the atmosphere and the real essence of the poem.

I cannot better introduce the few poems which I shall present for your consideration, than by the citation of the Pröem to Mr. Longfellow's "Waif:"

> The day is done, and the darkness
>   Falls from the wings of Night,
> As a feather is wafted downward
>   From an Eagle in his flight.
>
> I see the lights of the village
>   Gleam through the rain and the mist,
> And a feeling of sadness comes o'er me,
>   That my soul cannot resist;
>
> A feeling of sadness and longing,
>   That is not akin to pain,
> And resembles sorrow only
>   As the mist resembles the rain.
>
> Come, read to me some poem,
>   Some simple and heartfelt lay,
> That shall soothe this restless feeling,
>   And banish the thoughts of day.
>
> Not from the grand old masters,
>   Not from the bards sublime,
> Whose distant footsteps echo
>   Through the corridors of time.
>
> For, like strains of martial music,
>   Their mighty thoughts suggest
> Life's endless toil and endeavour;
>   And to-night I long for rest.
>
> Read from some humbler poet,
>   Whose songs gushed from his heart,

> As showers from the clouds of summer,
>   Or tears from the eyelids start;
>
> Who through long days of labour,
>   And nights devoid of ease,
> Still heard in his soul the music
>   Of wonderful melodies.
>
> Such songs have power to quiet
>   The restless pulse of care,
> And come like the benediction
>   That follows after prayer.
>
> Then read from the treasured volume
>   The poem of thy choice,
> And lend to the rhyme of the poet
>   The beauty of thy voice.
>
> And the night shall be filled with music,
>   And the cares that infest the day,
> Shall fold their tents, like the Arabs,
>   As they silently steal away.

With no great range of imagination, these lines have been justly admired for their delicacy of expression. Some of the images are very effective. Nothing can be better than—

> ——The bards sublime,
> Whose distant footsteps echo
> Down the corridors of Time.[7]

The idea of the last quatrain is also very effective. The poem, on the whole, however, is chiefly to be admired for the graceful *insouciance* of its metre, so well in accordance with the character of the sentiments, and especially for the *ease* of the general manner. This "ease," or naturalness, in a literary style, it has long been the fashion to regard as ease in appearance alone—as a point of really difficult attainment. But not so:—a natural manner is difficult only to him who should never meddle with it—to the unnatural. It is but the result of writing with the understanding, or with the instinct, that *the tone,* in composition, should always be that which the mass of mankind would adopt—and must perpetually vary, of course, with the occasion. The author who, after the fashion of "The North American Review," should be, upon *all* occasions, merely "quiet," must necessarily upon *many* occasions, be simply silly, or stupid; and has no more right to be considered "easy," or "natural," than the Cockney exquisite, or than the sleeping Beauty in the wax-works.

---

[7]Note that in stanza 5 of this poem, which Poe has just quoted, Longfellow's actual word is "Through," rather than "Down."

Among the minor poems of Bryant, none has so much impressed me as the one which he entitles "June." I quote only a portion of it:

> There through the long, long summer hours,
>   The golden light should lie,
> And thick young herbs and groups of flowers
>   Stand in their beauty by.
> The oriole should build and tell
> His love-tale, close beside my cell;
>   The idle butterfly
> Should rest him there, and there be heard
> The housewife-bee and humming bird.
>
> And what, if cheerful shouts at noon,
>   Come, from the village sent,
> Or songs of maids, beneath the moon,
>   With fairy laughter blent?
> And what, if in the evening light,
> Betrothed lovers walk in sight
>   Of my low monument?
> I would the lovely scene around
> Might know no sadder sight nor sound.
>
> I know, I know I should not see[8]
>   The season's glorious show,
> Nor would its brightness shine for me,
>   Nor its wild music flow;
> But if, around my place of sleep,
> The friends I love should come to weep,
>   They might not haste to go.
> Soft airs, and song, and light, and bloom
> Should keep them lingering by my tomb.
>
> These to their softened hearts should bear
>   The thought of what has been,
> And speak of one who cannot share
>   The gladness of the scene;
> Whose part in all the pomp that fills
> The circuit of the summer hills,
>   Is—that his grave is green;
> And deeply would their hearts rejoice
> To hear again his living voice.

The rhythmical flow, here, is even voluptuous—nothing could be more melodious. The poem has always affected me in a remarkable manner. The intense melancholy which seems to well up, perforce, to the surface of all the poet's cheerful sayings about his grave, we

---

[8]Rather than "I know, I know I should not see," William Cullen Bryant's poem reads "I know that no more should see" (*Poetical Works*).

find thrilling us to the soul—while there is the truest poetic elevation
in the thrill. The impression left is one of a pleasurable sadness.

And if, in the remaining compositions which I shall introduce to
you, there be more or less of a similar tone always apparent, let me
remind you that (how or why we know not) this certain tint of sadness is inseparably connected with all the higher manifestations of
true Beauty. It is, nevertheless,

> A feeling of sadness and longing
>   That is not akin to pain,
> And resembles sorrow only
>   As the mist resembles the rain.

The taint of which I speak is clearly perceptible even in a poem so
full of brilliancy and spirit as the "Health" of Edward Coote Pinkney:

> I fill this cup to one made up
>   Of loveliness alone,
> A woman, of her gentle sex
>   The seeming paragon;
> To whom the better elements
>   And kindly stars have given
> A form so fair, that, like the air,
>   'Tis less of earth than heaven.
>
> Her every tone is music's own,
>   Like those of morning birds,
> And something more than melody
>   Dwells ever in her words;
> The coinage of her heart are they,
>   And from her lips each flows
> As one may see the burdened bee
>   Forth issue from the rose.
>
> Affections are as thoughts to her,
>   The measures of her hours;
> Her feelings have the fragrancy,
>   The freshness of young flowers;
> And lovely passions, changing oft,
>   So fill her, she appears
> The image of themselves by turns,—
>   The idol of past years!
>
> Of her bright face one glance will trace
>   A picture on the brain,
> And of her voice in echoing hearts
>   A sound must long remain;
> But memory, such as mine of her,
>   So very much endears,
> When death is nigh, my latest sigh
>   Will not be life's but hers.

> I filled this cup to one made up
>   Of loveliness alone,
> A woman, of her gentle sex
>   The seeming paragon—
> Her health! and would on earth they stood
>   Some more of such a frame,
> That life might be all poetry,
>   And weariness a name.

It was the misfortune of Mr. Pinkney[9] to have been born too far south. Had he been a New Englander, it is probable that he would have been ranked as the first of American lyrists, by that magnanimous cabal which has so long controlled the destinies of American Letters, in conducting the thing called "The North American Review." The poem just cited is especially beautiful; but the poetic elevation which it induces, we must refer chiefly to our sympathy in the poet's enthusiasm. We pardon his hyperboles for the evident earnestness with which they are uttered.

It was by no means my design, however, to expatiate upon the *merits* of what I should read you. These will necessarily speak for themselves. Boccalini, in his "Advertisements from Parnassus," tells us that Zoilus once presented Apollo a very caustic criticism upon a very admirable book:—whereupon the god asked him for the beauties of the work. He replied that he only busied himself about the errors. On hearing this, Apollo, handing him a sack of unwinnowed wheat, bade him pick out *all the chaff* for his reward.

Now this fable answers very well as a hit at the critics—but I am by no means sure that the god was in the right. I am by no means certain that the true limits of the critical duty are not grossly misunderstood. Excellence, in a poem especially, may be considered in the light of an axiom, which need only be properly *put*, to become self-evident. It is *not* excellence if it require to be demonstrated as such:—and thus, to point out too particularly the merits of a work of Art, is to admit that they are *not* merits altogether.

Among the "Melodies" of Thomas Moore,[10] is one whose distinguished character as a poem proper, seems to have been singularly left out of view. I allude to his lines beginning—"Come, rest in this bosom." The intense energy of their expression is not surpassed by anything in Byron. There are two of the lines in which a sentiment is conveyed that embodies the *all in all* of the divine passion of love—a sentiment which, perhaps, has found its echo in more, and in more

---

[9]Edward Coote Pinkney (1802–1828), American poet. He was, in fact, born in London, not in the South—he did not live in the South until the age of nine.
[10]Thomas Moore (1779–1852), prolific and celebrated Irish poet who also published many prose works, some of them pseudonymously.

passionate, human hearts than any other single sentiment ever
embodied in words:

> Come, rest in this bosom, my own stricken deer,
> Though the herd have fled from thee, thy home is still here;
> Here still is the smile that no cloud can o'ercast,
> And a heart and a hand all thy own to the last.
>
> Oh! what was love made for, if 'tis not the same
> Through joy and through torment, through glory and shame?
> I know not, I ask not, if guilt's in that heart,
> I but know that I love thee, whatever thou art.
>
> Thou hast called me thy angel in moments of bliss,
> And thy angel I'll be, 'mid the horrors of this,—
> Through the furnace, unshrinking, thy steps to pursue,
> And shield thee, and save thee,—or perish there too!

It has been the fashion, of late days, to deny Moore imagination,
while granting him fancy—a distinction originating with Coleridge,
than whom no man more fully comprehended the great powers of
Moore. The fact is, that the fancy of this poet so far predominates
over all his other faculties, and over the fancy of all other men, as to
have induced, very naturally, the idea that he is fanciful *only*. But
never was there a greater mistake. Never was a grosser wrong done
the fame of a true poet. In the compass of the English language I can
call to mind no poem more profoundly—more wierdly *imaginative*, in
the best sense, than the lines commencing—"I would I were by that
dim lake,"—which are the composition of Thomas Moore. I regret
that I am unable to remember them.

One of the noblest—and, speaking of fancy, one of the most singularly fanciful of modern poets, was Thomas Hood.[11] His "Fair Ines"
had always, for me, an inexpressible charm.

> O saw ye not fair Ines?
>   She's gone into the West,
> To dazzle when the sun is down,
>   And rob the world of rest;
> She took our daylight with her,
>   The smiles that we love best,
> With morning blushes on her cheek,
>   And pearls upon her breast.
>
> O turn again, fair Ines,
>   Before the fall of night,
> For fear the moon should shine alone,
>   And stars unrivalled bright;

---

[11]English poet and humorist Thomas Hood (1799–1845).

And blessed will the lover be
　　That walks beneath their light,
And breathes the love against thy cheek
　　I dare not even write!

Would I had been, fair Ines,
　　That gallant cavalier,
Who rode so gaily by thy side,
　　And whispered thee so near!
Were there no bonny dames at home,
　　Or no true lovers here,
That he should cross the seas to win
　　The dearest of the dear?

I saw thee, lovely Ines,
　　Descend along the shore,
With bands of noble gentlemen,
　　And banners waved before;
And gentle youth and maidens gay,
　　And snowy plumes they wore;
It would have been a beauteous dream,
　　—If it had been no more!

Alas, alas, fair Ines,
　　She went away with song,
With music waiting on her steps,
　　And shoutings of the throng;
But some were sad and felt no mirth,
　　But only Music's wrong,
In sounds that sang farewell, farewell,
　　To her you've loved so long.

Farewell, farewell, fair Ines;
　　That vessel never bore
So fair a lady on its deck,
　　Nor danced so light before,—
Alas, for pleasure on the sea,
　　And sorrow on the shore!
The smile that blest one lover's heart
　　Has broken many more?

"The Haunted House," by the same author, is one of the truest poems ever written—one of the *truest*—one of the most unexceptionable—one of the most thoroughly artistic, both in its theme and in its execution. It is, moreover, powerfully ideal—imaginative. I regret that its length renders it unsuitable for the purposes of this Lecture. In place of it, permit me to offer the universally appreciated "Bridge of Sighs."

One more Unfortunate,
Weary of breath,
Rashly Importunate,
Gone to her death!

Take her up tenderly,
Lift her with care;—
Fashioned so slenderly,
Young, and so fair!

Look at her garments
Clinging like cerements;
Whilst the wave constantly
Drips from her clothing;
Take her up instantly,
Loving, not loathing.—

Touch her not scornfully;
Think of her mournfully,
Gently and humanly;
Not of the stains of her,
All that remains of her
Now, is pure womanly.

Make no deep scrutiny
Into her mutiny
Rash and undutiful;
Past all dishonour,
Death has left on her
Only the beautiful.

Still, for all slips of hers,
One of Eve's family—
Wipe those poor lips of hers
Oozing so clammily.

Loop up her tresses
Escaped from the comb,
Her fair auburn tresses;
Whilst wonderment guesses
Where was her home?

Who was her father?
Who was her mother?
Had she a sister?
Had she a brother?
Or was there a dearer one
Still, and a nearer one
Yet, than all other?

Alas! for the rarity
Of Christian charity

Under the sun!
Oh! it was pitiful!
Near a whole city full,
Home she had none.

Sisterly, brotherly,
Fatherly, motherly,
Feelings had changed;
Love, by harsh evidence,
Thrown from its eminence;
Even God's providence
Seeming estranged.

Where the lamps quiver
So far in the river,
With many a light
From window and casement,
From garret to basement,
She stood, with amazement,
Houseless by night.

The bleak wind of March
Made her tremble and shiver;
But not the dark arch,
Or the black flowing river:

Mad from life's history,
Glad to death's mystery,
Swift to be hurled—
Anywhere, anywhere
Out of the world!

In she plunged boldly,
No matter how coldly
The rough river ran,—
Over the brink of it,
Picture it,—think of it,
Dissolute Man!
Lave in it, drink of it
Then, if you can!

Take her up tenderly,
Lift her with care;
Fashioned so slenderly,
Young, and so fair!
Ere her limbs frigidly
Stiffen too rigidly,
Decently,—kindly,—
Smooth, and compose them;
And her eyes, close them,
Staring so blindly!

Dreadfully staring
Through muddy impurity,
As when with the daring
Last look of despairing
Fixed on futurity.

Perishing gloomily,
Spurred by contumely,
Cold inhumanity,
Burning insanity,
Into her rest,—
Cross her hands humbly,
As if praying dumbly,
Over her breast!
Owning her weakness,
Her evil behaviour,
And leaving, with meekness,
Her sins to her Saviour!

The vigour of this poem is no less remarkable than its pathos. The versification, although carrying the fanciful to the very verge of the fantastic, is nevertheless admirably adapted to the wild insanity which is the thesis of the poem.

Among the minor poems of Lord Byron, is one which has never received from the critics the praise which it undoubtedly deserves:

Though the day of my destiny's over,
    And the star of my fate hath declined,
Thy soft heart refused to discover
    The faults which so many could find;
Though thy soul with my grief was acquainted,
    It shrunk not to share it with me,
And the love which my spirit hath painted
    It never hath found but in *thee*.

Then when nature around me is smiling,
    The last smile which answers to mine,
I do not believe it beguiling,
    Because it reminds me of thine;
And when winds are at war with the ocean,
    As the breasts I believed in with me,
If their billows excite an emotion,
    It is that they bear me from *thee*.

Though the rock of my last hope is shivered,
    And its fragments are sunk in the wave,
Though I feel that my soul is delivered
    To pain—it shall not be its slave.
There is many a pang to pursue me:
    They may crush, but they shall not contemn—

They may torture, but shall not subdue me—
    'Tis of *thee* that I think—not of them.

Though human, thou didst not deceive me,
    Though woman, thou didst not forsake,
Though loved, thou forborest to grieve me,
    Though slandered, thou never couldst shake,—
Though trusted, thou didst not disclaim me,
    Though parted, it was not to fly,
Though watchful, 'twas not to defame me,
    Nor mute, that the world might belie.

Yet I blame not the world, nor despise it,
    Nor the war of the many with one—
If my soul was not fitted to prize it,
    'Twas folly not sooner to shun:
And if dearly that error hath cost me,
    And more than I once could foresee,
I have found that whatever it lost me,
    It could not deprive me of *thee*.

From the wreck of the past, which hath perished,
    Thus much I at least may recall,
It hath taught me that which I most cherished
    Deserved to be dearest of all:
In the desert a fountain is springing,
    In the wide waste there still is a tree,
And a bird in the solitude singing,
    Which speaks to my spirit of *thee*.

Although the rhythm, here, is one of the most difficult, the versification could scarcely be improved. No nobler *theme* ever engaged the pen of poet. It is the soul-elevating idea, that no man can consider himself entitled to complain of Fate while, in his adversity, he still retains the unwavering love of woman.

From Alfred Tennyson—although in perfect sincerity I regard him as the noblest poet that ever lived—I have left myself time to cite only a very brief specimen. I call him, and *think* him the noblest of poets— *not* because the impressions he produces are, at *all* times, the most profound—*not* because the poetical excitement which he induces is, at *all* times, the most intense—but because it *is*, at all times, the most ethereal—in other words, the most elevating and the most pure. No poet is so little of the earth, earthy. What I am about to read is from his last long poem, "The Princess:"

    Tears, idle tears, I know not what they mean,
    Tears from the depth of some divine despair
    Rise in the heart, and gather to the eyes,
    In looking on the happy Autumn-fields,
    And thinking of the days that are no more.

Fresh as the first beam glittering on a sail,
That brings our friends up from the underworld,
Sad as the last which reddens over one
That sinks with all we love below the verge;
So sad, so fresh, the days that are no more.

Ah, sad and strange as in dark summer dawns
The earliest pipe of half-awakened birds
To dying ears, when unto dying eyes
The casement slowly grows a glimmering square;
So sad, so strange, the days that are no more.

Dear as remembered kisses after death,
And sweet as those by hopeless fancy feigned
On lips that are for others; deep as love,
Deep as first love, and wild with all regret;
O Death in Life, the days that are no more.

Thus, although in a very cursory and imperfect manner, I have endeavoured to convey to you my conception of the Poetic Principle. It has been my purpose to suggest that, while this Principle itself is, strictly and simply, the Human Aspiration for Supernal Beauty, the manifestation of the Principle is always found in *an elevating excitement of the Soul*—quite independent of that passion which is the intoxication of the Heart—or of that Truth which is the satisfaction of the Reason. For, in regard to Passion, alas! its tendency is to degrade, rather than to elevate the Soul. Love, on the contrary—Love—the true, the divine Eros—the Uranian, as distinguished from the Dionæan Venus—is unquestionably the purest and truest of all poetical themes. And in regard to Truth—if, to be sure, through the attainment of a truth, we are led to perceive a harmony where none was apparent before, we experience, at once, the true poetical effect—but this effect is referable to the harmony alone, and not in the least degree to the truth which merely served to render the harmony manifest.

We shall reach, however, more immediately a distinct conception of what the true Poetry is, by mere reference to a few of the simple elements which induce in the Poet himself the true poetical effect. He recognises the ambrosia which nourishes his soul, in the bright orbs that shine in Heaven—in the volutes of the flower—in the clustering of low shrubberies—in the waving of the grain-fields—in the slanting of tall, Eastern trees—in the blue distance of mountains—in the grouping of clouds—in the twinkling of half-hidden brooks—in the gleaming of silver rivers—in the repose of sequestered lakes—in the star-mirroring depths of lonely wells. He perceives it in the songs of birds—in the harp of Æolus—in the sighing of the night-wind—in the repining voice of the forest—in the surf that complains to the shore—in the fresh breath of the woods—in the scent of the violet—in the voluptuous perfume of the hyacinth—in the suggestive odour that comes to him, at eventide, from far-distant, undiscovered islands, over dim oceans, illimitable and unexplored. He owns it in all noble thoughts—in all unworldly motives—in all holy impulses— in all chivalrous, generous, and self-sacrificing deeds. He feels it in the beauty of woman—in the grace of her step—in the lustre of her eye—in the melody of her voice—in her soft laughter—in her sigh— in the harmony of the rustling of her robes. He deeply feels it in her winning endearments—in her burning enthusiasms—in her gentle charities—in her meek and devotional endurances—but above all— ah, far above all—he kneels to it—he worships it in the faith, in the purity, in the strength, in the altogether divine majesty—of her *love*.

Let me conclude—by the recitation of yet another brief poem— one very different in character from any that I have before quoted. It is by Motherwell,[12] and is called "The Song of the Cavalier." With our modern and altogether rational ideas of the absurdity and impiety of warfare, we are not precisely in that frame of mind best adapted to sympathize with the sentiments, and thus to appreciate the real excellence of the poem. To do this fully, we must identify ourselves, in fancy, with the soul of the old cavalier.

> Then mounte! then mounte, brave gallants, all,
>   And don your helmes amaine:
> Deathe's couriers, Fame and Honour, call
>   Us to the field againe.
>
> No shrewish teares shall fill our eye
>   When the sword-hilt is in our hand,—
> Heart-whole we'll part, and no whit sighe
>   For the fayrest of the land;
> Let piping swaine, and craven wight,
>   Thus weepe and puling crye,
> Our business is like men to fight,
>   And hero-like to die!

---

[12]Scottish poet William Motherwell (1797–1835).

A CATALOG OF SELECTED
DOVER BOOKS
IN ALL FIELDS OF INTEREST

A CATALOG OF SELECTED DOVER
BOOKS IN ALL FIELDS OF INTEREST

CONCERNING THE SPIRITUAL IN ART, Wassily Kandinsky. Pioneering work by father of abstract art. Thoughts on color theory, nature of art. Analysis of earlier masters. 12 illustrations. 80pp. of text. 5⅜ x 8½.　　　　　23411-8 Pa. $4.95

ANIMALS: 1,419 Copyright-Free Illustrations of Mammals, Birds, Fish, Insects, etc., Jim Harter (ed.). Clear wood engravings present, in extremely lifelike poses, over 1,000 species of animals. One of the most extensive pictorial sourcebooks of its kind. Captions. Index. 284pp. 9 x 12.　　　　　23766-4 Pa. $14.95

CELTIC ART: The Methods of Construction, George Bain. Simple geometric techniques for making Celtic interlacements, spirals, Kells-type initials, animals, humans, etc. Over 500 illustrations. 160pp. 9 x 12. (USO)　　　　　22923-8 Pa. $9.95

AN ATLAS OF ANATOMY FOR ARTISTS, Fritz Schider. Most thorough reference work on art anatomy in the world. Hundreds of illustrations, including selections from works by Vesalius, Leonardo, Goya, Ingres, Michelangelo, others. 593 illustrations. 192pp. 7⅛ x 10¼.　　　　　20241-0 Pa. $9.95

CELTIC HAND STROKE-BY-STROKE (Irish Half-Uncial from "The Book of Kells"): An Arthur Baker Calligraphy Manual, Arthur Baker. Complete guide to creating each letter of the alphabet in distinctive Celtic manner. Covers hand position, strokes, pens, inks, paper, more. Illustrated. 48pp. 8¼ x 11.　　　　　24336-2 Pa. $3.95

EASY ORIGAMI, John Montroll. Charming collection of 32 projects (hat, cup, pelican, piano, swan, many more) specially designed for the novice origami hobbyist. Clearly illustrated easy-to-follow instructions insure that even beginning papercrafters will achieve successful results. 48pp. 8¼ x 11.　　　　　27298-2 Pa. $3.50

THE COMPLETE BOOK OF BIRDHOUSE CONSTRUCTION FOR WOODWORKERS, Scott D. Campbell. Detailed instructions, illustrations, tables. Also data on bird habitat and instinct patterns. Bibliography. 3 tables. 63 illustrations in 15 figures. 48pp. 5¼ x 8½.　　　　　24407-5 Pa. $2.50

BLOOMINGDALE'S ILLUSTRATED 1886 CATALOG: Fashions, Dry Goods and Housewares, Bloomingdale Brothers. Famed merchants' extremely rare catalog depicting about 1,700 products: clothing, housewares, firearms, dry goods, jewelry, more. Invaluable for dating, identifying vintage items. Also, copyright-free graphics for artists, designers. Co-published with Henry Ford Museum & Greenfield Village. 160pp. 8¼ x 11.　　　　　25780-0 Pa. $10.95

HISTORIC COSTUME IN PICTURES, Braun & Schneider. Over 1,450 costumed figures in clearly detailed engravings–from dawn of civilization to end of 19th century. Captions. Many folk costumes. 256pp. 8⅜ x 11¾.　　　　　23150-X Pa. $12.95

STICKLEY CRAFTSMAN FURNITURE CATALOGS, Gustav Stickley and L. & J. G. Stickley. Beautiful, functional furniture in two authentic catalogs from 1910. 594 illustrations, including 277 photos, show settles, rockers, armchairs, reclining chairs, bookcases, desks, tables. 183pp. 6½ x 9¼.   23838-5 Pa. $11.95

AMERICAN LOCOMOTIVES IN HISTORIC PHOTOGRAPHS: 1858 to 1949, Ron Ziel (ed.). A rare collection of 126 meticulously detailed official photographs, called "builder portraits," of American locomotives that majestically chronicle the rise of steam locomotive power in America. Introduction. Detailed captions. xi + 129pp. 9 x 12.   27393-8 Pa. $13.95

AMERICA'S LIGHTHOUSES: An Illustrated History, Francis Ross Holland, Jr. Delightfully written, profusely illustrated fact-filled survey of over 200 American light-houses since 1716. History, anecdotes, technological advances, more. 240pp. 8 x 10¾.
25576-X Pa. $12.95

TOWARDS A NEW ARCHITECTURE, Le Corbusier. Pioneering manifesto by founder of "International School." Technical and aesthetic theories, views of indus-try, economics, relation of form to function, "mass-production split" and much more. Profusely illustrated. 320pp. 6⅛ x 9¼. (USO)   25023-7 Pa. $9.95

HOW THE OTHER HALF LIVES, Jacob Riis. Famous journalistic record, expos-ing poverty and degradation of New York slums around 1900, by major social reformer. 100 striking and influential photographs. 233pp. 10 x 7⅞.
22012-5 Pa. $11.95

FRUIT KEY AND TWIG KEY TO TREES AND SHRUBS, William M. Harlow. One of the handiest and most widely used identification aids. Fruit key covers 120 deciduous and evergreen species; twig key 160 deciduous species. Easily used. Over 300 photographs. 126pp. 5⅜ x 8½.   20511-8 Pa. $3.95

COMMON BIRD SONGS, Dr. Donald J. Borror. Songs of 60 most common U.S. birds: robins, sparrows, cardinals, bluejays, finches, more–arranged in order of increasing complexity. Up to 9 variations of songs of each species.
Cassette and manual 99911-4 $8.95

ORCHIDS AS HOUSE PLANTS, Rebecca Tyson Northen. Grow cattleyas and many other kinds of orchids–in a window, in a case, or under artificial light. 63 illus-trations. 148pp. 5⅜ x 8½.   23261-1 Pa. $5.95

MONSTER MAZES, Dave Phillips. Masterful mazes at four levels of difficulty. Avoid deadly perils and evil creatures to find magical treasures. Solutions for all 32 exciting illustrated puzzles. 48pp. 8¼ x 11.   26005-4 Pa. $2.95

MOZART'S DON GIOVANNI (DOVER OPERA LIBRETTO SERIES), Wolfgang Amadeus Mozart. Introduced and translated by Ellen H. Bleiler. Standard Italian libretto, with complete English translation. Convenient and thoroughly portable–an ideal companion for reading along with a recording or the performance itself. Introduction. List of characters. Plot summary. 121pp. 5¼ x 8½.
24944-1 Pa. $3.95

TECHNICAL MANUAL AND DICTIONARY OF CLASSICAL BALLET, Gail Grant. Defines, explains, comments on steps, movements, poses and concepts. 15-page pictorial section. Basic book for student, viewer. 127pp. 5⅜ x 8½.
21843-0 Pa. $4.95

AUTOBIOGRAPHY: The Story of My Experiments with Truth, Mohandas K. Gandhi. Boyhood, legal studies, purification, the growth of the Satyagraha (nonviolent protest) movement. Critical, inspiring work of the man responsible for the freedom of India. 480pp. 5⅜ x 8½. (USO) 24593-4 Pa. $8.95

CELTIC MYTHS AND LEGENDS, T. W. Rolleston. Masterful retelling of Irish and Welsh stories and tales. Cuchulain, King Arthur, Deirdre, the Grail, many more. First paperback edition. 58 full-page illustrations. 512pp. 5⅜ x 8½. 26507-2 Pa. $9.95

THE PRINCIPLES OF PSYCHOLOGY, William James. Famous long course complete, unabridged. Stream of thought, time perception, memory, experimental methods; great work decades ahead of its time. 94 figures. 1,391pp. 5⅜ x 8½. 2-vol. set.
Vol. I: 20381-6 Pa. $13.95
Vol. II: 20382-4 Pa. $14.95

THE WORLD AS WILL AND REPRESENTATION, Arthur Schopenhauer. Definitive English translation of Schopenhauer's life work, correcting more than 1,000 errors, omissions in earlier translations. Translated by E. F. J. Payne. Total of 1,269pp. 5⅜ x 8½. 2-vol. set.
Vol. 1: 21761-2 Pa. $12.95
Vol. 2: 21762-0 Pa. $12.95

MAGIC AND MYSTERY IN TIBET, Madame Alexandra David-Neel. Experiences among lamas, magicians, sages, sorcerers, Bonpa wizards. A true psychic discovery. 32 illustrations. 321pp. 5⅜ x 8½. (USO) 22682-4 Pa. $9.95

THE EGYPTIAN BOOK OF THE DEAD, E. A. Wallis Budge. Complete reproduction of Ani's papyrus, finest ever found. Full hieroglyphic text, interlinear transliteration, word-for-word translation, smooth translation. 533pp. 6½ x 9¼.
21866-X Pa. $11.95

MATHEMATICS FOR THE NONMATHEMATICIAN, Morris Kline. Detailed, college-level treatment of mathematics in cultural and historical context, with numerous exercises. Recommended Reading Lists. Tables. Numerous figures. 641pp. 5⅜ x 8½.
24823-2 Pa. $11.95

THEORY OF WING SECTIONS: Including a Summary of Airfoil Data, Ira H. Abbott and A. E. von Doenhoff. Concise compilation of subsonic aerodynamic characteristics of NACA wing sections, plus description of theory. 350pp. of tables. 693pp. 5⅜ x 8½. 60586-8 Pa. $14.95

THE RIME OF THE ANCIENT MARINER, Gustave Doré, S. T. Coleridge. Doré's finest work; 34 plates capture moods, subtleties of poem. Flawless full-size reproductions printed on facing pages with authoritative text of poem. "Beautiful. Simply beautiful."–*Publisher's Weekly.* 77pp. 9¼ x 12. 22305-1 Pa. $7.95

NORTH AMERICAN INDIAN DESIGNS FOR ARTISTS AND CRAFTSPEOPLE, Eva Wilson. Over 360 authentic copyright-free designs adapted from Navajo blankets, Hopi pottery, Sioux buffalo hides, more. Geometrics, symbolic figures, plant and animal motifs, etc. 128pp. 8⅜ x 11. (EUK) 25341-4 Pa. $8.95

SCULPTURE: Principles and Practice, Louis Slobodkin. Step-by-step approach to clay, plaster, metals, stone; classical and modern. 253 drawings, photos. 255pp. 8⅛ x 11.
22960-2 Pa. $11.95

BRASS INSTRUMENTS: Their History and Development, Anthony Baines. Authoritative, updated survey of the evolution of trumpets, trombones, bugles, cornets, French horns, tubas and other brass wind instruments. Over 140 illustrations and 48 music examples. Corrected and updated by author. New preface. Bibliography. 320pp. 5⅜ x 8½. 27574-4 Pa. $9.95

HOLLYWOOD GLAMOR PORTRAITS, John Kobal (ed.). 145 photos from 1926-49. Harlow, Gable, Bogart, Bacall; 94 stars in all. Full background on photographers, technical aspects. 160pp. 8⅜ x 11¼. 23352-9 Pa. $12.95

MAX AND MORITZ, Wilhelm Busch. Great humor classic in both German and English. Also 10 other works: "Cat and Mouse," "Plisch and Plumm," etc. 216pp. 5⅜ x 8½. 20181-3 Pa. $6.95

THE RAVEN AND OTHER FAVORITE POEMS, Edgar Allan Poe. Over 40 of the author's most memorable poems: "The Bells," "Ulalume," "Israfel," "To Helen," "The Conqueror Worm," "Eldorado," "Annabel Lee," many more. Alphabetic lists of titles and first lines. 64pp. 5³⁄₁₆ x 8¼. 26685-0 Pa. $1.00

PERSONAL MEMOIRS OF U. S. GRANT, Ulysses Simpson Grant. Intelligent, deeply moving firsthand account of Civil War campaigns, considered by many the finest military memoirs ever written. Includes letters, historic photographs, maps and more. 528pp. 6⅛ x 9¼. 28587-1 Pa. $12.95

AMULETS AND SUPERSTITIONS, E. A. Wallis Budge. Comprehensive discourse on origin, powers of amulets in many ancient cultures: Arab, Persian Babylonian, Assyrian, Egyptian, Gnostic, Hebrew, Phoenician, Syriac, etc. Covers cross, swastika, crucifix, seals, rings, stones, etc. 584pp. 5⅜ x 8½. 23573-4 Pa. $15.95

RUSSIAN STORIES/PYCCKNE PACCKA3bl: A Dual-Language Book, edited by Gleb Struve. Twelve tales by such masters as Chekhov, Tolstoy, Dostoevsky, Pushkin, others. Excellent word-for-word English translations on facing pages, plus teaching and study aids, Russian/English vocabulary, biographical/critical introductions, more. 416pp. 5⅜ x 8½. 26244-8 Pa. $9.95

PHILADELPHIA THEN AND NOW: 60 Sites Photographed in the Past and Present, Kenneth Finkel and Susan Oyama. Rare photographs of City Hall, Logan Square, Independence Hall, Betsy Ross House, other landmarks juxtaposed with contemporary views. Captures changing face of historic city. Introduction. Captions. 128pp. 8¼ x 11. 25790-8 Pa. $9.95

AIA ARCHITECTURAL GUIDE TO NASSAU AND SUFFOLK COUNTIES, LONG ISLAND, The American Institute of Architects, Long Island Chapter, and the Society for the Preservation of Long Island Antiquities. Comprehensive, well-researched and generously illustrated volume brings to life over three centuries of Long Island's great architectural heritage. More than 240 photographs with authoritative, extensively detailed captions. 176pp. 8¼ x 11. 26946-9 Pa. $14.95

NORTH AMERICAN INDIAN LIFE: Customs and Traditions of 23 Tribes, Elsie Clews Parsons (ed.). 27 fictionalized essays by noted anthropologists examine religion, customs, government, additional facets of life among the Winnebago, Crow, Zuni, Eskimo, other tribes. 480pp. 6⅛ x 9¼. 27377-6 Pa. $10.95

FRANK LLOYD WRIGHT'S HOLLYHOCK HOUSE, Donald Hoffmann. Lavishly illustrated, carefully documented study of one of Wright's most controversial residential designs. Over 120 photographs, floor plans, elevations, etc. Detailed perceptive text by noted Wright scholar. Index. 128pp. 9¼ x 10¾. 27133-1 Pa. $11.95

THE MALE AND FEMALE FIGURE IN MOTION: 60 Classic Photographic Sequences, Eadweard Muybridge. 60 true-action photographs of men and women walking, running, climbing, bending, turning, etc., reproduced from rare 19th-century masterpiece. vi + 121pp. 9 x 12.   24745-7 Pa. $10.95

1001 QUESTIONS ANSWERED ABOUT THE SEASHORE, N. J. Berrill and Jacquelyn Berrill. Queries answered about dolphins, sea snails, sponges, starfish, fishes, shore birds, many others. Covers appearance, breeding, growth, feeding, much more. 305pp. 5¼ x 8¼.   23366-9 Pa. $9.95

GUIDE TO OWL WATCHING IN NORTH AMERICA, Donald S. Heintzelman. Superb guide offers complete data and descriptions of 19 species: barn owl, screech owl, snowy owl, many more. Expert coverage of owl-watching equipment, conservation, migrations and invasions, etc. Guide to observing sites. 84 illustrations. xiii + 193pp. 5⅜ x 8½.   27344-X Pa. $8.95

MEDICINAL AND OTHER USES OF NORTH AMERICAN PLANTS: A Historical Survey with Special Reference to the Eastern Indian Tribes, Charlotte Erichsen-Brown. Chronological historical citations document 500 years of usage of plants, trees, shrubs native to eastern Canada, northeastern U.S. Also complete identifying information. 343 illustrations. 544pp. 6½ x 9¼.   25951-X Pa. $12.95

STORYBOOK MAZES, Dave Phillips. 23 stories and mazes on two-page spreads: Wizard of Oz, Treasure Island, Robin Hood, etc. Solutions. 64pp. 8¼ x 11.
                                                     23628-5 Pa. $2.95

NEGRO FOLK MUSIC, U.S.A., Harold Courlander. Noted folklorist's scholarly yet readable analysis of rich and varied musical tradition. Includes authentic versions of over 40 folk songs. Valuable bibliography and discography. xi + 324pp. 5⅜ x 8½.
                                                     27350-4 Pa. $9.95

MOVIE-STAR PORTRAITS OF THE FORTIES, John Kobal (ed.). 163 glamor, studio photos of 106 stars of the 1940s: Rita Hayworth, Ava Gardner, Marlon Brando, Clark Gable, many more. 176pp. 8⅜ x 11¼.   23546-7 Pa. $14.95

BENCHLEY LOST AND FOUND, Robert Benchley. Finest humor from early 30s, about pet peeves, child psychologists, post office and others. Mostly unavailable elsewhere. 73 illustrations by Peter Arno and others. 183pp. 5⅜ x 8½. 22410-4 Pa. $6.95

YEKL and THE IMPORTED BRIDEGROOM AND OTHER STORIES OF YIDDISH NEW YORK, Abraham Cahan. Film Hester Street based on Yekl (1896). Novel, other stories among first about Jewish immigrants on N.Y.'s East Side. 240pp. 5⅜ x 8½.   22427-9 Pa. $6.95

SELECTED POEMS, Walt Whitman. Generous sampling from *Leaves of Grass.* Twenty-four poems include "I Hear America Singing," "Song of the Open Road," "I Sing the Body Electric," "When Lilacs Last in the Dooryard Bloom'd," "O Captain! My Captain!"—all reprinted from an authoritative edition. Lists of titles and first lines. 128pp. 5¾₆ x 8¼.   26878-0 Pa. $1.00

THE BEST TALES OF HOFFMANN, E. T. A. Hoffmann. 10 of Hoffmann's most important stories: "Nutcracker and the King of Mice," "The Golden Flowerpot," etc. 458pp. 5⅜ x 8½. 21793-0 Pa. $9.95

FROM FETISH TO GOD IN ANCIENT EGYPT, E. A. Wallis Budge. Rich detailed survey of Egyptian conception of "God" and gods, magic, cult of animals, Osiris, more. Also, superb English translations of hymns and legends. 240 illustrations. 545pp. 5⅜ x 8½. 25803-3 Pa. $13.95

FRENCH STORIES/CONTES FRANÇAIS: A Dual-Language Book, Wallace Fowlie. Ten stories by French masters, Voltaire to Camus: "Micromegas" by Voltaire; "The Atheist's Mass" by Balzac; "Minuet" by de Maupassant; "The Guest" by Camus, six more. Excellent English translations on facing pages. Also French-English vocabulary list, exercises, more. 352pp. 5⅜ x 8½. 26443-2 Pa. $9.95

CHICAGO AT THE TURN OF THE CENTURY IN PHOTOGRAPHS: 122 Historic Views from the Collections of the Chicago Historical Society, Larry A. Viskochil. Rare large-format prints offer detailed views of City Hall, State Street, the Loop, Hull House, Union Station, many other landmarks, circa 1904-1913. Introduction. Captions. Maps. 144pp. 9⅜ x 12¼. 24656-6 Pa. $12.95

OLD BROOKLYN IN EARLY PHOTOGRAPHS, 1865-1929, William Lee Younger. Luna Park, Gravesend race track, construction of Grand Army Plaza, moving of Hotel Brighton, etc. 157 previously unpublished photographs. 165pp. 8⅞ x 11¾. 23587-4 Pa. $13.95

THE MYTHS OF THE NORTH AMERICAN INDIANS, Lewis Spence. Rich anthology of the myths and legends of the Algonquins, Iroquois, Pawnees and Sioux, prefaced by an extensive historical and ethnological commentary. 36 illustrations. 480pp. 5⅜ x 8½. 25967-6 Pa. $10.95

AN ENCYCLOPEDIA OF BATTLES: Accounts of Over 1,560 Battles from 1479 B.C. to the Present, David Eggenberger. Essential details of every major battle in recorded history from the first battle of Megiddo in 1479 B.C. to Grenada in 1984. List of Battle Maps. New Appendix covering the years 1967-1984. Index. 99 illustrations. 544pp. 6½ x 9¼. 24913-1 Pa. $16.95

SAILING ALONE AROUND THE WORLD, Captain Joshua Slocum. First man to sail around the world, alone, in small boat. One of great feats of seamanship told in delightful manner. 67 illustrations. 294pp. 5⅜ x 8½. 20326-3 Pa. $6.95

ANARCHISM AND OTHER ESSAYS, Emma Goldman. Powerful, penetrating, prophetic essays on direct action, role of minorities, prison reform, puritan hypocrisy, violence, etc. 271pp. 5⅜ x 8½. 22484-8 Pa. $7.95

MYTHS OF THE HINDUS AND BUDDHISTS, Ananda K. Coomaraswamy and Sister Nivedita. Great stories of the epics; deeds of Krishna, Shiva, taken from puranas, Vedas, folk tales; etc. 32 illustrations. 400pp. 5⅜ x 8½. 21759-0 Pa. $12.95

BEYOND PSYCHOLOGY, Otto Rank. Fear of death, desire of immortality, nature of sexuality, social organization, creativity, according to Rankian system. 291pp. 5⅜ x 8½. 20485-5 Pa. $8.95

A THEOLOGICO-POLITICAL TREATISE, Benedict Spinoza. Also contains unfinished Political Treatise. Great classic on religious liberty, theory of government on common consent. R. Elwes translation. Total of 421pp. 5⅜ x 8½. 20249-6 Pa. $9.95

PERSPECTIVE FOR ARTISTS, Rex Vicat Cole. Depth, perspective of sky and sea, shadows, much more, not usually covered. 391 diagrams, 81 reproductions of drawings and paintings. 279pp. 5⅜ x 8½. 22487-2 Pa. $7.95

DRAWING THE LIVING FIGURE, Joseph Sheppard. Innovative approach to artistic anatomy focuses on specifics of surface anatomy, rather than muscles and bones. Over 170 drawings of live models in front, back and side views, and in widely varying poses. Accompanying diagrams. 177 illustrations. Introduction. Index. 144pp. 8⅜ x11¼. 26723-7 Pa. $8.95

GOTHIC AND OLD ENGLISH ALPHABETS: 100 Complete Fonts, Dan X. Solo. Add power, elegance to posters, signs, other graphics with 100 stunning copyright-free alphabets: Blackstone, Dolbey, Germania, 97 more–including many lower-case, numerals, punctuation marks. 104pp. 8⅛ x 11. 24695-7 Pa. $8.95

HOW TO DO BEADWORK, Mary White. Fundamental book on craft from simple projects to five-bead chains and woven works. 106 illustrations. 142pp. 5⅜ x 8. 20697-1 Pa. $5.95

THE BOOK OF WOOD CARVING, Charles Marshall Sayers. Finest book for beginners discusses fundamentals and offers 34 designs. "Absolutely first rate . . . well thought out and well executed."–E. J. Tangerman. 118pp. 7¾ x 10⅝. 23654-4 Pa. $7.95

ILLUSTRATED CATALOG OF CIVIL WAR MILITARY GOODS: Union Army Weapons, Insignia, Uniform Accessories, and Other Equipment, Schuyler, Hartley, and Graham. Rare, profusely illustrated 1846 catalog includes Union Army uniform and dress regulations, arms and ammunition, coats, insignia, flags, swords, rifles, etc. 226 illustrations. 160pp. 9 x 12. 24939-5 Pa. $10.95

WOMEN'S FASHIONS OF THE EARLY 1900s: An Unabridged Republication of "New York Fashions, 1909," National Cloak & Suit Co. Rare catalog of mail-order fashions documents women's and children's clothing styles shortly after the turn of the century. Captions offer full descriptions, prices. Invaluable resource for fashion, costume historians. Approximately 725 illustrations. 128pp. 8⅜ x 11¼. 27276-1 Pa. $11.95

THE 1912 AND 1915 GUSTAV STICKLEY FURNITURE CATALOGS, Gustav Stickley. With over 200 detailed illustrations and descriptions, these two catalogs are essential reading and reference materials and identification guides for Stickley furniture. Captions cite materials, dimensions and prices. 112pp. 6½ x 9¼. 26676-1 Pa. $9.95

EARLY AMERICAN LOCOMOTIVES, John H. White, Jr. Finest locomotive engravings from early 19th century: historical (1804–74), main-line (after 1870), special, foreign, etc. 147 plates. 142pp. 11⅜ x 8¼. 22772-3 Pa. $10.95

THE TALL SHIPS OF TODAY IN PHOTOGRAPHS, Frank O. Braynard. Lavishly illustrated tribute to nearly 100 majestic contemporary sailing vessels: Amerigo Vespucci, Clearwater, Constitution, Eagle, Mayflower, Sea Cloud, Victory, many more. Authoritative captions provide statistics, background on each ship. 190 black-and-white photographs and illustrations. Introduction. 128pp. 8⅞ x 11¾. 27163-3 Pa. $14.95

THE INFLUENCE OF SEA POWER UPON HISTORY, 1660–1783, A. T. Mahan. Influential classic of naval history and tactics still used as text in war colleges. First paperback edition. 4 maps. 24 battle plans. 640pp. 5⅜ x 8½. 25509-3 Pa. $14.95

THE STORY OF THE TITANIC AS TOLD BY ITS SURVIVORS, Jack Winocour (ed.). What it was really like. Panic, despair, shocking inefficiency, and a little heroism. More thrilling than any fictional account. 26 illustrations. 320pp. 5⅜ x 8½. 20610-6 Pa. $8.95

FAIRY AND FOLK TALES OF THE IRISH PEASANTRY, William Butler Yeats (ed.). Treasury of 64 tales from the twilight world of Celtic myth and legend: "The Soul Cages," "The Kildare Pooka," "King O'Toole and his Goose," many more. Introduction and Notes by W. B. Yeats. 352pp. 5⅜ x 8½. 26941-8 Pa. $8.95

BUDDHIST MAHAYANA TEXTS, E. B. Cowell and Others (eds.). Superb, accurate translations of basic documents in Mahayana Buddhism, highly important in history of religions. The Buddha-karita of Asvaghosha, Larger Sukhavativyuha, more. 448pp. 5⅜ x 8½. 25552-2 Pa. $12.95

ONE TWO THREE . . . INFINITY: Facts and Speculations of Science, George Gamow. Great physicist's fascinating, readable overview of contemporary science: number theory, relativity, fourth dimension, entropy, genes, atomic structure, much more. 128 illustrations. Index. 352pp. 5⅜ x 8½. 25664-2 Pa. $8.95

ENGINEERING IN HISTORY, Richard Shelton Kirby, et al. Broad, nontechnical survey of history's major technological advances: birth of Greek science, industrial revolution, electricity and applied science, 20th-century automation, much more. 181 illustrations. ". . . excellent . . ."–*Isis.* Bibliography. vii + 530pp. 5⅜ x 8¼. 26412-2 Pa. $14.95

DALÍ ON MODERN ART: The Cuckolds of Antiquated Modern Art, Salvador Dalí. Influential painter skewers modern art and its practitioners. Outrageous evaluations of Picasso, Cézanne, Turner, more. 15 renderings of paintings discussed. 44 calligraphic decorations by Dalí. 96pp. 5⅜ x 8½. (USO) 29220-7 Pa. $4.95

ANTIQUE PLAYING CARDS: A Pictorial History, Henry René D'Allemagne. Over 900 elaborate, decorative images from rare playing cards (14th–20th centuries): Bacchus, death, dancing dogs, hunting scenes, royal coats of arms, players cheating, much more. 96pp. 9¼ x 12¼. 29265-7 Pa. $12.95

MAKING FURNITURE MASTERPIECES: 30 Projects with Measured Drawings, Franklin H. Gottshall. Step-by-step instructions, illustrations for constructing handsome, useful pieces, among them a Sheraton desk, Chippendale chair, Spanish desk, Queen Anne table and a William and Mary dressing mirror. 224pp. 8⅛ x 11¼. 29338-6 Pa. $13.95

THE FOSSIL BOOK: A Record of Prehistoric Life, Patricia V. Rich et al. Profusely illustrated definitive guide covers everything from single-celled organisms and dinosaurs to birds and mammals and the interplay between climate and man. Over 1,500 illustrations. 760pp. 7½ x 10⅛. 29371-8 Pa. $29.95

Prices subject to change without notice.

Available at your book dealer or write for free catalog to Dept. GI, Dover Publications, Inc., 31 East 2nd St., Mineola, N.Y. 11501. Dover publishes more than 500 books each year on science, elementary and advanced mathematics, biology, music, art, literary history, social sciences and other areas.